PENGUIN BOOKS

DEEP BLUES

Robert Palmer was born in 1945 and educated in Little Rock, Arkansas, where he began writing about music and played the saxophone and clarinet in blues, rock, soul, and jazz bands. A founder and organizer of the Memphis Blues festivals in the middle and late 1960s, he moved to New York City in 1970 and was chief pop-music critic for *The New York Times* and a frequent contributor to *Rolling Stone* and *Penthouse*. His articles appeared in *Atlantic Monthly*, *Saturday Review*, the *Journal of American Folklore*, *Ethnomusicology*, and many other publications, and he taught American music at Yale, Bowdoin, the Smithsonian Institution, Brooklyn College, and Memphis State University. He was also the author of *Rock & Roll: An Unruly History*. Robert Palmer died in 1997.

Deep Blues

ROBERT PALMER

PENGUIN BOOKS

PENGUIN BOOKS
Published by the Penguin Group
Penguin Group (USA) Inc., 375 Hudson Street, New York, New York 10014, U.S.A.
Penguin Books Ltd, 80 Strand, London WC2R 0RL, England
Penguin Books Australia Ltd, 250 Camberwell Road, Camberwell, Victoria 3124, Australia
Penguin Books Canada Ltd, 10 Alcorn Avenue, Toronto, Ontario, Canada M4V 3B2
Penguin Books India (P) Ltd, 11 Community Centre, Panchsheel Park, New Delhi – 110 017, India
Penguin Group (NZ), cnr Airborne and Rosedale Roads, Albany, Auckland 1310, New Zealand
Penguin Books (South Africa) (Pty) Ltd, 24 Sturdee Avenue,
Rosebank, Johannesburg 2196, South Africa

Penguin Books Ltd, Registered Offices: 80 Strand, London WC2R 0RL, England

First published in the United States of America by
Viking Penguin Inc. 1981
Published in Penguin Books 1982

50

LIBRARY OF CONGRESS CATALOGING IN PUBLICATION DATA
Palmer, Robert.
Deep blues.
Discography: p.
Bibliography: p.
Includes index.
1. Blues (Songs, etc.) – United States – History and
criticism. 2. Afro-American musicians – Biography.
I. Title.
ML3521.P34   1982   784.5′3′009   82-382
ISBN 0 14 00.6223 8   AACR2

Printed in the United States of America
Set in CRT Primer

Grateful acknowledgment is made to the following for permission to reprint copyrighted material.

Arc Music: Lyrics from "Feel Like Going Home," words and music by McKinley Morganfield; copyright © Arc Music Corp., 1964, 1977. Lyrics from "I Can't Be Satisfied," words and music by Muddy Waters; copyright © Arc Music Corp., 1959, 1974. Lyrics from "Louisiana Blues," words and music by Muddy Waters; copyright © Arc Music Corp., 1959. Lyrics from "Gypsy Woman," words and music by McKinley Morganfield; copyright © Arc Music Corp., 1966. Lyrics from "Clouds in My Heart," words and music by McKinley Morganfield; copyright © Arc Music Corp., 1959, 1965.

Knox Music, BMI: Portions of lyrics from "Cotton Crop Blues" by James Cotton.

THIS BOOK IS DEDICATED TO
Harriett Tyson Palmer

ACKNOWLEDGMENTS

A number of people contributed so much assistance, energy, and thought to the writing of this book that it wouldn't have been possible without them. Harriett Tyson Palmer endured the writing not only of the present manuscript but of an earlier, unpublished attempt to grapple with some of the same materials. She was also of inestimable help in getting the finished work in shape. Mary Katherine Aldin compiled the basic discography and offered encouragement, good advice, blues talk, and more. Maude Schuyler Clay opened doors in the Delta that would otherwise have remained closed to me and taught me a great deal about the land and its people. David Evans, director of regional music studies at Memphis State University and a veteran of almost fifteen years of anthropological fieldwork in Mississippi, provided access to some of the unpublished fruits of his research and was always ready with ideas and advice. William Ferris, director of the Center for the Study of Southern Culture at the University of Mississippi, provided inspiration with his films of the Delta's blues life, his uniquely sympathetic fieldwork, and his occasional summonses to various academic conferences and revels. Bruce Iglauer and Mindy Giles of Alligator records provided contacts and assistance above and beyond the call of duty in Chicago. Jim and Amy O'Neal of *Living Blues* magazine provided me with a basic data bank before I began my own researches by giving me access to their archive, which includes a complete set of back issues of their magazine and *Blues Unlimited, Blues World,* and other blues publications. Dick Shurman and Steve Thomashefsky were also helpful when I was working in Chicago. Sid and Shirley Selvidge and Jerry Pillow furnished introductions and orientation in Helena. Once I had written most of the book, it was difficult to find a way of ending it, and Debra Rae Cohen provided the key that enabled me to do that.

I owe a special debt of gratitude to the musicians I interviewed for their time, their encouragement, and of course their music. Muddy Waters introduced me to the concept of deep blues. Hayes McMullen entertained me graciously by the light of a Coleman lantern during a vicious Delta ice storm; when we'd talked enough he huddled with his wife and some neighbors and sang spirituals to keep us all warm. Many other musicians went out of their way to tell their stories—Sunnyland Slim drove halfway across Chicago in the middle of a blizzard and talked with me for hours in the basement of Bob Koester's Jazz Record Mart, Robert Lockwood dropped the guarded manner he's displayed in other interviews and reminisced about his Delta days in depth. Each of the dozens of musicians I talked to should be thanked individually, along with the other people, like Joe Rice Dockery and Sonny Payne, whose lives are such an important part of the Delta blues story, but there isn't the space.

Vicky Stein, my editor, was enthusiastic and in love with the music even before I began writing and was a source of encouragement all the way through. And several musician friends contributed to my understanding of the blues years before I thought of writing this book, including Bill Barth, Ornette Coleman, Leo Smith, Marion Brown, Jim Dickinson, Joe Callicott, and Furry Lewis.

Robert Palmer
August 1980

CONTENTS

PROLOGUE
"It Wasn't No Big Money, but We's Doin' It"

"For the past six weeks," a high school student in the Missis-sippi Delta town of Clarksdale wrote in her composition book in May 1943, "Miss Waddell's Sixth Grade English classes have been having a unit on poetry. To understand it better, we have answered questions about it and learned meanings of new and poetic words. Also we have found out how much thought can be hidden in a few short lines of poetry."

MANY OF THE STUDENTS' FATHERS were off fighting the war; their mothers soldiered on that warm, bright May with a combined celebration of National Poetry Week and National Music Week. "Poetry, music, and flowers joined hands and rendered a most delightful program," the Clarksdale *Register* reported.

Ballads and folksongs were ably discussed by Mrs. Stovall Lowrey, Chairman of the literary department of the club. Music literally played its part in the afternoon schedule through the medium of a phonograph, graciously loaned the club by the Clarksdale Office Supply Company, and records furnished by the Library of Congress, Archives Division. As a beautiful background for the stirring lyrics, the clubhouse was artistically decorated in Talisman roses, purple iris, mock orange, and narcissi. As an opening for the program, a new poem by Jan Strothers, "The American Way," was charmingly read by Mrs. C. E. Mount. In the ballad class, Mrs. Lowrey discussed "The Lady of Carlisle," a song of ancient origin now sung in the Kentucky mountains, and played it on the phonograph. Similarly treated were sailor ballads, miners' songs and English folksongs. An ice course was served by the hostess.

Two folk-song collectors from the Library of Congress, Alan Lomax and John Work, had been through Clarksdale in the summer of 1941. They were looking for Robert Johnson, a blues singer and guitarist who'd often performed in the area, mostly on the huge cotton plantations outside town that employed thousands of black tenant farmers and day laborers and were the real seat of the Delta's wealth and power. Lomax and Work were aware that black musicians who lived and performed in the Delta tended to drift from plantation to plantation and town to town, moving in circles that local whites neither knew nor cared much about, so they didn't bother to talk to any of the members of the Woman's Club of Clarksdale or to call at the planters' rambling, comfortable manor houses. Instead, they drove out into Coahoma County and stopped at crossroads, where two thin ribbons of asphalt met on the flat plane of the Delta land under skies bleached white by the sun.

Black men in overalls and floppy straw hats could usually be found sitting on chairs or crates on the shaded front porches of crossroads gas stations and grocery stores, talking and laughing softly among themselves. Most of the time they responded to questions about Robert Johnson and other blues singers with oblique, noncommittal mumbles and, if pressed, drifted away in sullen twos and threes, but once in a while one would volunteer some information and Lomax and Work would follow it up. They'd leave the blacktop behind and follow dusty, rutted roads out into the country, past mile after mile of perfectly level fields that were alive with bulging green cotton bolls. In a few weeks the cotton would burst through the bolls and the fields would turn blindingly white, the same color as the sky. Then the store porches would be almost deserted except at lunchtime and after dark, and black men, women, and children would be moving across the fields, dragging long canvas sacks and stuffing them with cotton. Already, as Lomax and Work drove along at the head of a great cloud of reddish dust, they could see a number of blacks at work weeding and hoeing in preparation for the harvest. These people might know something about Robert Johnson.

The two folk-song collectors didn't know it yet, but somebody had served Robert Johnson an ice course—a cool drink of poisoned whiskey. Nobody who was willing to discuss the incident was very clear about the details. It was widely rumored that Johnson had been the victim of powerful, malignant conjury, that he'd spent his last hours crawling around on his hands and knees and barking like a dog. Most of the folks who repeated these tales didn't know whether to believe them or not, and most of them really didn't care very much. If they'd known Robert Johnson at all, chances are they knew him as another no-good rambler who never stayed in one place too long, never put in an honest day's work, and made too many passes at married women. Other musicians in the area played about as well as Johnson had and commanded a similarly devoted following among the kind of people who spent their weekends drinking white lightning, gambling, dancing the snake hips, and looking for casual sexual liaisons. As a matter of fact, one of them played a lot like Robert Johnson. He lived on the Stovall plantation, three or four miles outside Clarksdale, in a cabin that doubled as a good-time place, a juke house, on weekends. He made the best moonshine whiskey in the vicinity. Sometimes he played guitar in a little country string band, sometimes he played with a partner, and sometimes he played alone. His name was McKinley Morganfield but everybody knew him as Muddy Waters.

Muddy was a vigorous twenty-six-year-old with high cheekbones and cool, hooded eyes, features that lent him a certain Oriental inscrutability. By the modest economic standards of his peers, he was a success. His juke house cleared a small but dependable profit that nicely supplemented the 22½ cents an hour he was getting for driving a tractor on the plantation. Some of the white overseers regularly bought his whiskey, and he picked up loose change playing at parties in their houses, which were usually one-story frame structures, more comfortable than the black sharecroppers' shacks but not nearly as imposing as the big frame house that belonged to Colonel William Howard Stovall.

Alan Lomax came driving up the narrow dirt road, stopped, waited for the dust to settle, got out, and introduced himself. Muddy greeted him the same way he greeted any business proposition—he listened, saying little, sizing up the young white Southerner and his talk of Washington and folk songs. The prospect of recording was exciting, but Muddy was less than enthralled when Lomax told him the discs were for a library and not for jukebox and store sales. Several of Muddy's friends—Robert Nighthawk, Son House—had made commercial phonograph records up north. They hadn't seen any money after being paid for the initial sessions, but having a record on a neighborhood jukebox or for sale in town had done wonders for their local reputations. Lomax was only paying ten dollars a song, but he promised to send a disc copy if the recording turned out well, and although Muddy didn't let on, he had wanted to make a record ever since he'd first heard Leroy Carr and Memphis Minnie and the Delta's own Charley Patton on a neighbor's windup phonograph, back when he was in his early teens. So he watched intently while Lomax set up the bulky portable recording rig, which picked up sound waves and engraved impressions of them, in the form of circular grooves, directly onto aluminum discs. By the time Lomax was ready, Muddy had taken out his steel-bodied guitar and the bottleneck (actually the neck of a glass bottle, with the jagged broken end melted smooth in a high flame) that he wore on one of the fingers of his left hand when he played.

After he'd fooled around enough for Lomax to set a recording level, Muddy settled down to making some real music. He ran the bottleneck lightly over the bass strings as he picked them to get a dark, moaning sound and sang, at a loping pace, a song that consisted of two lines, a repeat, two more lines, a repeat, and so on, his voice sliding easily from note to note in the crabbed, chantlike melody. It was his version of a song (actually a loose collection of verses and a guitar part) that musicians sang and played the length and breadth of the Mississippi Delta. Son House had recorded it as "My-Black Mama," Robert Johnson as "Walkin' Blues"; Muddy called his "Country Blues."

It's gettin' late on in the evenin' child, I feel like, like blowin' my horn
I woke up this mornin', found my, my little baby gone
(repeat)

Well now, some folks say the worried, woah, blues ain't bad
That's the meanest old feelin' I most ever had
(repeat)

Brooks run into the ocean, ocean run into the sea
If I don't find my baby, somebody sure gonna bury me
(repeat)

Minutes seem like hours, hours seem like days
Seems like my baby would stop her lowdown evil ways
(repeat)

I'm leavin' this mornin' if I have to, to ride the blinds
I'm feelin' mistreated, and I don't mind dyin'
(repeat)

He could have gone on and on, making up new lyrics, adding verses from Son House or Robert Johnson, or filling the song out with some of the countless floating verses that were the common property of all blues singers. But the verse about leaving was as good a place to stop as any, and Lomax had signaled to him that one side of an aluminum disc was almost filled. He put down the guitar. It was a hot, quiet Saturday afternoon; most of Stovall's hundreds of blacks were off in Clarksdale, shopping and mingling with blacks from neighboring plantations, and there wasn't any traffic on the winding dirt road outside the house. Muddy sat listening to the stillness for a few moments and then he heard those first glancing guitar notes and his rich, booming voice playing back, boldly lifelike, on Lomax's machine. The first thing he thought was that he sounded as good as anybody's records. "I can *do* it," he said to himself. "I can *do* it." In his heart he'd always known he could. He'd always hated farming, always thought he could do better as a musician. Maybe that had something to do with his choice of a second blues to sing for Lomax.

> If I'm feelin' tomorrow
> Like I feel today

I'm gonna pack my suitcase
And make my getaway
'Cause I'm troubled
I'm all worried in mind
And I never been satisfied
And I just can't keep from cryin'

"What do you want to call that?" Lomax asked, and Muddy replied, "I Be's Troubled." In the months that followed he *was* troubled; somehow, after hearing his confident singing and razor-sharp guitar playing come bouncing back at him that Saturday afternoon, he couldn't settle down. He had to drive his tractor; had to keep playing his music for people while they danced and drank and screamed, "Oooh, shit, man, play it!"; had to keep making his whiskey and running his gambling games. But he began drinking and gambling more himself, and his temper flared more often. One day he impulsively caught a train for St. Louis, taking a young woman from a neighboring town and leaving his wife on Stovall.

A few brief visits to Memphis had been Muddy's only contact with city life; he didn't even know much of the Delta countryside except for Coahoma and parts of nearby counties. He wanted to like St. Louis, but he found it disturbing that people didn't stop and speak on the street and tended to treat him like a country bumpkin. Soon he was back on Stovall. He told his wife to move out, moved his new girl friend in, and went back to his tractor, his moonshine, his cards and dice and policy wheel, and his blues. Lomax eventually sent two discs, each with "Country Blues" on one side and "I Be's Troubled" on the other, and Muddy proudly put one of them on the jukebox in his joint. In July and August of 1942 Lomax came back, and this time he recorded quite a few songs—Muddy alone, Muddy with second guitar by Charles Berry or an older musician named Son Sims, Muddy with Sims's little string band.

By this time, Muddy was profoundly dissatisfied. He would have left, gone anywhere, but his grandmother, who'd brought him up to Stovall from the lower Delta when he was a baby, needed help, and Chicago, where most of the black people who left the Delta headed, seemed as cold and foreign as the North Pole. Still, he began to think, maybe Chicago wouldn't be so bad. Conditions on the Stovall place seemed to be deteriorating. Colonel Stovall was away fighting in the war, and although the overseer, Mr. Fulton, bought Muddy's whiskey and hired him to play from time to time, there was something about the man, a certain patronizing aloofness, that none of the sharecroppers liked very much.

Gradually Muddy began to smart under what he perceived as discrimination directed specifically at him. For example, the top hands on the plantation were getting 27½ cents an hour for driving tractors, and he was only getting 22½ cents. So one Monday morning in May 1943, while the students at Clarksdale's white high school were studying poetry and their mothers were planning programs for National Music Week, Muddy Waters walked into his overseer's office and asked, respectfully he thought, for a raise to 25 cents. Mr. Fulton stomped around the room in his hip boots, cussing and fuming. Muddy stood, hat in hand, not saying anything, but his mind was talking. It told him, "Go to Chicago."

The more he thought about it, the more he felt that first impulse was right. He went to see his grandmother, who still lived in the cabin where he had grown up, in a remote area of the Stovall place several miles from most of the other croppers' shacks. "Well," she said, "If you think you're going to have some problem, you better go. I ain't going to let it whup me." He worked the rest of Monday afternoon, Tuesday, Wednesday, and Thursday. Thursday night a heavy rain came, turning the rich flatlands into seas of mud, but the sun began drying things out early the next morning. Muddy sent word to Mr. Fulton that he was sick, put on his one suit, packed a few belongings in a suitcase, said good-bye to his grandmother, told his girl friend he'd send for her, and caught the Illinois Central train out of Clarksdale at four that afternoon.

A LITTLE MORE THAN A YEAR LATER, in the summer of 1944, *Time* magazine estimated that since the beginning of the decade 50,000 black people had left Mississippi for the North. This exodus had been going on since World War I, with some interruption during the worst years of the Depression, yet in the Delta the population was still overwhelmingly black. In Coahoma County, where Clarksdale and the Stovall plantation are located, there were three blacks for every white; in Tunica County, directly to the north, the ratio was seven to one. The figures for the Delta as a whole were approximately 293,000 blacks to 98,000 whites.

The "Delta" isn't really the Mississippi's delta, which lies several hundred miles farther south at the river's mouth. It's a flat, fertile, leaf-shaped plain that stretches from just south of Memphis down to Vicksburg, a distance of around two hundred miles, with the river on the west and the state's central hills some eighty-five miles to the east at the widest point. The Delta's early settlers were mostly planters and planters' sons from the southeastern United States. Around 1820, when the Treaty of Doak's Stand opened up some Choctaw Indian lands to settlers, and especially after 1830, when the Choctaws ceded the rest of their lands east of the Mississippi to the United States, these relatively well-to-do pioneers began moving into the area, which was mostly forest and swamp, with their families and their slaves. They bought up huge tracts of land and put the slaves to work clearing and draining it, and most of them were ready to plant their first crop within a year or two. They found the dark alluvial soil, which lay on the Delta plain in deep, even deposits, perfect for cotton.

The plantation that was being run by William Howard Stovall when Muddy was growing up there had been passed down through the women of the family since the early 1840s. Other early settlers lost their plantations in the Civil War, and some were lost soon after; during this period more than a few Delta plantations were won and lost in poker games. But whether the owners were from old families or from more humble backgrounds, during the years after the war they faced the same predicament. Even if a family owned an impressive parcel of land, they couldn't farm it by themselves; they needed labor. The Southern economy was in such shambles that in many cases they couldn't even afford to buy seed and farm implements, much less to pay hired hands. At the same time, most of the blacks who'd been shackled to the land before the Civil War were still there, living in the old slave quarters or in shacks they'd built themselves, trying to raise enough food to keep from starving, getting by from one day to the next.

A bargain was struck. The white landowners, through mortgaging their property or through credit connections, scraped together enough cash to provide seed, implements, provisions, and basic shelter for the blacks who were willing to stay on and work. In return, the blacks planted and harvested the crops, under the supervision of a handful of salaried white overseers on the larger plantations and under the watchful eye of the owner himself if the farm was smaller. It was up to the plantation owners to sell each year's cotton harvest, compute each black family's fair share of the proceeds, deduct the market value of the food, clothing, and other necessities that had been provided to that family, and pay them the difference in cash. In theory, the system was fair enough, but in practice it was heavily weighted against the blacks. The price of cotton on the open market fluctuated wildly. At the end of a good year, a large, hardworking black family might expect to see some cash, perhaps enough to buy new clothes and even an automobile. At the end of a bad year, and most years seemed bad to some degree, the blacks wound up in debt. Their debts were duly entered in the record books the planters kept for each black family and carried over into the following year. Families that stayed on the same plantation year after year found that they sank deeper into debt regardless of how hard they worked.

This was the sharecropping system. It was shaped by mutual dependency in the years immediately following the Civil War, but it rapidly developed into a kind of modern-day feudalism. The larger plantations printed their own paper money and minted their own coins and advanced these to their tenant farmers against the next year's crop rather than giving them real cash. Plantation money was as good as the real thing at plantation stores, which sometimes charged exorbitant prices for necessities. Usually the stuff was accepted as legal tender in the closest town, but it wasn't much good in the next county or in a large city, and it tended to keep blacks tied to the plantation. Other abuses were possible. Planters could shortchange their sharecroppers when totaling up the cotton harvest, or quote them a price lower than the cotton's actual market value. After a time, an informal system of checks and balances developed. Blacks who were heavily indebted or thought they were being treated unfairly simply packed up in the dead of night and hit the road; planters who were particularly exploitative or whose overseers were cruel often found themselves critically shorthanded at harvest time.

Large tracts of Delta land had remained wooded and undeveloped at the time of the Civil War, and it was only after the roughest years of Reconstruction that the area began to attract significant investment capital again. During the early decades of the twentieth century, Delta land was still being cleared, and the year-round black population wasn't large enough to handle both the clearing and the annual cotton harvests. Seasonal migrants were welcomed, and there was plenty of work for any who decided to stay. Throughout the late nineteenth and early twentieth centuries, blacks migrated up into the Delta from the hills, plains, and small farms to the south and east. They were attracted not only by the promise of work but by the fluidity an expanding labor market made possible; if conditions on one plantation were too hard, there was always another one up the road.

There was little room in the sharecropping system for small landowners or poor white renters. The stronghold of northern Mississippi's poor whites was the hill country to the east of the Choctaw ridge, which marks the abrupt end of the Delta for most of its eastern expanse. In the Delta towns there were a few jobs for enterprising hill whites—on the police force, perhaps, or in the stores, though many businesses were run by Italian, Chinese, or Jewish settlers. On the big plantations poor whites were decidedly unwelcome, unless there happened to be an opening for an overseer. The landowners found black workers stronger, healthier, and more tractable, and the blacks learned to consider "white trash" their natural enemy. If blacks were rambunctious or hot-tempered, they were liable to run afoul of white-trash lawmen in the towns. When there were outbreaks of night riding or lynchings, poor whites were the perpetrators; planters often stepped in to protect "their" blacks.

Sharecropping may have been born out of mutual dependency, but it endured by playing on mutual distrust. The blacks tended to assume that plantation owners were duplicitous and exploitative by nature, but preferred them to the virulently racist poor whites. The planters tended to consider the blacks a race of chronic liars and malingerers, but they also distrusted the poor whites, who were moving into the Delta's towns in increasing numbers during the early twentieth century; unlike blacks, who had been effectively disenfranchised by poll tax or literacy requirements or both, poor whites could vote and were thus a threat to the planters' political hegemony. But the poor whites, who found that the planters and blacks were effectively allied against them, didn't trust each other, either; they were competing among themselves for tenuous footholds in a hostile environment. The social situation in the Mississippi Delta was extremely volatile, but there was a balance of power; the system worked. It could not extend into the hill country, where there were smaller farms, fewer big landowners, and fewer blacks; it could and did extend west into the Arkansas counties that were close enough to the river to have Delta characteristics—flat, rich land, large plantations, predominantly black populations.

Even before the turn of the century, the Delta was acting as a kind of funnel for blacks. On the one hand, they were being drawn into the area from the south and east. On the other hand, many of them were already leaving and heading north, a trend that accelerated dramatically during and after the First World War. Most of those who left took the Illinois Central Railroad, which ran all the way from New Orleans up through the Delta to Chicago in just twenty-four hours; the fare in 1940 was $16.95 from New Orleans, $11.10 from Memphis. Chicago was the home of the *Defender*, the outspoken and widely read black newspaper that encouraged Southern sharecroppers to escape economic servitude by moving north. And in Chicago, especially during World War I and World War II and the periods of prosperity that followed them, jobs were plentiful, with Southern blacks given preference over northern-born blacks because, again, they were considered stronger, healthier, and more tractable.

Of course most of these jobs were of the roughest, dirtiest sort, work not even Eastern European immigrants wanted, but a man could make enough money to eat and keep a tenement apartment in a black neighborhood on the city's South Side. He didn't have to wait until the cotton harvest every year to find out how much his crop was worth, how much debt he had accumulated at the plantation store, and whether he'd come out in the red or in the black. Nor did he have to worry about being arrested, beaten, and fined in a town like Clarksdale for having a good time on Saturday night.

Women could find domestic jobs that did not require live-in arrangements, and children could go to school instead of having to help plant, fertilize, hoe, and pick cotton.

Chicago was cold, expensive, dirty, and dangerous. Some people found they didn't like it, turned around and went back home. But most of the migrants stayed. By 1930 the city had more Mississippi-born residents than any other municipality outside Mississippi: 38,356 according to census figures that are probably much too low. In the decade 1940–1950, the census reports, 154,000 blacks arrived in Chicago from the South, around half of them coming from Mississippi and many more coming from the Delta counties in Arkansas. And again the figure is probably too low.

THIRTY-FIVE YEARS AFTER he caught the Illinois Central to Chicago, Muddy Waters sat in the kitchen of his white, two-story frame house, an hour from the Loop in a tree-shaded suburb. The house isn't grand by any means, but it's almost grandiose compared to the dwellings most of Chicago's 1.5 million black people live in. There are deep carpeting and modern furniture in the living room and several pleasant bedrooms upstairs. The kitchen is big, modern, and all-electric, with a kitchen table near the screen door that's a favorite conversation spot, as kitchen tables are in the Delta. In fact, this particular spring afternoon smelled and sounded and felt like Mississippi. Muddy's grandchildren and a few neighborhood kids would run in the screen door, circle around the kitchen floor, and whoop and holler their way back outdoors. His right-hand man, Bo, who grew up with him on Stovall, was in the corner at the kitchen range, frying up some shrimp.

Muddy's wife (not the woman he ran off to St. Louis with and later brought to Chicago; "they get along no kind of way"); had died a few years before, but there were subtle signs of a woman's touch all around the house. Muddy was courting; in 1979, at the age of sixty-four, he would take time off from a tour with rock star Eric Clapton to marry twenty-five-year-old Marva Jean Brooks. Signs of Muddy's country roots and city triumphs were scattered around the house. Outside, in garden plots that skirted the foundation and ran along a concrete driveway, he kept his own personal patches of tomatoes, red and green chili peppers, okra, cabbage, and turnip greens. Inside, in the little anteroom to his den, were discreet framed portraits of the two outstanding harmonica soloists who played in his band and helped shape modern electric blues during the fifties—Little Walter and James Cotton. There weren't many phonograph records, and his guitars, including some expensive gifts from well-heeled white admirers, were locked away; there had been several break-ins in the neighborhood recently.

Muddy poured himself a glass of Piper Heidseck champagne and shoved the bottle across the kitchen table. His doctor had taken him off the hard stuff, he explained, and this was what he drank now. He looked his sixty-three years, but he looked energetic, too, and everything he did, from the way he lifted his champagne glass to the gesture with which he gently but firmly shooed the children away, radiated an imposing, irrefutable authority. Looking out through those heavy-lidded eyes, smiling ever so slightly, and rendering definite opinions in his deep, rolling voice, he was every inch the Muddy Waters who sang, "I'm the hoochie coochie man, everybody knows I am."

Blues wasn't particularly popular in 1978, but Muddy's career was riding high. He'd won so many of the Grammy awards bestowed annually by the National Academy of Recording Arts and Sciences competitors were muttering that the "Best Ethnic or Traditional Recording" category must have been created especially for him. He was in the movies, singing a smoldering "Mannish Boy" in Martin Scorsese's "The Last Waltz." His albums on the Blue Sky label, sympathetically produced by rock guitarist Johnny Winter and distributed by Columbia, were outselling all his previous records. He was performing as often as he wanted to (which was almost constantly) and commanding increasingly substantial fees. Sometimes he played nightclubs, but often he headlined in theaters or opened shows for rock stars in stadiums and arenas. Still, he remembered coming to Chicago at the age of twenty-eight as the single most momentous event of his life.

The Illinois Central cuts through the heart of the South Side, where most Chicago blacks lived in 1943 and most still do. The passenger's first look at the city consists of mile after mile of weatherbeaten two- and three-story frame and brick buildings with dilapidated back porches that reach right to the edge of the tracks. They march sullenly past the train's windows for what seems like an hour, and then the rhythmic clickclack of the pistons slows down and the engine pulls into Central Station.

The station was noisy and crowded with disembarking black Southerners, shouting porters, and anxiously waiting relatives on the Saturday morning of Muddy's arrival. "Boy, I wish you could have seen me," he laughed to Bo, who turned away from the stove momentarily, revealing a broad expanse of chest draped in a fuchsia "Save the Whales" T-shirt. "I got off that train and it looked like this was the fastest place in the world—cabs dropping fares, horns blowing, the peoples walking so fast. And then trying to get in a taxicab, and he whooshes up and drives fast, and big buildings. I made him pull up and I wouldn't let him leave till I see do my sister and her husband Dan live in this house. All the buildings on the South Side then looked just alike. So he looked on the door and he say, 'Yeah, they live here, but they on the fourth floor and there ain't no bell.' So I walked up and knocked and they said, 'What you doing here?' and I walked back and paid the taxicab and got my suitcase.

"That was during the wartime, and there wasn't no rooms for rent, wasn't no nothing. People come, lot of people come. But I changed my luck all the way around when I moved up here. I should have made that change a long time ago. I lived with Dan and his wife and slept on this steel couch for about a week, and then down on the second floor, somebody moved out of there and I got a room just that quick. And there was jobs all over. I got a job in a container factory just about as soon as I got here, and then after about two or three weeks I found out I had a bunch of cousins here; they come got me and brought me over to the West Side. I stayed with them about two or three months and then I got myself a four-room apartment. Things was clicking for me, man."

Soon after he got to Chicago, Muddy began playing the blues for his friends in relaxed moments, and that led to work playing at rent parties, for small tips and all the whiskey he could drink. "You know," he said, refilling his glass with champagne, "I wanted to go to Chicago in the late thirties, 'cause Robert Night-hawk came to see me and said he was goin' and get a record. He says, you go along and you might get on with me. I thought, oh, man, this cat is just jivin', he ain't goin' to Chicago. I thought goin' to Chicago was like goin' out of the world. Finally he split, and the next time I heard he had a record out. So I started asking some of my friends that had went to Chicago, Can I make it with my guitar? 'Naww, they don't listen to that kind of old blues you're doin' now, don't nobody listen to that, not in Chicago.' So when I finally come to Chicago, the same person that told me that"—he flashed his eyes at Bo—"Dan's wife, my sister, that's the same person I started playin' every Saturday night for, at the rent party in her apartment. Peoples is awful funny." He chuckled, savoring the irony. "So I started playing for these rent parties, and then I run into Blue Smitty and Jimmy Rogers and we got somethin' goin' on. We started playing little neighborhood bars on the West Side, five nights a week, five dollars a night. It wasn't no big money, but we's doin' it." They were doing it, all right; they were creating modern blues and laying the groundwork for rock and roll.

THE ELECTRIC GUITAR was introduced on jazz and blues records in the late 1930s and was still something of a novelty when Muddy bought his first one, in 1944. He didn't enjoy playing it as much as he'd enjoyed his old acoustic models, but it helped him cut through the noise in ghetto taverns, and by 1946 he was gigging regularly in a little electric band with Claude Smith, a guitarist from the Arkansas Delta, and Jimmy Rogers, who'd learned harmonica and guitar while growing up in the Mississippi Delta near Greenwood. A little later, Baby Face Leroy, who was from Mobile, Alabama, but also seems to have learned guitar in Mississippi, joined the band, doubling guitar and drums, and after him came Little Walter Jacobs, who was from Louisiana but matured musically in the vicinity of the Delta town of Helena, Arkansas. By 1949 Smitty had dropped out and Muddy, with Walter on harp, Leroy on drums, and Jimmy on second guitar, had graduated from small-time tavern gigs to packing the Du Drop Lounge and making records for a company called Aristocrat, soon to be re-named Chess.

Muddy and his associates can't claim to have invented electric blues, but they were the first important electric band, the first to use amplification to make their ensemble music rawer, more fero-cious, more physical, instead of simply making it a little louder. And they spearheaded the transformation of Delta blues from a regional folk music into a truly popular music that developed first a large black following, then a European white following, and fi-nally a worldwide following of immense proportions. Before Muddy Waters established himself in Chicago, Delta blues was a music by and for Delta blacks. Chicago in the twenties, thirties, and forties had its own blues stars, and they came from all over— Tampa Red, Georgia Tom, Big Maceo from Alabama, John Lee "Sonny Boy" Williamson from Tennessee. By the early fifties, Chicago blues was amplified Delta blues, with Muddy leading the way and setting the pace. And even though there still was consid-erable blues activity in the Delta itself, including live radio pro-gramming and recording, the music's cutting edge was no longer to be found there. The most popular Delta blues records were being made in Chicago, and musicians who lived in the Delta were beginning to copy these records, especialy the Chess records of Muddy Waters, Little Walter, and Jimmy Rogers.

The significance of Delta blues is often thought to be synony-mous with its worldwide impact. According to this line of reason-ing, the music is important because some of the world's most popular musicians—the Rolling Stones, Bob Dylan, Eric Clap-ton—learned to sing and play by imitating it and still revere the recorded works of the Delta masters. It's important because rock guitarists everywhere play with a metal or glass slider on their fin-gers, a homage, acknowledged or not, to Delta musicians like Muddy Waters and Elmore James. It's important because Delta guitarists were the first on records to deliberately explore the uses of feedback and distortion. It's important because almost everyone who picks up a harmonica, in America or England or France or Scandinavia, will at some stage in his development emulate either Little Walter or a Little Walter imitator. It's important because bass patterns, guitar riffs, and piano boogies invented in the Delta course through a broad spectrum of Western popular music, from hard rock to singer-songwriter pop to disco to jazz to movie soundtracks. It's important because Delta bluesmen like Muddy Waters and Robert Johnson have become icons, larger-than-life figures who seem to have articulated some of contemporary America's highest aspirations and darkest secrets with incomparable immediacy in music they made thirty or forty years ago.

These are all good reasons for listening to and learning about Delta blues, but they're neither the only reasons nor the best reasons. The music has never needed interpreters or popularizers; it's always been strong enough to stand on its own. Its story, from the earliest shadowy beginnings to the Chicago migration to the present worldwide popularity of Muddy Waters and some younger Delta-born bluesmen, is an epic as noble and as essentially American as any in our history. It's the story of a small and deprived group of people who created, against tremendous odds, something that has enriched us all.

The odds are worth considering. Blues in the Delta, which may or may not have been the first blues anywhere but is certainly the first blues we know much about, was created not just by black people but by the poorest, most marginal black people. Most of the men and women who sang and played it could neither read nor write. They owned almost nothing and lived in virtual serfdom. They were not considered respectable enough to work as house servants for the whites or to hold responsible positions within their own communities. Blues was so disreputable that even its staunchest devotees frequently found it prudent to disown it. If you asked a black preacher, schoolteacher, small landowner, or faithful churchgoer what kind of people played and listened to blues, they would tell you, "cornfield niggers."

On the other hand, blues singers didn't have to respect social conventions or the church's shopworn homilies; they were free to live the way they wanted and to tell the truth as they saw it. They could find a paying audience in the tiniest hamlet, in a rural sawmill or café, or on any downtown street corner; they didn't have to devote their lives to backbreaking farm work or stay in one place too long. They were the life of the party, the toast of the back of town; they got as much to drink and as many women as they could handle, and sometimes more. They knew the worst of times, but during the best of times they sported eye-catching clothes, jewelry, a wad of greenbacks, even a fancy automobile. To the people who danced and drank and courted and made love to their music, they were stars.

Despite continuing attacks from the black middle class and aspirants thereto, blues endured. Obviously it served a purpose, filled a need. For one thing, it was unbeatable dance music; one or two guitarists or a pianist were enough to get a whole barrelhouse rocking. Bluesmen gave their audience a music they could relate to in the most intensely personal manner, a music that was theirs and theirs alone. Blues lyrics could be light, mocking, risqué, or could deal forthrightly with the most highly charged subject matter—intimate details of love, sex, and desire; a fascination with travel for its own sake that was rooted in the years of black captivity; the hypocrisies and foibles of preachers and other upstanding folks; the fantastic and often disturbing imagery of dreams; the practice and tools of magic and conjury; aggressive impulses that had to be severely repressed in everyday life; and in some blues, particularly the Delta blues of Robert Johnson, an unabashed identification with the leader of the world's dark forces, the ultimate Other.

Most writing on the blues has concentrated on the lyrics, or on the more colorful eccentricities of the performers. But Delta blues, the purest and most deeply rooted of all blues strains, is also significant as music. It seems simple enough—two identical lines and a third answering line make up a verse, there are no more than three chords and sometimes only one, melodies are circumscribed, rhythms are propulsively straightforward. Yet countless white musicians have tried to master it and failed, and Delta bluesmen often laugh among themselves, remembering black musicians from Alabama or Texas who just couldn't learn to play acceptably in the Delta style.

The fact of the matter is, Delta blues is a refined, extremely subtle, and ingeniously systematic musical language. Playing and especially singing it right involve some exceptionally fine points that only a few white guitarists, virtually no white singers, and not too many black musicians who learned to play and sing anywhere other than the Delta have been able to grasp. These fine points have to do with timing, with subtle variations in vocal timbre, and with being able to hear and execute, vocally and instrumentally, very precise gradations in pitch that are neither haphazard waverings nor mere effects. We're talking here about techniques that are learned and methodically applied, are meaningful in both an expressive and a purely musical sense, and are absolutely central to the art.

Paul Garon, paraphrasing André Breton, writes that the blues "represents a fusion of music and poetry accomplished at a very high emotional temperature." If one takes poetry to mean something truer and more genuinely of the spirit than the verse Miss Waddell's Clarksdale English class was studying, then Garon's description is a good one. The operative word in it is "fusion"; functionally speaking the poetry and the music are of equal importance. For the musical language of the blues expresses, in a way the words cannot, something profoundly important about the depth, vitality, and continuity of African-American culture. In fact, some of the earliest Delta bluesmen often indulged in wordless singing, or allowed musical values to take such precedence that words, lines, and entire verses became virtually indecipherable, not just to outsiders but to the core audience and to other blues musicians as well. Delta blacks often danced and listened with pleasure to blues singing that had little or no verbal content, but it's difficult to imagine them appreciating crisply enunciated blues verses set to melodies from Mozart or Tin Pan Alley.

Blues can't be adequately understood if we confine our analysis to phonograph records or to the music that's sung in nightclub and concert situations by blues musicians today. We need to understand what blues came from, where it grew, how it changed, what sorts of camouflage it had to adopt in order to preserve its identity. And we need to understand the people who made and listened to blues, not just as blacks or oppressed Americans or romantic archetypes or clever technicians or successful entertainers but as particular people who made particular personal and artistic choices in a particular place at a particular time. In seeking to arrive at these various understandings we'll concentrate on Delta blues, which creatively absorbed elements from other locales and other kinds of music and survived transplantation from an isolated rural environment to an urban and eventually an international milieu without losing either its essential musical and poetic identity or its particular inner fire. We'll pay especially close attention to Muddy Waters because he best illustrates the places Delta blues has been and the places it's gone.

PART
I

CHAPTER 1
Beginnings

C harles Peabody of Harvard's Peabody Museum arrived in Coahoma County in June 1901 to begin archaeological excavations at some Indian mounds in the vicinity of the Stovall and Carson plantations. His first stop was Clarksdale, then a typical Delta town with a flat, dusty, treeless business district and oak- and maple-lined residential streets that ended in cotton fields. He stocked up on provisions, hired some wagons, and recruited a gang of black workmen, and one sunny morning his party set off for the first dig, fifteen miles outside town. To Peabody's surprise, his workmen immediately burst into rhythmic song, and they kept it up all the way to the campsite. One strong-voiced man would take the lead, improvising short lines that touched on scenes along the road, women everyone seemed to know or know about, Biblical themes, and the romantic involvements and recreational habits of certain men on the crew. The others would answer with a refrain—"the time ain't long," or "goin' down the river"—sung in rough unison.

The mounds Peabody was interested in were imposing structures up to fifty feet in height. A few were burial mounds, but most had served the practical purpose of keeping Indian homes and community buildings dry during the periodic rampages of the Mississippi, their "father of waters." Many of the planters who first cleared the land for farming built their homes on the tops of

Indian mounds, the only high ground around. But Peabody's sites had remained untouched, and he suspected that once he penetrated down to the earliest strata in the mounds, he would find cast-off bits of pottery, arrowheads, and other artifacts indicative of how some of the earliest Mound Builders had lived.

Peabody put his crew to work scooping deep trenches out of the moist soil, and they kept right on singing, timing their call and response to the rhythm of the digging. Before long, he found he was being worked into the songs. On a Saturday that had been declared a half-holiday, he was startled to hear Ike Antoine, the group's robust song leader, singing "mighty long half-day Captain" from deep down in the trench. On another occasion, when quitting time was at hand and Peabody and a white compatriot were sitting in front of their tent idly flipping a knife into the ground, he heard the men sing, "I'm so tired I'm most dead / Sittin' up there playin' mumbley-peg."

Peabody wasn't a folklorist, but he'd had some musical training and he thought enough of what he was hearing to jot down lyrics and impressions and even attempt musical transcriptions. The transcriptions weren't very successful—much of the music, he admitted, was "singularly hard to copy in notes"—but his descriptions, published in the 1903 *Journal of American Folk-Lore,* are the first we have of black music in the Delta. He seems to have been particularly struck by the differences he perceived between the music of the countryside and the music of his workmen from Clarksdale. The "autochthonous music," as he called it, puzzled him. He referred to the unaccompanied hollers of a man working in a nearby field as "strains of apparently genuine African music"; a lullaby he overheard coming from a cabin near his tent was "quite impossible to copy, weird in interval and strange in rhythm; peculiarly beautiful." An elderly ex-slave who lived on the Stovall plantation and was called in to entertain Peabody one night displayed a remarkable singing voice, with "a timbre resembling a bagpipe played pianissimo or a Jew's-harp played legato, and to some indistinguishable words he hummed a rhythm of no regularity and notes apparently not more than three or more in number at intervals within a semi-tone."

The singing of the men from Clarksdale seemed less alien, especially when they accompanied themselves on guitars. Their repertoires included ragtime and minstrel songs they had picked up from visiting tent shows, tunes that were popular throughout the South. In style these songs were close cousins to white country music. For the most part they were black in origin, but from the 1840s on they had been picked up by white minstrel entertainers and imitated by professional songwriters. After the Civil War, black minstrel and medicine show performers sang both the originals and the Tin Pan Alley facsimiles, and these songs were absorbed back into the black folk tradition. "Some folks say preachers won't steal," went one of the ditties Peabody heard, "But I found two in my cornfield / One with a shovel and t'other with a hoe / A-diggin' up my taters row by row." The song's original culprits had been "niggers," not preachers, and the field had been full of watermelons.

But along with these songs, which Peabody's men loosely called "ragtime," there were other songs, closer in character to the chants of the country blacks. These were sung unaccompanied as work songs or hollers, or accompanied by guitars for dancing and partying. To Peabody they tended to blur into "hours-long ululation of little variety," but he was struck by some of the words. The most common subjects were hard luck, women, and "favorite occupations and amusements," and among the lines Peabody wrote down were "They had me arrested for murder / And I never harmed a man" and "The reason I loves my baby so / 'Cause when she gets five dollars she give me fo'." These are, or were in the process of becoming, blues lines. Peabody visited the Delta just when blues was beginning to emerge as a distinct musical genre out of the loose, partially improvised music country blacks sang to make their work go faster or to entertain themselves in moments of leisure. The music probably wasn't referred to as "the blues" yet, although "having the blues," a slang expression descriptive of melancholia that can be traced back to the "blue devils" of Elizabethan England, was a phrase and a state of mind with which both blacks and whites were familiar.

THE AFRICAN MUSIC from which the blues ultimately derives came to what is now the southern United States with the first

African slaves. These Africans had belonged to a number of different tribal and linguistic groups, each of which had its own musical traditions. Most of the earliest arrivals were from a stretch of the West African coast the slave traders called Senegambia. it extended from present-day Senegal and the Gambia down to the northern coastline of Guinea, an area which was forested toward the south but whose northern extremities edged into the Sahara. For centuries Senegambia had been dominated by powerful empires, but during the sixteenth century the Wolof empire splintered into warring city states and in the decades of turmoil that followed many prisoners were taken and sold into slavery. Islam was already making headway in the region, and its coming contributed to the general unrest that made Senegambia particularly attractive to European slave traders. The slavers were not above kidnapping, but it was more efficient and less risky to deal with Senegambian kings and princes who had prospered in war and owned more slaves than they could profitably use.

As the slave trade gathered momentum, it tended to shift farther south, to the immense stretch of coastline Europeans loosely referred to as the slave coast—present day Sierra Leone, Liberia, the Ivory Coast, Ghana, Togo, Dahomey, Nigeria, and Cameroon. A third area south of the Congo River's mouth, along the coast of what is now Angola, also became an important slaving center. By 1807, when Great Britain and the United States officially outlawed the trade, slaving in Senegambia had dropped off dramatically and most of the activity was centered along the slave coast and the Angolan coastline.

Between 1807 and the outbreak of the American Civil War slaving continued clandestinely. The Congo-Angola region became more and more important because the many channels and small islands at the Congo River's broad mouth made it easier for the slavers to skulk out of sight of patrolling English and American warships. Other slave traders managed to operate in the vicinity of what is now Nigeria, especially in the Bight of Benin where there was considerable political turmoil during the first half of the nineteenth century. And some ventured around Cape Horn to trade for slaves in Mozambique and at the Arab slave markets on the island of Madagascar.

Senegambia, the slave coast, and Congo-Angola differed markedly in terms of topography, political organization, and material culture; musically each area had—and to a considerable extent still has—a distinct personality of its own. There are no great forests in the relatively dry Senegambia, so there aren't as many large wooden drums as in the more southerly areas. But one encounters a wealth of stringed instruments, from the humblest one-stringed gourd fiddles to guitarlike lutes with two, three, or four strings to elaborate harp-lutes with more than twenty strings. Because of Senegambia's many centuries of contact with the Berber and Arab cultures north of the desert, the vocal music tends to reflect the Middle East's predilection for long, tortuous melodic lines. And there's a fondness for formal solo singing, which is relatively unusual in most African music.

In many Senegambian societies, singers and musicians belong to a particular social caste, the *griots*. They sing the praises of wealthy and powerful men and memorize long epic genealogies that constitute a kind of oral history of their people. Some of them are attached to royal courts, while others sing in the streets, or play in groups that encourage farmers and other workers by setting rhythms for their tasks. One would expect the griots to be valued members of their societies, but in fact they are both admired, for they often attain considerable reputations and amass wealth, and despised, for they are thought to consort with evil spirits, and their praise songs, when not properly rewarded, can become venomous songs of insult. Some of the earliest European visitors to Senegambia remarked that when griots died they were not buried with the respectable people of their communities; instead, their bodies were left to rot in hollow trees.

Village music making in Senegambia involves drumming, hand clapping, and group singing in call and response form; usually an improvising vocal soloist is answered by a chorus singing a repeating refrain in unison. This kind of communal music making, which was much more prevalent in Senegambia in the days of the slave trade than it is now, is also characteristic of much of the slave coast, but there the drumming and percussion tend to be more elaborate. Often villages mount orchestras of drums, rattles, bells, and other percussion instruments that play polyrhythmic music of dazzling complexity. In group singing the parts of the lead vocalist and chorus often overlap, or even blend in a kind of polyphony—music that consists of several different but simultaneous melodies. There is harmony in slave-coast vocal music, too—not the periodic resolving harmony of European music but the parallel melodies sung a third, fourth, or fifth away from each other.

The people of Bantu stock who are the dominant population group in much of the Congo-Angola region also play drums and percussion instruments, but for the most part their rhythms aren't as complex as, say, Ewe or Akan or Yoruba drumming from Ghana and Nigeria. Bantu choral music, however, is the most highly developed in Africa. Even in call and response singing the leader and chorus tend to overlap, and there are local traditions of exceptionally refined vocal polyphony; sometimes solos, duets, and trios emerge from a dense choral backdrop that pits two sections of singers against each other. Some Bantu vocal music includes whooping, or sudden jumping into the falsetto range, which seems to derive from the pygmies who were the area's original inhabitants.

Despite their differences, the musics of these three areas also have certain broad, basic features in common, features that are characteristic of African and African-derived music wherever it's found. For one thing, African music is usually participative. Shepherds do serenade their flocks with lonely flutes, and the musically inclined sometimes play small instruments like the sansa or hand piano to entertain themselves, but most music making is group music making, and in group situations the distinction between performers and audience that is so basic in Western music tends to blur or disappear entirely. Whole villages take part, with musical specialists handling the more demanding roles and everyone else chiming in with choral responses or simple hand-clapping patterns. There are plenty of opportunities to practice, for almost every group activity—religious rituals, planting, hoeing, pounding grain, building dwellings, partying—has its own body of music. The structure of the music actively encourages participation, whether it's call and response, in which anyone can join the response, or a method of organization called hocketing, especially prevalent among the Bantu and the pygmies, which involves the building of a multitude of individual one- or two-note parts into a dense polyphony.

Both call and response and hocketing are forms of musical conversation. Even professional instrumental ensembles that organize their music in a more complex manner play conversationally; the master drummer "talks" to his accompanying drummers, one xylophone player addresses another, two flutes entwine in a sputtering, partially vocalized dialogue, and so on. Sometimes these musical conversations involve the exchange of actual verbal information. The Yoruba, the Akan, and many other African peoples speak pitch-tone languages in which a single syllable or word has several meanings, and one indicates the desired meaning by speaking at an appropriate pitch level, usually high, middle, or low. Among these people, speech has melodic properties, and the melodies found in music suggest words and sentences. By using generally understood correspondences between pitch configurations in speech and in music, musicians can make their instruments talk. This is the secret of the celebrated West African talking drums, which literally drum up trade for merchants by announcing wares and prices and can also send messages, announce visitors, and flatter or revile public figures. Horns, flutes, xylophones, and other instruments are also capable of talking. When they are played in groups, the music consists of layers of melodies and rhythms, some of which may have verbal meaning while others do not.

Speech and music are closely related even where pitch-tone languages are not spoken. The use of musical instruments for signaling is found everywhere, and drummers learn rhythms by imitating either meaningful verbal phrases or onomatopoeic nonsense syllables. Instrumentalists, especially flutists, sing or hum while blowing in order to produce grainy, voicelike textures. One fascinating group of instruments, singing horns and singing gourds, can be played as horns, with the lips vibrating, or simply used as megaphones to amplify the voice. The Luba of Zaire lip their singing gourds as if they were playing trumpets, and the instrumets contribute propulsive bass parts to ensemble music. The playing technique, and the instrument's musical function, were preserved by the jug blowers in black American jug bands.

Gunther Schuller has defined the rhythmic quality familiarly called swing as "forward-propelling directionality." That's a mouthful, but until a description comes along that is equally accurate and rolls off the tongue more readily, it will have to do. African rhythms don't always swing in a jazz sense; sometimes the polyrhythm is too dense and complex. But they always have that quality of forward-propelling directionality—they're driving, "hot." And it doesn't take a battery of drummers to drive the music along; a single musician playing a stringed instrument or even a flute or horn can generate plenty of heat. As one would expect, the African instruments with the most highly developed solo traditions tend to be instruments like the widely distributed hand piano or the harp-lutes of Senegambia that can simultaneously produce driving ostinatos (repeating patterns) and chording or melody lines that answer or comment on the player's singing. The persistence of this principle in America helps explain the alacrity with which black musicians in the rural South took up the guitar once white musicians and mail order catalogues introduced it to them.

European and American visitors to Africa have often been puzzled by what they perceived as an African fondness for muddying perfectly clean sounds. African musicians will attach pieces of tin sheeting to the heads of drums or the necks of stringed instruments in order to get a noisy, rattling buzz. When confronted with a wooden flute, which naturally produces a relatively pure tone, they will sing or hum while they play. And their solo singing makes use of an extravagant variety of tonal effects, from grainy falsetto shrieks to affected hoarseness, throaty growls, and guttural grunting. This preference for what western musicology tells us are impure sounds has always been evident in black American music, from the rasp in so much folk, blues, and popular singing—think of Mahalia Jackson, or James Brown—to the gutbucket sounds of early New Orleans jazz trumpeters, who sometimes played into brass spitoons or crammed homemade mutes made out of kazoos into the bells of their horns.

THERE'S A LOT MORE TO AFRICAN MUSIC than these generalities, of course, but this should be enough background for us to return to the music's gradual transformation in the American

South. At first, Africans from different cultures were thrown together by slave traders and planters without regard for their dis-
parate origins, but as time went on the planters developed definite
preferences for slaves from certain areas. In seventeenth and
eighteenth century Virginia and the Carolinas the favorites were
Senegambians, who were thought to be more civilized and thus
more adaptable than pastoralists and hunter-gatherers from farther south. Some of these Senegambian slaves had been city
dwellers and were converts to Islam—there are cases of trusted
slaves keeping plantation records in Arabic—but most of them
were from backcountry tribal cultures. There were Bambara, Ma-
linke or Mandingo, Hausa, and many others, but the Wolof seem
to have played a particularly important and perhaps a culturally
dominant role in the early slave culture of the southern United
States.

"The Wolof are famous for their good looks," writes the anthropologist David Ames. "They are a tall, slender, black-skinned people, who stand straight and are proud and dignified in their
posture." The earliest English slavers to visit Senegambia found
that the Wolof language (which is not a pitch-tone language) was
widely spoken, probably because so many tribes had been vassals
of the medieval Wolof empire. So Wolof speakers were sought out
as interpreters and guides, and it was during this period that
Wolof terms for several foodstuffs—banana, yam—passed into
English usage. The linguist David Dalby has suggested that several American slang terms with strong musical association also derive from Wolof. In his article "Americanisms That May Once
Have Been Africanisms," Dalby compares the American slang
verb "dig" to the Wolof *dega*, pronounced something like "digger"
and meaning to understand. He relates "jive" to the Wolof *jev*, to
talk disparagingly, and "hip cat" to the Wolof verb *hipi*, "to open
one's eyes," and agentive suffix -*kat*; in Wolof, a *hipi-kat* is "a
person who has opened his eyes."

The Wolof are also a likely source of the most popular American
musical instrument to have originated among the slaves—the
banjo. The word, which was variously reported in accounts from
the colonial period as *banjer*, *banshaw*, *banza*, and *bandore*,
seems to be a corruption of *bania*, a generic name for a similar
type of instrument found in Senegal, but there are particularly

close connections between black American banjo music and music played on the Wolof *halam*. Like the banjo, the halam has five strings, one of which vibrates openly as a drone string, and it is played in what American folk musicians call frailing or claw hammer style—which the minstrel banjo instruction books of the nineteenth century referred to as brushless, drop-thumb frailing. In frailing, the fingernail (or nails) picks various strings in a rhythmic, fast-moving pattern while the ball of the thumb repeatedly strikes down at the drone string, providing an insistent ostinato. It's a purely rhythmic-melodic style; the adjective "brushless" means that the fingers don't brush several strings at once to produce a chord.

Most Senegambian lutes have fewer strings than the halam, but the frailing technique is widespread. One hears it today in Morocco and Tunisia among the descendants of Senegambian blacks who were brought there centuries ago as slaves. It survives in only a handful of recordings of black American music; it was passé if not positively archaic by the 1920s, when black folk music first found its way onto discs. But it was still popular among white musicians in Kentucky, Tennessee, and other Southern states, especially in the mountains. A number of white mountaineers have reported learning to play the banjo from blacks who lived in or visited their localities, and the instrument and the frailing style were also spread by traveling minstrel shows whose performers, whites in blackface, copied slave musicians they'd heard on Deep South plantations.

Long after the Senegambian slave trade had declined, blacks from that area continued to enjoy special status on many plantations. New Senegambian arrivals were given relatively light work to do around the house, while blacks from the slave coast and especially Bantu from the Congo-Angola region were sent to the fields. Senegambians who had played bowed stringed instruments would not have had too much trouble adapting to the European violin, their homemade banjos would not have sounded too harsh to European ears, and small percussion instruments like bone clappers and triangles would also have been acceptable. Slave orchestras consisting of various combinations of these instruments, sometimes with flutes or fifes, became a fixture of plantation life almost from the first. These plantation house musicians, many of whom learned some European music and probably combined it with African playing habits, inspired the blackface minstrel troupes that dominated the American entertainment scene from the 1840s until some years after the Civil War.

Musically inclined blacks from the slave coast and Congo-Angola, where complex drumming was indispensable to much music making, found themselves at a distinct disadvantage. Drums were banned everywhere in North America except French Louisiana by the middle of the eighteenth century, and so were horns, which are made from wood or animal horns and played in hocketing ensembles in the slave coast and Congo-Angola regions. Plantation owners had learned, sometimes the hard way, that such loud instruments could be used to signal slave insurrections. The range of musical expression that was left to Africans from south of Senegambia was cruelly circumscribed. Their lives were filled with backbreaking labor, with little time left for making instruments or practicing. Since they were forbidden drums and horns, and since more elaborate instruments such as harps or xylophones required too many special materials and took too much time to construct, all these instruments eventually died out after making early appearances on a few Southern plantations. The music that was left utilized mankind's most basic musical resources, the voice and the body.

The slaves who toiled in Southern fields came from every part of Africa that was touched by the slave trade. Through singing to themselves, hollering at each other across the fields, and singing together while working and worshiping, they developed a hybridized musical language that distilled the very essence of innumerable African vocal traditions. In parts of Senegal, Upper Volta, Ghana, and the Cameroons, and undoubtedly in other areas where few field recordings have been made, African singing has many of the characteristics of this American hybrid. Such singing tends to sound vaguely familiar to the European ear, as if the melodies were based on the major scale but with flattening or wavering in pitch around the third and sometimes the fifth and seventh notes. On closer examination, it becomes evident that the singers' intonation—their manner of singing "in tune"—is determined by natural harmonic resonances and not by the more arbitrary tempered scale of European music. The solo singers indulge in considerable sliding, gliding, and quivering between pitches, and in a group all the singers evidence an acute sense of timing and rhythmic drive. The group answers the lead vocalist's musical and verbal improvisations with a fixed refrain, sung in unison with perhaps some relatively simple harmonizing or polyphonic elaboration.

This description may seem detailed, but it's general enough to apply equally well to field recordings from many parts of West Africa or to recordings of black work songs made on Southern prison farms in the 1930s. One feature demands additional comment: the flattened third, which is referred to as a "blue note" in most jazz literature but is really a melodic tendency and not a note with a fixed pitch relationship to its neighbors. This is the expressive core of the hollers, work songs, spirituals that have not been substantially influenced by white church music, and later the blues, especially Delta blues. You can hear it, or suggestions of it, in African vocal music from Senegambia to the Congo, and it has special significance among the Akan-speaking people of Ghana, who suffered the depredations of English and American slavers through most of the period of the slave trade. Akan is a pitch-tone language in which rising emotion is expressed by falling pitch, and in Akan song rising emotion is often expressed by flattening the third. There seems to be a direct continuity between this tendency and blues singing, for blues singers habitually use falling pitches to raise the emotional temperature of a performance. Usually these falling pitches are thirds, but Muddy Waters and other vocalists and guitarists from the Delta tradition also employ falling fifths, often with shattering emotional effect.

Whooping, a kind of yodeling that's traditional among the pygmies and their neighbors in the Congo-Angola region, is an example of a specific African vocal technique that survived in the rural South well into the twentieth century, especially in field hollers and blues. Originally, hollers and blues were almost exclusively the province of field workers; house servants had no need to holler. Blues, as almost any Mississippian will tell you, came "from the cotton patch," and Bantu slaves were almost invariably put to work in the field and not in the house. Bantu were being brought into the South in large numbers long after the Senegambian and slave coast trade had dwindled. All these factors help explain the whooping tradition's long life. Texas Henry Thomas, whose 1874 birthdate makes him one of the oldest black singers captured on recordings, played a set of panpipes whooping style, alternately vocalizing and blowing into his pipes so as to produce a continuous melody line. Panpipes and whooping have also been recorded in other Southern states, including Alabama and Mississippi, and the instrument as well as the technique can be traced directly to African prototypes. But as a purely vocal technique, whooping or octave-jumping seems to have survived most strongly in the hollers and blues of Mississippi. One hears it in the work of early bluesmen like Tommy Johnson and in the later Chicago recordings of Delta-bred singers like Muddy Waters and Howlin' Wolf.

Voice masking is another African vocal technique with some bearing on blues singing. The finest African masks are now valued as precious art objects, but in village rituals these masks were simply the visual aspect of a masking procedure that also involved modifying the voice. The masker was often believed to be possessed by a god or spirit, so his voice had to change along with his appearance. Some masks had mirliton membranes mounted in their mouthpieces and the maskers sang through them, producing a buzzing timbre not unlike that of a kazoo. Other masked singers, especially in the slave coast region, mastered deep chest growls, false bass tones produced in the back of the throat, strangulated shrieks, and other deliberately bizarre effects.

Since such extreme voice modification had primarily religious or ritual associations in West Africa, it's interesting to note that it figured more prominently in black American sacred singing than in secular music. One encounters it with particular frequency in the early recordings of guitar-playing evangelists such as the Texan Blind Willie Johnson. The recordings of Charley Patton, Son House, and Rubin Lacy, three seminal figures in the first decades of Mississippi Delta blues, also contain frequent examples of techniques that are possibly related to voice masking, and all three men were preachers and religious singers at one time or another. Lacy was permanently converted not long after he made his only blues recording, Son House wavered back and forth between preaching and the blues life, and Patton made commercial recordings of religious material (as Elder J. J. Hadley) and reserved some of his most spectacular vocal displays for these occasions.

An African-American continuity can be discerned in the subject matter of song lyrics too. In Africa, and in the South both during and after slavery, song leaders who were quick-witted improvisers were highly valued. The improvisations Charles Peabody heard from his Clarksdale work crew were typical in their ironic humor, their overriding concern with relations between the sexes, and their unselfconscious mixing of imagery from the church and the bedroom. Several European explorers in precolonial Africa documented the trading of insults in song; often such insults constituted a kind of socially sanctioned censure directed at specific members of the community. This practice survived in a slave custom known as putting someone "on the banjo" and its spirit was often present in pre-blues and blues singing. Charley Patton's recordings, for example, include frequent jabs at real individuals, including several wives and girl friends and the "high sheriff" who often arrested him.

Man-woman relationships, probaby the most persistent concern of blues lyrics, are also important in traditional African villages, where social harmony is often considered synonymous with or dependent on harmony in the home. And the mixing of the sacred and the profane in black American song lyrics is more easily understood once one realizes that in precolonial Africa these two fields of human activity were not generally thought of as polar opposites. There's a telling photograph from a Nigerian Tiv village in Charles Keil's book *Tiv Song*. A man is squatting on the ground holding a ritual object, a very large clay penis, while a group of male children looks on. It's tale-telling night, a serious occasion when stories having to do with important spiritual concepts and behavioral norms are repeated for the benefit of the young. But the penis is awfully big and awfully stiff, and the man is smirking.

THE STUDY OF RHYTHM AND PERCUSSION in slave music and in the black music of the post–Civil War period has been severely hampered until recently by a lack of documentation and by some unwarranted assumptions. For many years conventional wisdom had it that the Black Codes which banned slave drumming effectively eliminated African polyrhythm from black music in the United States; phenomena such as the very rapid development of jazz drumming after 1900 could be explained by "natural rhythm." But such explanations will no longer wash. The consensus among anthropologists is that cultural intangibles such as a feel for complicated rhythms are learned, not innate.

During the last decade, scholarly detective work on several fronts has finally begun to give us a more complete picture of the fate of African polyrhythms in North America. To begin with, the passage of the Black Codes, which in most states actually predated the Revolutionary War, did not automatically stamp out all slave drumming. An exhaustive analysis of diaries, letters, and travelers' journals from colonial times up to the Civil War, undertaken by Dena J. Epstein and detailed in her book *Sinful Tunes and Spirituals,* yielded a surprising number of references to slave music that was primarily percussive. Usually such music was associated with annual festivals, when the year's crop was harvested and several days were set aside for celebration. As late as 1861, a traveler in North Carolina saw dancers dressed in costumes that included horned headdresses and cows' tails and heard music provided by a sheepskin-covered "gumbo box," apparently a frame drum; triangles and jawbones furnished the auxiliary percussion. Such late accounts are not plentiful, but there are quite a few from the southeastern states and Louisiana dating from the period 1820–1850. Most of the Delta was still Indian territory and wilderness at the time, but it was settled by planters and cleared by slaves who came from these states. Some of the earliest Delta settlers came from the vicinity of New Orleans, where drumming was never actively discouraged for very long and handmade drums were used to accompany public dancing until the outbreak of the Civil War.

Where slaves could not make or play drums they could at least pat juba. "The patting," an ex-slave reported in 1853, "is performed by striking the right shoulder with one hand, the left with the other—all the while keeping time with the feet, and singing." Undoubtedly there were any number of personal variations on this formula. And anyone who has heard the work of a master jazz drummer like Max Roach or Elvin Jones will be well aware that a single gifted musician can muster enough coordination to execute elaborate rhythm patterns in several different meters simultaneously.

The ring shout, a black "holy dance" in which worshipers shuffled rhythmically in a circle, clapping and stamping, seems to have developed with the widespread conversion of slaves to Christianity during the revival fervors of the eighteenth and early nineteenth centuries. The earliest accounts date from the 1840s; more vivid descriptions from the twentieth century leave little doubt that the dancing and stamping constituted a kind of drumming, especially when the worshipers had a wooden church floor to stamp on. "It always rouses my imagination," wrote Lydia Parrish of the Georgia Sea Islands in 1942, "to see the way in which the McIntosh County 'shouters' tap their heels on the resonant board floor to imitate the beat of the drum their forebears were not allowed to have." A recording of a ring shout, made by John Work and Alan Lomax for the Library of Congress in 1934, sounds like a percussion ensemble, with hand clapping furnishing a crisp counter-rhythm to the thudding beat of feet on the floor. This tradition is surely older than the earliest white accounts of it.

In 1942, when Alan Lomax was in Coahoma County recording Muddy Waters and other musicians, he heard about a black band from the Mississippi hill country that had recently visited Clarksdale. This group, led by a multi-instrumentalist named Sid Hemphill, could perform as either a country string band, a brass band, or a fife and drum band. Lomax went looking for Hemphill and his musicians and found them near the little hamlet of Sledge, where the northern Delta country meets the central hills. They were professionals who traveled around Mississippi performing for both whites and blacks, and they had a repertoire for just about any occasion. With Hemphill blowing a homemade fife and the other three musicians on two snare drums and a bass drum, they gave an admirable approximation of a white fife and drum band, playing period pop tunes like "After the Ball Is Over" and "The Sidewalks of New York" in straight march tempo with very little syncopation. But Hemphill, who was born in 1876 and probably played most comfortably in styles that were current around 1900, also played panpipes in the African whooping style, as well as both white country music and blueslike music on fiddle, guitar, mandolin, banjo, and harmonica.

After Emancipation, drumming was no longer forbidden, and many black brass bands and fife and drum bands that included store-bought snare and bass drums were formed. Some of these bands must have approximated white music, but some clearly did not. In 1959 Lomax returned to northern Mississippi, and in the hills east of the Delta he found and recorded some elderly fife and drum musicians who performed in a much more African or at least a much blacker style. Ed Young played repeating, hollerlike melodies with flattened thirds and sevenths on his fife, fluttering one of his fingers rapidly back and forth across a finger hole to produce a voicelike quavering and affecting a hoarse, grainy sound. He also sang out snatches of hollers, spirituals, and popular blues. The snare and bass drummers played syncopated cross-rhythms that rarely fell directly on the downbeats and were designed to stimulate uninhibited, improvisational group and solo dancing. This tradition must have dated back to the latter half of the nineteenth century, and it could not have developed in the first place if there hadn't been a reservoir of polyrhythmic sophistication in the culture that nurtured it. David Evans, an anthropologist who has done extensive fieldwork in the hill country of northern Mississippi, recorded black families there who play polyrhythmic music in their homes on chairs, tin cans, and empty bottles. He reports that among the area's older black fife and drum musicians, making the drums "talk it"—that is, playing rhythm patterns that conform to proverbial phrases or the words of popular fife and drum tunes—"is considered the sign of a good drummer." This enduring tradition of folk polyrhythm played an important part in the development of Mississippi blues.

BLACK AMERICAN MUSIC as it was sung and played in the rural South was both a continuation of deep and tenacious African traditions and a creative response to a brutal, desperate situation. But while some of the earliest slave musicians were making purely African music, others were learning European dance music in an attempt to better their positions in the slave hierarchy, and some became adept performers of European classical music. Dena Epstein has unearthed accounts of gatherings at which some slaves danced to music played on African instruments and sung in African languages while others danced approximations of the minuet to European-style music.

Over the nearly three centuries between the first accounts of slave music in North America and the earliest recordings of black folk music in the South, blendings of innumerable kinds and degrees took place. By the period of the Civil War, almost every conceivable hue of the musical spectrum must have been present to some degree in black folk culture, from the almost purely African to the almost purely white American. And while one would expect to find field workers whose parents were born in Africa playing more African music and blacks whose forebears had been house servants for generations playing in a more acculturated style, this was not always the case. Black musicians, especially professionals whose music is also their livelihood, have always been pragmatic. There must have been a number of musicians who, like Sid Hemphill, could play anything from African whooping music to folk ballads to fiddle and banjo breakdowns to the latest Tin Pan Alley hits, as required.

Long before the Civil War, black professional musicians in the North were playing white classical and dance music and, probably, some early forms of syncopated dance music as well. In the rural South even the musicians who played in plantation orchestras were less than fully professional; they had other duties around the house. Emancipation gave the plantation musician mobility, making true professionalism possible. At the same time, most of the plantation orchestras disappeared due to the harsh economic exigencies of the Reconstruction period. So countless black musicians—fiddlers, banjo players, mandolinists, fife and panpipe players—took to the roads. The great majority of Southern blacks stayed on the land, often on the very plantations where they had been slaves or on other plantations in the neighborhood, but musicians found that they could walk or ride horses, mules, wagons, and trains from plantation to plantation and hamlet to hamlet, playing on town street corners for tips on Saturday afternoons, when the plantation hands crowded in to shop and socialize, and out in the country later, at all-night frolics.

These traveling musicians of the Reconstruction period were called songsters, musicianers, or musical physicianers by their people. (The songsters were wandering balladeers, while musicianers and physicianers were particularly adept as instrumentalists.) Some of them may have played a kind of blues, but the evidence, incomplete though it is, strongly suggests otherwise. If they performed blueslike material, it was almost certainly either narrative ballads with a melodic flavor that approximated what later became known as blues, or songs called jump-ups that strung together more or less unrelated lines, most of them of a proverbial nature, over a simple chorded accompaniment. "See, they had these little old jump-up songs," LeDell Johnson, a Mississippi bluesman-turned-preacher born in 1892 told David Evans when he was asked about the music of his parents' generation. "The little old blues they had to my idea wasn't worth fifteen cents."

For the most part, the songsters' repertoires consisted of country dance tunes, songs from the minstrel stage (some black in origin, some white, some of impossibly tangled pedigree), spirituals, and narrative ballads, all of which reflected considerable affinities with the white country music of the period. But one should think twice about calling this material white-influenced; after all, early white music had drawn heavily on black fiddle and banjo styles and on plantation songs composed by blacks. It would be fairer to say that from the time of the Civil War until the early twentieth century, the music of the songsters and musicianers shared a number of traits with white country music, with musicians of each race borrowing freely from the other.

But even though many white and black *songs* were similar or the same, black performing style, with its grainy vocal textures and emphasis on rhythmic momentum, remained distinctive. And gradually the songsters developed a body of music that diverged more and more radically from the interracial common stock. They made up their own ballads about events in black life, ballads like "Frankie and Albert," which was probably composed in St. Louis in the 1890s when so many Southern blacks were pouring in to look for work that at night the sidewalks and the levee were littered with their sleeping forms. There were songs that celebrated black badmen, like "Looking for the Bully of the Town" and "Stackolee," who was so bad that in some versions he died, went to hell, fought with the Devil and came out on top. There were songs about black heroes like "John Henry," the steel-driving man who challenged a steam drill and won a Pyrrhic victory. And there were more localized ballads, like "The Carrier Line," a song recorded by Sid Hemphill in 1942 but only recently issued that dissected the follies of various whites with cool, pitiless accuracy. Most black ballads were of their time and place and did not outlast it, but a few proved remarkably resilient. "Stack-a-Lee" was a rhythm and blues hit in 1950 for the New Orleans pianist Archibald, and as "Stagger Lee" it became a 1958 rock and roll hit for Lloyd Price.

Jump-ups like the ones Charles Peabody heard his workers from Clarksdale singing in 1901 were much closer to the blues than these ballads. They were already popular in the early 1890s. In 1892, W. C. Handy, who was to achieve fame as a songwriter and popularizer of blues but was then an out-of-work cornet player with experience in black minstrel shows and brass bands, heard "shabby guitarists" in St. Louis playing a tune that began, "I walked all the way from old East St. Louis / And I didn't have but one po' measly dime." "It had numerous one-line verses," Handy recalled in his autobiography, "and they would sing it all night."

Was this a jump-up or a true blues? The question is of some academic interest, but in the context of black folk culture it's meaningless. Handy called the song he heard in St. Louis "East St. Louis Blues." He didn't indicate whether the people who sang it called it that in 1892, but we know that the term "blues" came into currency as a description of a particular kind of music sometime around 1900 and that it was applied very loosely from the very beginning. One can try to be as specific as possible and insist that only songs with recognizable blues melodies and three-line verses in an AAA or AAB format are true blues. These songs, at least the ones with AAB formats, in which each line or thought is stated, repeated, and then answered, developed later than "East St. Louis Blues" and the other early jump-ups, or "one-verse songs" as they were sometimes called. But the black songsters of the early twentieth century weren't particularly discriminating in their terminology; they called several kinds of songs blues. In "Hesitation Blues," which was popular as early as the first decade of the century and was widely recorded beginning in the 1920s, each verse consists of two lines and a refrain, and the melody is ragtime or minstrel influenced. Delta bluesman Charley Patton recorded dozens of blues in an AAB, roughly twelve-bar format, but he also called ballads with eight-bar verses blues—"Elder Green Blues," for example.

One can't even say with certainty that blues was simply a more evolved version of the earlier jump-ups or one-verse songs. Blues is a musical idiom that has drawn on numerous sources, including jump-ups, field hollers (which it most closely resembles melodically), songster ballads (from which it borrowed some imagery and some guitar patterns), church music (which influenced the singing of many blues musicians), and African-derived percussive music (which furnished some rhythmic ideas). Each blues performer draws on a mix of these sources and on the influence of other blues performers and comes up with something that is distinctively his or her own; the only way to define blues with any real precision would be to take the repertoire of every blues performer into account.

THIS IS WHERE REGIONAL DISTINCTIONS come in handy. We can't successfully define blues in a very specific way; we have to be content to talk about a *tendency* toward twelve-bar, AAA or AAB verse forms, or a tendency toward pentatonic melodies with a flattened third. But we can define Delta blues, or the blues of the Carolinas, Virginia, and Georgia, or the blues of East Texas in an acceptably concrete manner, taking as our raw data the work of all the blues singers who learned their music from oral tradition in these regions. And once we take this approach, we can begin to appreciate what made Delta blues unique. Early southeastern blues was lilting and melodic and included more songs of a ballad or ragtime nature than straight twelve-bar, AAB blues. In East Texas, where blues probably developed around the same time as in Mississippi, guitar-accompanied blues tended to be rhythmically diffuse, with guitarists like Blind Lemon Jefferson playing elaborate melodic flourishes to answer their vocal lines. At the same time, the lumber and turpentine camps of Texas and Louisiana spawned a black piano tradition that emphasized driving dance rhythms. Boogie-woogie probably developed out of this kind of playing, which was sometimes called fast western.

The Mississippi Delta's blues musicians sang with unmatched intensity in a gritty, melodically circumscribed, highly ornamented style that was closer to field hollers than it was to other blues. Guitar and piano accompaniments were percussive and hypnotic, and many Delta guitarists mastered the art of fretting the instrument with a slider or bottleneck; they made the instrument "talk" in strikingly speechlike inflections. Eventually Delta blues became firmly established in Chicago and had a profound and direct impact on American popular music. Texas blues migrated to California and became closely associated with the bluesier styles of big-band jazz; the influence of Texas on the Delta, and of the Delta on Texas and California, constitutes a continuing subplot.

Since blues was so firmly rooted in earlier black folk music that it's difficult to say with any certainty at what point it became blues, one would expect the professional black musicians of the period to have found it somewhat familiar. But two of the earliest accounts we have come from the professional entertainers Gertrude "Ma" Rainey and W. C. Handy, and they did not find the new music called blues at all familiar; they found it "strange" and "weird." Rainey was a vaudeville entertainer who sang minstrel and popular songs with a black tent show, the Rabbit Foot Minstrels. In a small Missouri town around 1902 she heard a girl who was hanging around the tent sing a "strange and poignant" song about how her man had left her. The entertainers in the troupe had never heard anything quite like it before and Rainey decided to work it into her act. The response she got from rural black audiences was overwhelming, so she began looking for similar songs as she traveled. When John Work interviewed her in the early thirties, she recalled that she frequently heard such songs after this initial incident but that they were not then called blues.

Handy's reaction to his first encounter with blues in the Delta seems even more curious. He had grown up near Florence, Alabama, not far from the Mississippi line, and his experience as a traveling band musician, playing for tent shows that roamed the length and breadth of the Deep South, had been extensive. He had heard the "East St. Louis Blues" and other jump-ups and one-verse songs as early as 1892, and by the early 1900s he was leading the most successful and progressive black dance orchestra in the Delta; operating out of Clarksdale, his group played ragtime, cakewalks, and other popular and light-classical music from written scores. But when he happened on the blues while waiting for a train in Tutwiler in 1903, it struck him as "the weirdest music I had ever heard."

Tutwiler, which is fifteen miles southeast of Clarksdale on Highway 49, had only a few hundred citizens in the early 1900s, and in the middle of the night the train depot, with closed-up stores in forbidding lines on either side of it, must have been a lonely place. Looking down the tracks, which ran straight off into the flat Delta countryside, Handy could probably hear the ghostly rustle of cypress and willow trees that were watered by nearby Hobson Bayou. The darkened stores, the trees bending and swaying over the track, a stray dog or two—it wasn't much to see, and Handy had seen it all innumerable times. He stretched, contorted his body to try to make it fit the hard contour of the bench, relaxed, and fell asleep.

The train was nine hours late, and sometime during the night a black man in ragged clothes sat down beside him and began playing a guitar, pressing a knife against the strings to get a slurred, moaning, voicelike sound that closely followed his singing. Handy woke up to this music, and the first words he heard the man sing were "Goin' where the Southern cross the Dog." The line was repeated three times, answered in each case by the slide guitar. Politely, Handy asked what it meant, and the guitarist rolled his eyes mirthfully. In Moorehead, farther south near the Sunflower River in the heart of the Delta, the tracks of the Yazoo & Mississippi Valley Railroad, known to the locals as the Yellow Dog, crossed the tracks of the Southern at right angles. The man was on his way to Moorehead, and he was singing about it.

Handy had heard jump-ups with train lyrics in the cotton fields and around the levee camps, where black day laborers shored up the earthworks that protected the Delta's rich farmland from the

Mississippi. But as a schooled musician who could swing a rag-time tune and follow it with a crisp "Poet and Peasant Overture," Handy had paid "primitive music," as he called it, scant attention. Now, suddenly, he was intrigued. *This* music was different. The singing was freely ornamented and the melodic range was narrow—it sounded like a field holler. The guitar part wasn't the sort of strummed accompaniment he'd heard so many black guitarists using since the 1890s, when Sears Roebuck and other mail order concerns had first begun offering guitars at prices even poor people could afford. Nor was it steady, regular picking, as in the fancier ragtime guitar and banjo styles. Instead, the guitar set up an intricate pattern of rhythmic accents and talked back to the singer. It was both a drum orchestra in miniature and another voice.

The voicelike sound of the slider was particularly novel. The slide technique was originally associated with an African instrument that has been reported from time to time in the American South, the single-stringed musical bow. One-stringed instruments played with sliders seem to have survived principally among black children, who would nail a length of broom wire to a wall and play it with a rock or pill bottle slider. The appearance of black slide guitarists in the early 1900s has often been linked to the popularization of a similar technique by Hawaiian guitarists, but slide guitar wasn't native to Hawaii; it was introduced there between 1893 and 1895, reputedly by a schoolboy, Joseph Kekuku. It did not spread from Hawaii to the mainland until 1900, when it was popularized by Frank Ferera, and by that time black guitarists in Mississippi were already fretting their instruments with knives or the broken-off necks of bottles.

Gus Cannon, who was born in northern Mississippi in 1883 and settled in the Delta near Clarksdale in 1895, first heard slide guitar "around 1900, maybe a little before." The guitarist was Alec or Alex Lee, who had been born around 1870 and spent most of his life in the vicinity of Coahoma County. The songs he played with a knife included "John Henry," probably one of the earliest slide guitar pieces, and "Poor Boy Long Ways from Home," a melodious one-verse song in which each line was repeated three times (AAA) and answered by the slider. In Coahoma County in 1900 this was unusual music. Cannon played country dance tunes, jigs, reels, minstrel songs, and a few light-classical pieces on his banjo and fiddle, and the black music he remembers hearing around Clarksdale at the time was made by banjo and fiddle groups, or by guitarists who played ballads, minstrel and medicine show songs, and an occasional jump-up, or by workers and worshipers who sang without instrumental accompaniment. Handy's band, which was all the rage among local blacks who considered themselves sophisticates, featured a fiddler named Jim Turner who did hilarious imitations of barnyard animals on his violin and knew plenty of reels in addition to more sedate dance and concert music. Only Alec or Alex Lee was playing music that could be said to resemble blues.

Cannon's memories of turn-of-the-century music making in Coahoma County confirm the reports of Charles Peabody and W. C. Handy. There was a rich and astonishingly varied music scene—hollers, work songs, spirituals, country string bands, fife and drum and brass bands, homemade percussion, guitar-accompanied ballads and jump-up songs, and upwardly mobile dance bands like Handy's. But with the possible exception of a few songs like "Poor Boy Long Ways from Home" in the repertoires of a few singer-guitarists, there wasn't blues, not before the early 1900s. The earliest Delta blues seems to have originated a little farther south, in the vicinity of the Will Dockery plantation—five thousand acres of bottomland on the Sunflower River about halfway between Tutwiler and the junction where the Southern crosses the Dog.

CHAPTER 2
Heart Like Railroad Steel

People whispered that Charley Patton wasn't his father's natural child, and it was easy enough to see why. Bill Patton, a dependable farm worker and stern Bible thumper who sometimes preached in backcountry churches, was a big man with a dark brown complexion. Charley was small and scrawny—between five feet five and five eight and around a hundred and forty pounds when full grown—and had light, yellowish skin, wavy hair, and almost Caucasian features. "He looked like a Mexican," says Hayes McMullen, who often saw Patton play the blues around the Will Dockery plantation in the 1920s. "He wasn't what you'd call a real colored fellow."

Bill and Annie Patton and their twelve children farmed in southern Mississippi, about halfway between Jackson and Vicksburg near the small hamlets of Bolton and Edwards, when Charley was growing up. It was an area of pebbled soil, occasional hills, stretches of flat prairielike grassland, patches of dense woods, and small farms that were largely devoted to food crops and dairy products. Some of the land was owned by blacks—generally the poorest, rockiest land. The larger farms were owned by whites and employed a few black families as field laborers and domestic servants. For a large black family, living was precarious. In the mid-1890s, when Charley was probably in his early teens (his most likely birthdate is around 1881, though 1885 and 1887 have also been suggested), Bill Patton began to hear about opportunities in the Delta, a hundred miles to the north, and he listened with interest.

For as long as Bill Patton could remember, that northern country had been mostly wilderness. Still farther north, up around Coahoma and Tunica counties, folks had been farming for several decades before the Civil War. They were close enough to the river there to bring in supplies and market their cotton crops without undue inconvenience and expense. The southernmost part of the Delta had been under cultivation for a while, too. But up around the Sunflower River, the land was heavily forested and studded with cypress swamps and dense canebrakes. Alligators slithered through the murky bottoms and panthers stalked deer among the cane.

There were some tentative settlements along the Sunflower, a sluggish yellow river lined with cypress, oak, holly, and tangled willows. But there were few roads, and provisions had to come inching up the Yazoo and Sunflower rivers all the way from Vicksburg, a distance of more than a hundred miles. Finally, toward the end of the nineteenth century, railroads began penetrating the area, and lumbering interests set to work cutting down some of the forests. A few men of means saw the land's potential and bought up huge tracts; one of them was Will Dockery.

Will's ancestors on both his mother's and father's sides had left the Carolinas with their slaves sometime before the Civil War. They settled near Hernando, Mississippi, just south of Memphis in the hill country, and for a while they lived very well, but the Civil War left both families practically destitute. Before the war, they would have sent a particularly bright son to one of the best eastern colleges, but Will's father and mother had a difficult time paying for his education at nearby Ole Miss.

Around 1885, fresh out of college and ready to make his mark in the world, Will left his parents' farm. With the help of his grandmother ("Will," she told him, "here's a thousand dollars and the world to make a living in, and that's all we can do for you") and credit from an uncle who was in the cotton business in Memphis, he established himself in Cleveland, Mississippi, a little settlement that had sprung up not far from the Sunflower River. First he bought land and a sawmill and went into the burgeoning local lumber business. By 1895 he owned a tract of forty square miles that was bisected by the river. Optimistically, for much of the land was wooded and wild, he called it Dockery Farms. He built a home—a frame structure, not ostentatious but pleasant enough and subject to incessant additions—and moved in; soon after that, he took a young wife.

Malaria-carrying mosquitoes bred without interference in the swampland on the property, and the Dockerys were sick so much they couldn't tell half the time whether they had malaria, colds, influenza, or simple exhaustion from the effort of wresting a plantation out of the wilderness. But they persevered. "My father was a pioneer, strictly a pioneer, and a very hard worker," says Joe Rice Dockery, who took over the management of Dockery Farms in 1926. "He was not a playboy in any sense of the word. He loved to develop things and would have loved to just go on and on developing for the rest of his life."

It didn't take long for word to get around that Will Dockery needed manpower (and womanpower) and was willing to pay for it. Like the other landowners in the area, he paid very little: "Many a day has been worked down here for fifty cents a day," says Joe Rice Dockery. But to many Mississippi blacks, even the lowest daily wage was better than trying to eke out a living farming rocky ground or working on a small white-owned farm for room and board. And the system that prevailed in the Delta was flexible enough to offer a variety of options. You could work by the day and be ready to move on at any time, you could work your way up to a more remunerative position, you could enter into one of a number of possible sharecropping arrangements. As blacks from southern Mississippi began drifting north, they found that Will Dockery wasn't interested in tricking them out of their wages or otherwise mistreating them, unlike some other white men, and they told their friends. Bill Patton figured he was in a good position to get a better deal than a common day laborer—he had a big family and could provide plenty of hands at cotton picking time—so in 1897 he and Annie and the children packed up their few belongings and trekked north to Dockery's.

Bill was worried about his son Charley, who had already been playing the guitar for around two years. To a man of God, guitar picking was a sin, and playing reels and other sinful tunes at parties and picnics where gambling and fornication were rampant was tantamount to selling one's soul to the Devil. So when Bill caught his son making music, he considered it his Christian duty to deliver stern warnings and, as the warnings continued to go unheeded, increasingly severe corporal punishment. But Charley kept playing. He would slip away and perform at various social affairs in and around Bolton with members of the Chatmon family, almost all of whom seemed to play at least one instrument. His early jobs were probably mostly for black audiences, but the Chatmons preferred playing syncopated dance music for whites, who paid better and didn't make them work as hard. The family repertoire included just about every kind of music that was popular in the rural South at the time—ballads, ragtime tunes, spirituals, minstrel show and Tin Pan Alley hits, white country dance music, and perhaps a few semiclassical pieces. Charley may have learned some jump-ups during his apprenticeship with the Chatmons, but in southern Mississippi in the 1890s there was no such thing as blues.

Charley was seen with the Chatmons so frequently that people began to say he was really Henderson Chatmon's son. He certainly looked more like the light-skinned Chatmons than like his father; perhaps he encouraged the rumors, stung as he must have been by Bill Patton's harsh words and beatings. The Chatmons themselves have claimed Patton as a relative, at least since his recording successes in the 1920s, but surviving Pattons dispute the claim, pointing out that Annie Patton looked very much like Charley. Her mother was an Indian with some black blood and her father was a white man who made his living trading in the rough and tumble frontier towns along the Mississippi.

If Bill Patton hoped that getting Charley away from the Chatmons would discourage his musical ambitions, and perhaps squelch the rumors about his parentage, those hopes were quickly dashed. Several guitarists were living on the Dockery plantation and at least one of them, Henry Sloan, played a rough, rhythmic sort of music Bill Patton must have found positively barbaric compared to the hot but polite playing of the southern Mississippi string bands. Charley loved the new music and began following Sloan everywhere, watching, listening, and learning. Bill and Annie Patton won the admiration of the community, assumed some responsibility for the running of the plantation, and rejoiced when one of their daughters married a man who worked his way up to a top managerial position, but Charley was soon entirely beyond their control.

Bill Patton probably never understood why a young man who'd had several years of schooling—that was several years more than most of the Delta's sharecroppers and day laborers had had—would want to perform at dances frequented by the most superstitious and illiterate field hands, stay drunk much of the time, live off women who worked in white kitchens, and avoid farming and other work unless it was absolutely necessary for survival. Charley himself wasn't entirely committed to this life-style. Throughout his life he would periodically repent, renounce loose women and alcohol, and take to studying his Bible in preparation for a preaching career. Once, when he was still a young man, he volunteered to preach in a little country church, and although he ran out the back door in a blind panic after coming face to face with the congregation, he later managed to deliver a number of successful sermons. But his conversions never lasted very long. An old friend would show up with a guitar and news of a house party or a big picnic a few miles down the road, and Charley would bottle up and go.

During the two decades following the Pattons' arrival, cheap black labor and Will Dockery's business acumen and determination built the plantation into a large self-contained agricultural empire, linked by horse and river and later by rail and road to holdings he acquired elsewhere in Mississippi and in Arkansas. He left the trees that grew near the banks of the Sunflower River standing, and other stands of timber remained as havens for wildlife, but his laborers systematically cleared and put into cultivation most of the rest of the land. He sold the logs to nearby sawmills and had the stumps and undergrowth burned off; practically every day, year after year, the air was hazy with wood smoke. It hung over the gray-brown earth, refracting the intense sunlight into blindingly bright orange rays so that the whole landscape seemed to be swimming in mud and fire.

Dockery also sent gangs of men out to clear a right-of-way and lay tracks for a railroad link to the outside world. The train that ran on the completed line out to Dockery's was dubbed the Pea Vine by the locals, probably because of its serendipitous route. It started its run in Cleveland around four in the morning, traveled two miles south to Boyle, and then backed out to the plantation's railroad depot, which employed a full-time ticket agent and provided living quarters for his family. Passengers and supplies were unloaded; passengers and, if it was the right season, bales of cotton were taken aboard; and then the train ran west all the way to Rosedale, the largest town on the Mississippi River between Memphis and Greenville. By that time it would be evening, and the Pea Vine would return to Cleveland. At every stage of its journey, the train was crowded with local blacks, and although the connection between Cleveland and Dockery's wasn't used after the late twenties, when improved roads and automobiles rendered it obsolete, the Pea Vine continued to make the rest of the run. In 1929 Charley Patton recorded a "Pea Vine Blues," and it became one of his most popular discs.

I think I heard the Pea Vine when she blowed
I think I heard the Pea Vine when she blowed
Blowed just like my rider getting on board

If you're livin' single then babe you . . . (*phrase finished by
   Patton's guitar*)
      (*Spoken:* Babe, you know I can't stay)
You're livin' single, Lord, you know I ain't gonna stay
I'm goin' up the country, mama, in a few more days

Yes, you know it you know it, you know you done me wrong
Yes, you know it you know it, you know you done done me wrong
Yes, you know it you know it, you know you done done me wrong

Yes, I cried last night and I ain't gonna cry no more
Yes, I cried last night and I ain't gonna cry no more
But the good book tells us you got to reap just what you sow

Stop your way of livin', and you won't . . . (*finished by guitar*)
      (*Spoken:* You won't have to cry no more, baby)
Stop your way of livin', and you won't have to cry no more
Stop your way of livin', and you won't have to cry no more

I think I heard the Pea Vine when she blowed
I think I heard the Pea Vine when she blowed
She blowed just like she wasn't gonna blow no more

NEAR HIS HOME, which overlooked the Sunflower just upriver
from a ferry landing, Will Dockery supervised the building of a
large cotton gin, a post office, and a two-story brick store that employed five full-time clerks and sold everything from seed, corn-
meal, and meat to four-wheel carriages and coffins. In order to
simplify his bookkeeping and avoid having to circulate large
amounts of cash, he issued his own paper money and coins. He
also instituted a system of burial insurance. "Daddy never made a
dollar from that," Joe Rice Dockery maintains. "He saw that the
undertakers were robbing the people blind, and he was just trying
to help his people out. Of course in helping them out, he was
helping himself out because he would've had to put the money
out. The boss man was the head doctor, he was the head burier, he
was the head feeder, he was everything as far as they were concerned."

When I visited Joe and his wife, Keith Sommerville Dockery, in
1979, they were still living in the rambling white frame house on
the Sunflower River. The gin had long since been shut down, but
the lettering on the side of it that faced the road was being scru-
pulously maintained. It said

DOCKERY FARMS

EST. 1895 BY
WILL DOCKERY 1865–1936

JOE RICE DOCKERY OWNER

The elegantly appointed sitting room included a piano, a stereo
system, and a shelf of records, mostly opera. "We do love music,"
said Joe Dockery, a balding, heavyset Cornell graduate with a cor-
dially authoritative manner who was then in his seventies. "Keith
is so enthused about working with the Metropolitan Opera, and
our daughter Douglass has perfect pitch. She finished in music at

Sweetbriar and then studied in Indiana awhile and played the piano for the Houston Ballet." The Dockerys also had a cassette of a television special on Mississippi blues that the state's educational television network produced, with narration by B.B. King. Joe Dockery is on the network's board of directors and took a keen interest in the program. During the early sixties he'd gradually become aware that the blues may actually have begun on his plantation, first through detailed and sometimes eccentric letters from young blues record collectors and later through correspondence with the Jazz Archive at Tulane. "None of us really gave much thought to this blues thing until a few years ago," Keith Dockery said, a little wistfully. "In other words, we never heard these people sing. We were never the type of plantation owners who invited their help to come in and sing for parties. I wish we had realized that these people were so important."

"A lot of the blues singers lived in what they called the quarters," Joe Dockery said, "and that's not a name we gave it. They called it 'quarters' after the term 'slave quarters.' The quarters was a group of maybe eight, ten, twelve boardinghouses and some other houses near the barn and the blacksmiths' shops. Now in many cases, a nigger—and I don't mean anything by that, it's just what they called themselves—had his own eighty acres or a hundred and twenty acres with his garden and his little duck pond and his stables for his own stuff. It just depended on . . . well, on how much effort he was willing to put into things himself. Most of the women wanted flowers, so they'd have flowers, a watermelon patch, whatever they had the energy to do. These were the men who'd taken up with a woman—they'd have what we called a 'plantation license,' they rarely were legally married in those days—and wanted to move out of the quarters and have their own setup. The boardinghouses were places where some old woman boarded half a dozen or so day hands who were bachelors. They came and went, and that's where the blues was played. I mean, you could tell what was going on by where the wagons were or the horses were, or where the automobiles were later on. There were killings, but really very few, and it was nothing premeditated. People would be drinking, and there'd be a spontaneous argument between men in the group. Women played a big part in that. You know the best thing B.B. King said in that program is that the blues means when a man has lost his woman. Which was all he had. He didn't have anything else.

"Now the blues was a Saturday night deal. The crap games started about noon Saturday, and then the niggers would start getting drunk. I've seen niggers stumbling around all over this place on a Saturday afternoon. And then they'd have frettin' and fightin' scrapes that night and all the next day. They made their own moonshine and all that kind of stuff. And of course some of them would end up in jail. There's a story about a psychologist from the North who comes down here and asks this big buck, this bachelor, 'Why do you work hard all week long and then get drunk and throw your money away and have a scrap and get put in jail? Why do you do that?' And he says, 'Boss, has you ever been a nigger on Saturday night?'" Joe Dockery allowed himself a deep chuckle. "Now Charley Patton was around playing on Saturday nights, or going from plantation to plantation, a new woman here and a new woman there, just having a party. Daddy could have told you more about that, because he was closer to it. I think they had to get Charley Patton out of jail about half the time."

Dockery Farms is mechanized now; the quarters and the little houses and shacks scattered around the property are abandoned. Instead of the five to eight hundred blacks who used to live and work there at any given time, a few specialists who live in nearby towns come in every day to drive and maintain a fleet of tractors and other agricultural machines. "The plantations used to have rivalries," said Joe Dockery. "You know, their own baseball teams and Fourth of July picnics and all. There was a certain amount of pride in this place, and it was never known for being savage toward its labor. We didn't exploit people, trick them out of their money because of their ignorance of mathematics and things like that. Some plantation owners did do that. But . . . the system was wrong. Daddy knew that, and I knew it. Everybody knew it." Perhaps, but the system endured until it became more profitable to replace men with machines.

Charley Patton saw a world of changes during the fifty-odd years of his life, but the system was in effect in the upper Delta before he was born, and it outlasted him by several decades. He adapted to it well enough despite his lingering rage, which he tended to take out on his women, sometimes by beating them with a handy guitar. He suffered his dark moods and his occasional repentances and conversions, but he also had fun, or something like it. He rarely worked for whites except to furnish a night's entertainment, and he was never tied to a menial job or a plot of land for very long. He went where he pleased, stayed as long as he pleased, stayed as intoxicated as he pleased, left when he wanted to, and had his pick of the women wherever he went. And he created an enduring body of American music, for he personally inspired just about every Delta bluesman of consequence, and some blueswomen as well. Along with Louis Armstrong, Elvis Presley, and a few others who created not just styles but dynasties, he is among the most important musicians twentieth century America has produced. Yet we know very little about his formative years, and practically nothing about how he learned his art.

WE KNOW EVEN LESS about Henry Sloan then we know about Charley Patton. We know that Sloan was already playing blues in 1897, making him one of the first blues musicians anywhere. We know that Patton dogged his every step, at least for a few years, and it's probably safe to surmise that Patton reworked Sloan's style to fit his own expressive needs, just as Tommy Johnson and Son House later devised very personal and very different reworkings of Patton. We know that Bill Patton once became so enraged when Charley slipped out of the house to play with Sloan that he went after his son with a bullwhip and that he later relented and actually bought Charley a guitar. We know that even though Charley had professional experience from his years in southern Mississippi, he "couldn't really pick a guitar," in the words of his sister Viola Cannon, until he began his "studies" with Sloan. And we know that by 1918, when Sloan followed the swelling tide of black migration north to Chicago, Patton had his own disciples and was the most celebrated bluesman in the vicinity of Dockery's. That was saying a lot, because Dockery's and nearby towns like Cleveland, Drew, and Ruleville already had a reputation. All over Mississippi, they were known as the place one went to learn to play blues.

Elsewhere in Mississippi, the older songster and string band traditions and a lilting, melodious sort of blues that still sounded a lot like nineteenth century ballads and jump-ups were popular. This was the kind of music the lanky, affable Tommy Johnson was singing and playing when he arrived in the area near Dockery's between 1912 and 1914. Tommy had been born in 1896 into a large and musical family that farmed near Crystal Springs, twenty miles south of Jackson. One of his uncles played guitar and harmonica, and other uncles were members of a brass band. They knew sentimental love songs, ballads, and jump-ups, and when Tommy took up the guitar, in 1910 or 1911, these were the tunes he learned. A year or two later he met an older woman, "old enough to be his mother," according to his older brother LeDell, and the two of them left southern Mississippi. They traveled north to the vicinity of Rolling Fork and then settled for a time near Boyle, which was two miles south of Cleveland and directly connected to Dockery's by the Pea Vine. Tommy, still an amateur musician, soon fell under the spell of Charley Patton and the man who was already Patton's almost constant companion, Willie Brown.

Brown, described by Hayes McMullen as "a little brownskin fellow," was born around 1890–95, probably in or near Robinsonville in the upper Delta. By the time he was in his teens he was living around Drew, principally on Jim Yeager's plantation, and learning guitar from Patton. He soon outstripped his mentor in terms of sheer technique. "Willie was a much better musician than Charley," says McMullen, and on the few recordings he made, Brown lived up to his reputation with fast, clean, aggressive picking, inventive bass patterns, extraordinary polyrhythmic dexterity, and such violent string snapping that he must have literally torn the strings off more than one guitar. But even though he made an invaluable contribution to Patton's music—he would keep those irresistible basses rumbling and deftly fill in chords while the older musician threw his guitar up in the air, caught it between his legs, and ran through his other tricks—he never really made a name for himself as a creator and singer of blues songs. His few recordings under his own name are musically excellent but stylistically derivative, primarily of Patton. For the most part, he seems to have been content to work as an indispensable sideman, though he often argued and fought with Charley and one suspects a bruised ego might have had something to do with it.

Tommy Johnson spent a year or two absorbing the music of the Patton-Brown juggernaut and of musicians like Dick Bankston and Ben Maree who played in a related style. When he returned to his family's home in southern Mississippi, he was no longer an amateur. His guitar technique was polished and persuasive, and although he rarely growled and moaned like Patton, he was singing strongly. He began teaching his new music, which included a version of "Pony Blues" and most of the tunes and lyrics he recorded between 1928 and 1930, to his older brother LeDell, who had never heard anything like them.

On the basis of his recordings, Johnson had been decisively influenced by Patton and Brown—their guitar patterns, melodies, and lyrics crop up again and again. But Tommy's style was very much his own. His guitar playing had a slippery, danceable swing that derived from his superbly controlled mixing of duple- and triple-meter picking and strumming patterns, and his voice had a unique crying quality that was particularly effective when he slid into his eerie falsetto, echoing the archaic sound of the field holler. Johnson's music stands next to Patton's as the most perfectly realized and most influential blues to have emerged from the Delta during this early period.

The new music wasn't all Johnson brought back from the vicinity of Dockery's. When he left Crystal Springs, he was a teenager who knew something about women but was otherwise fairly innocent in the ways of the world. He returned home a compulsive womanizer. He wasn't much of a drinker when he left, but after a couple of years in the Delta, he was already well settled into a pattern of acute alcoholism and would drink almost anything— Sterno, shoe polish, denatured alcohol. And he had acquired a sinister reputation to go with his new persona, a reputation he assiduously cultivated. When his credulous brother LeDell asked him how he had learned to play so well in such a short time, Tommy told him, with calculated dramatic flourishes, a story of having sold his soul to the Devil.

"He said the reason he knowed so much, said he sold hisself to the Devil," LeDell Johnson told researcher David Evans. "I asked him how. He said, 'If you want to learn how to play anything you want to play and learn how to make songs yourself, you take your guitar and you go to where a road crosses that way, where a cross-road is. Get there, be sure to get there just a little 'fore twelve o'clock that night so you'll know you'll be there. You have your guitar and be playing a piece sitting there by yourself. You have to go by yourself and be sitting there playing a piece. A big black man will walk up there and take your guitar, and he'll tune it. And then he'll play a piece and hand it back to you. That's the way I learned how to play anything I want."

This story is at least as old as the blues. Its roots are in the voo-doo lore that preserved some African religious beliefs and prac-tices long after the religions themselves had vanished. (In the Caribbean, African religions have survived strongly, and New Or-leans, which was part of the French Caribbean until 1803, is the undisputed center of voodoo in the United States.) The "black man" is recognizable as Legba, a Yoruba trickster god who "opens the path" for other supernatural powers and is traditionally asso-ciated with crossroads. As the only wholly unpredictable deity in the Yoruba pantheon—the rituals that are virtually guaranteed to bring a desired response from all others do not always work in his case—Legba became identified with the Devil of Christianity early on. Slave lore often depicted the Devil as a trickster figure, more like Legba with his mordant sense of humor and his delight in chaos and confusion than like the more somber and threatening Devil portrayed in hellfire-and-brimstone sermons.

Like many of the Delta blues singers who came after him, Tommy Johnson affected a trickster's personality. He took to car-rying a large rabbit's foot around with him and displaying it often, and his performances were spectacularly acrobatic. "He'd kick the guitar, flip it, turn it back of his head and be playin' it," re-members Houston Stackhouse, a bluesman who played with Johnson in the late twenties. "Then he get straddled over it like he was ridin' a mule, pick it that way. All that kind of rot. Oh, he'd tear it up, man. People loved to see that."

Tommy married a woman named Maggie in 1916, and the two of them, along with LeDell Johnson and his wife, headed for the Delta. They settled on Tommy Sanders's plantation near Drew, working as sharecroppers. Patton was living on Dockery's, eight miles away, and Brown was nearby on Jim Yeager's. All these men, who were then in their early twenties except for the somewhat older Patton, played together around the area, singly or in duos or ad hoc string bands. There were other musicians in their circle—Jake Martin, who was born near Patton's original home and followed the migration north to Dockery's around 1916; Jack Hicks, who was also from the country between Jackson and Vicksburg; Dick Bankston, Mott Willis, and Cap Holmes, three particularly adept guitarists; Fiddlin' Joe Martin, who played mandolin and fiddle as well as guitar and was a good man for string band jobs; and Jimmy Holloway, who later became a preacher in Memphis. There were more, too, most of them just names now, some of them highly regarded. They must have had individual styles, lyrics, and song ideas that were their own or became associated with them, and their own students and camp followers. But whatever their individual contributions were, they all learned from Patton, the elder statesman of the bunch, most of them at first hand. And basically they sang and played Patton's brand of music—on this much the survivors seem to agree.

By the mid-twenties, a still younger crop of bluesmen had come along. One of them was Roebuck Staples, who left for Chicago in 1930 and eventually molded his family into a successful gospel and pop group, the Staple Singers. "I was raised on the Will Dockery place from the time I was eight till I got to be twenty years old," he says. "Charley Patton stayed on what we called the lower Dockery place, and we stayed on the upper Dockery. And he was one of my great persons that inspired me to try to play guitar. He was really a great man. At first, I was too small to go hear him on Saturday night, but on Saturday afternoons everybody would go into town and those fellows like Charley Patton, Robert Johnson, and Howlin' Wolf would be playin' on the streets, standin' by the railroad tracks, people pitchin' 'em nickels and dimes, white and black people both. The train come through town maybe once that afternoon, and when it was time, everybody would gather around just to see that train pull up. They'd play around there, before and after the train came, and announce where they'd be that night. And that's where the crowd would go.

"They'd have a plank nailed across the door to the kitchen and be sellin' fish and chitlins, with dancin' in the front room, gamblin' in the side room, and maybe two or three gas or coal-oil lamps on the mantelpiece in front of the mirror—powerful light. It was different people's houses, no clubs or nothin'. And I finally grew up to play." Staples's music is very different now. His group keeps up with the latest trends, employing funk and disco rhythms and full orchestras. But when he picks his guitar by himself, echoes of Patton's playing are still evident.

Robert Johnson, perhaps the most celebrated and star-crossed of all the Delta bluesmen, began following Willie Brown from job to job and picking up pointers from him around 1926, when the two of them were living near Robinsonville, forty miles south of Memphis. Patton would visit the area frequently to play with Brown, and although Robert listened avidly to phonograph records by sophisticated bluesmen like Leroy Carr and Lonnie Johnson, Patton and Brown were his principal local inspirations until Son House settled in Robinsonville in 1930. House's major influences were several Coahoma County musicians who have otherwise remained obscure, but he borrowed at least one of his most characteristic guitar patterns from Patton, and after his rediscovery in the sixties, he told interviewer Jeff Titon that "I would listen to Charley's [records] way before I ever started to play or think about trying to play." Booker T. Washington "Bukka" White, whose early recordings had a decisive impact on Bob Dylan and many other urban folksingers of the sixties, also learned from Patton's recordings. In an interview, White recalled visiting Clarksdale just after the release of a new Patton record and being unable to squeeze into the crowded room where it was being played. When he was a young man, he would often tell friends and acquaintances, "I wants to come to be a great man like Charley Patton." It is striking how often similar phrases come up among Patton's successors. "Charley was heavy, see," says Hayes McMullen. "That's what heavy was. He was very famous then, to my eyes. And he was first."

Howlin' Wolf, one of the most popular Chicago bluesmen and Muddy Waters' chief competitor there during the fifties and sixties, moved to Dockery's from Tupelo in 1926, when he was sixteen. "It was [Patton] who started me off playing," he told Pete

Welding in a mid-sixties interview. "He took a liking to me, and I asked him would he learn me, and at night, after I'd get off work, I'd go and hang around." Wolf's first recording, made at a West Memphis radio station around 1948, was "Saddle My Pony," a version of Patton's "Pony Blues." Patton had been performing it for at least twelve years when Wolf learned it, for it was one of the pieces Tommy Johnson brought back from his first stay in the vicinity of Dockery's. It seems to have been disseminated more widely than any of Patton's other blues, and it is still the song most older Mississippians first think of when his name is mentioned. The version he performed at his first recording session in 1929 went like this:

> Hitch up my pony, saddle up my black mare
> Hitch up my pony, saddle up my black mare
> I'm gon' find a rider, baby, in the world somewhere
>
> Hello, Central, the matter with your line?
> Hello, Central, matter Lord wi' your line?
> Come a storm last night an' tore the wire down
>
> Got a brand new Shetland, man, already trained
> Brand new Shetland, baby, already trained
> Better get in the saddle, tighten up on your rein
>
> An' a brownskin woman like somethin' fit to eat
> Brownshin woman like, sometin' fit to eat
> But a jet black woman, don't put you' hand on me
>
> Took my baby, to meet the mornin' train
> Took my baby, meet that mornin' train
> An' the blues come down, baby, like showers of rain
>
> I've got somethin' to tell you when I gets the chance
> Somethin' to tell you, when I get a chance
> I don't wanna marry, just wanna be your man

"PONY BLUES" depends for its musical effect on an extraordinary rhythmic tension. The guitar part strongly accents the first beat of each measure, while the vocal is just as strongly accented on beat four. Furthermore, Patton carries the note that begins on each accented fourth beat over into the next measure, producing the polyrhythmic effect of a three-beat measure followed by a five-beat measure over the clearly delineated four-beat measures of the guitar part. The rhythmic picture is further complicated by the way both the vocal and guitar parts skillfully weave triplet figures into the piece's duple-meter flow and by Patton's use of off-beat accents, which he bangs out on the body of the guitar. The song's verses are each approximately thirteen and a half bars in length—three four-bar phrases, each followed by a two-bar fill, adding up to a structure that sounds perpetually off-balance and adds yet another dimension of rhythmic complexity.

Most of the rhythmic devices Patton uses have counterparts in West African drumming, and he uses them in an African manner, stacking rhythms on top of each other in order to build up a dense, layered rhythmic complexity. Blind Lemon Jefferson and other Texas bluesmen who were more or less Patton's contemporaries employed polyrhythmic effects in a manner that was essentially linear rather than layered; instead of stacking contrasting rhythm patterns they tended to join them end to end. In this respect, the Texans' work was closer to the period's popular dance music and jazz.

J. H. Kwabena Nketia, the Ghanaian musicologist, has written that "African music emphasizes rapid succession of durational values or changes in impulses and shows preference for this to rapid changes of tone. A piece of music with a narrow melodic range is felt to be dynamic and satisfying if it has a rhythmic drive." And Patton's blues do have a narrow melodic range. Some, "High Water Everywhere" and "Moon Going Down" for example, have three-note melodies. They're built around the tonic, the blue third, and the fifth, although Patton's use of microtonal waverings in pitch and of sliding tones complicates the picture somewhat. The music's harmonic content is almost nonexistent. In some of his blues, changes from the I chord to IV and V are sketched in, but Patton rarely strums a full chord, not even a triad. He picks propulsive bass runs, interjects hammered percussive effects in the treble, and hits the sound box with his palm much more often than he chords.

Patton's recordings of the songster ballad "Frankie and Albert," the hoedown number "Running Wild," and the sentimental ballad "Poor Me" show that he was perfectly capable of performing material with regular eight- and sixteen-bar verses, sedate rhythm patterns, and a broader melodic and harmonic range. Yet in his blues, as the Yazoo Records consortium of blues scholars has noted, "His rhythms assume such importance in each work that they ultimately become the work itself." This rhythmic emphasis was clearly a matter of choice, not of limitation.

The rhythmic density of Patton's music is exceptional, even in an idiom as rhythmically oriented as blues, and so is his frequent use of thirteen-and-a-half-bar verses. According to the anthropologist and blues researcher David Evans, these apparent idiosyncrasies are rooted in pre-blues music. Evans noticed that in the hill country just east of the Delta, where much archaic black music has been preserved, fife and drum bands, guitarists, and young musicians playing a homemade, one-stringed children's instrument called the jitterbug generally structure their performances around repeating one-measure patterns. "In blues with guitar or 'jitterbug' accompaniment," he writes in his article "Afro-American One-Stringed Instruments," "it is necessary to play the full one-measure figure twice after each vocal line. Since vocal lines in blues are usually two and one-half measures in length . . . three-line stanzas of thirteen and one-half measures each are produced."

Evans believes that the use of these one-measure figures as structural building blocks derives from folk drumming and was transferred to the guitar via the one-stringed jitterbug, the first stringed instrument mastered by many early blues guitarists. He has recorded reminiscences of "African-style drumming" taking place in southern Mississippi as late as the 1920s, and a black fife and drum tradition is known to have flourished in Franklin County, not far from where Patton grew up, in the early 1900s. If Evans is correct, the thirteen-and-a-half-bar verses and rhythmic density of Patton's music represent a direct link between the polyrhythmic folk drumming of the nineteenth century and the blues that came after him.

Patton's command of vocal nuance is equally noteworthy. He handled his voice like an instrument, so much so that even though there is no record of his having suffered a speech impediment, his diction was often almost impenetrable, even to his contemporaries. Several of the leading blues collectors of the sixties, having puzzled over certain passages for years, finally played some of their scratchy Patton records for Son House, who expressed complete bafflement and commented that he had always found Patton's lyrics difficult to understand.

Patton often seemed to alter the stresses of conventional speech for purely musical ends. In his recording of "Pony Blues," for example, he stretches certain syllables and inserts split-second pauses between words in order to achieve a desired rhythmic effect. "Come a sto-orm last night and to-o-re the [*pause*] wire down,' he sings, stretching the "down" into the next measure and playing with its timbre by alternately constricting and relaxing his throat muscles. These vocal techniques, along with the ability to hear and execute microtonal pitch shadings, are basic attributes of superior Delta blues singing. And Patton often used a slider to imitate his vocal timbre, timing, and diction on the guitar. In his recording of a "A Spoonful Blues," he repeatedly "says" the word "spoonful" with his guitar instead of singing it. The song can be heard as a conversation involving four voices—Patton's customary singing voice, a womanish falsetto, a lower speaking voice, and the voice of the slider. This is another aspect of Patton's work that seems strongly linked to African roots—music as call and response, as dialogue.

Patton's virtuosity wasn't necessarily evident to the bluesmen who knew him primarily as a live performer. "Everything Charley played, he played in the same tune," complained Hayes McMullen. "A musician, if he gonna make music, well, he need to change the tune sometime." According to Son House, Patton indulged in too much clowning with the guitar—throwing it in the air and catching it, banging on it, playing it behind his back or between his legs—and would often string together poorly enunciated lyrics in patterns that made no sense; he would "make a song out of anything." At least that was House's initial comment when he was discovered living in Rochester, New York, by a team of blues researchers more than twenty years after he had left the Delta. When he heard Patton's recordings again, he was genuinely startled by their excellence.

It's evident from Patton's recordings that he took himself seriously as a creative artist, but his original audience thought of him primarily as an entertainer, and he did most of his entertaining in the quarters on Dockery's, in the homes of enterprising sharecroppers, and perhaps in a few small town cafés or specially constructed juke joints in the country. In these situations, the talk was incessant and boisterous. The sound of the dancers' feet was loud and percussive on board floors, muffled but still rhythmic if the floor was packed earth. Potent white lightning flowed freely, and some drank more noxious concoctions like Canned Heat— Sterno strained through a handkerchief. Musical subtleties were entirely beside the point; Patton's listeners wanted to hear a strong-voiced singer shouting out words they could relate to, and they wanted to dance or at least feel a heady, insistent rush from the rhythmic momentum of the performance.

"I've seen Charley Patton just bump on his guitar, 'stead of pickin' it," says Hayes McMullen. "I bumped on it too. Colored folks dancin' gonna dance all night, and I'd get tired. So I'd get 'em good'n started, you know, I'd be hollerin', and then I'd just be knockin' on the box when the music get going." Musicians who were also visually appealing, like Patton with his acrobatic guitar stunts, were held in particularly high esteem by their audiences. Only the other musicians in the house would listen critically, faulting a bluesman who rapped rather than picked and sang "junk" instead of thoughtfully organized songs.

Patton was underrated by some of his contemporaries precisely *because* he was a consummate Saturday night entertainer. Often he would keep a single guitar pattern going for thirty minutes or more, building up a cumulative, almost hypnotic effect and stringing together verses that might or might not relate to each other in a literary, linear fashion. Some of his records reflect this casual method of organization, and certain melodies and guitar parts repeat from record to record, indicating that what appear to be separate songs because of the limits imposed by recording are in fact fragmentary examples of a kind of music making that could go on "in the same tune" as long as it held an audience's interest.

But when Patton went into the recording studio, he also thought in terms of concise song lyrics. A number of his recorded blues have a definite thematic unity, or at least a unity of feeling or perspective. In the first verse of "Pea Vine Blues," the sound of the Pea Vine train's whistle blowing triggers a sharp image in Patton's mind; he seems to see his rider (sexual partner) getting on board to leave him. In the second verse he counters this disturbing image with braggadocio, asserting that *he's* leaving, "goin' up the country, mama, in a few more days." In the third verse he explains, and reiterates three times for effect, his side of the problem that has been gnawing at the back of his mind: his rider has done him wrong. In the fourth verse he admits he's been crying, says he's determined not to cry anymore, and warns his rider with the biblical injunction, "you got to reap just what you sow," a warning that is made more imperative by the fifth verse ("Stop your way of livin', and you won't have to cry no more"). The sixth and final verse returns to the opening image of the Pea Vine whistle blowing, but this time the third line has the ring of finality: "She blowed just like she wasn't gonna blow no more." "Pea Vine Blues" is a careful, coherent creation that would have been especially meaningful to the people for whom Patton performed, since it not only conjures a complex of emotions that many of his listeners would have shared but makes a vivid mental association between these emotions and an experience that was, in the vicinity of Dockery's, virtually universal: hearing the Pea Vine whistle blow.

"Pea Vine Blues" is also a good example of the way Patton and other country blues singers personalize their creations. If the song is broken down into individual phrases it becomes evident that most and quite possibly all these phrases were unoriginal. They were floating formulas, some of which came from older ballads and spirituals while others were folk sayings or everyday figures of speech. Phrases like "I'm goin' up the country" or "you've got to reap just what you sow" were repeated by countless wandering songsters throughout the latter half of the nineteenth century and probably figured in black music before Emancipation. But while one singer might say, "I'm goin' up the country, mama, in a few more days," another would sing, "I'm goin' up the country, baby, don't you want to go," or "I'm goin' up the country where the water tastes like wine." Certain formulas were flexible enough to admit local references; Patton sang "I think I heard the Pea Vine when she blowed," while a singer elsewhere in the South would have inserted the name of a train from closer to home. Further-more, any formulaic or partly formulaic line could be placed at the beginning or the end of a verse and joined to another line that was either a formula, a combination of a formula and an original turn of phrase, or entirely original. Nobody has ventured to guess how many formulaic phrases, lines, and verses might have been cur-rent among blues singers at any given time; David Evans has written that there is "a vast body" of such material and that "a few dozen to a few hundred of these formulas comprise the repertoires of many blues singers."

Originality in the blues, then, is not a question of sitting down and making up songs out of thin air. Yet a blues singer whose songs consist entirely or almost entirely of borrowed phrases, lines, and verses will claim these songs as his own, and he will be right. From a lyrical point of view, the art of "writing" blues songs consists of combining phrases, lines, and verses with compatible emotional resonances into associational clusters that reflect the singer's own experiences, feelings, and moods and those of his lis-teners. And more often than not, the result is truly original. "Pea Vine Blues," as recorded by Charley Patton in 1929, had its own tune, rhythmic patterns, and guitar accompaniment and com-bined these musical materials in a particular way. Patton probably kept the melody, the rhythm, the guitar pattern, and the "core" verses that mentioned the Pea Vine train and inserted other verses each time he performed the song, adding to it as he went along according to how he felt and how he gauged the audience's re-sponse. "Pony Blues" and most of Patton's other pieces evolved from night to night in the same way, with the lyrics changing while the core verse or verses and the music remained basically the same. With the coming of recordings, which could be played over and over and thus tended to fix the content and order of verses in a song, audiences began to expect to hear roughly the same song every time.

Despite his extensive use of formulas, Patton sang about the way he lived, as his listeners, most of whom knew him at least by reputation, expected him to do. In "Elder Green Blues," he sat-irized whoring preachers, a popular blues theme that must have had particular meaning for him, and celebrated some of his favor-ite pastimes.

> I like to fuss and fight
> I like to fuss and fight
> Lord, and get sloppy drunk off a bottle and ball
> And walk the streets all night

Patton was known for having a "big mouth" and for occasionally provoking fights his slight build and height made him ill-equipped to win, but he did most of his fussing and fighting with his many women. As Joe Rice Dockery surmised, Patton was on intimate terms with women throughout the Mississippi Delta, and probably in north-central Mississippi, Arkansas, and Louisiana as well.

In his blues, Patton frequently criticized women for infidelity ("She's got a man on her man, got a kid on her kid / Baby done got so bold, Lord, she won't keep it hid," from "It Won't Be Long") or greed ("Well these evil women sure make me tired / Gotta handful gimme an' mouthful much obliged," from "Going to Move to Alabama") or cold indifference ("Baby got a heart like a piece of railroad steel / An' if I leave here this mornin' never say, Daddy, how you feel?" repeated in "Heart Like Railroad Steel" and "Rattlesnake Blues"). But his self-portraits were equally merciless. In "It Won't Be Long," he bragged of an affair with a married woman.

> I'll tell you something, keep it to yourself, baby
> I'm gonna tell you something, keep it to yourself, baby
> You don't tell your husband, Lord, and no one else
>
> She's a long tall woman, tall like a cherry tree, baby
> Got a long tall woman, tall like a cherry tree, baby
> She gets up 'fore day and she put the thing on me

"I say I'm just like a rattlesnake, baby, I sting every mare in this world," he sang in "Rattlesnake Blues." And the last line of "Pony Blues" can be taken as a kind of credo: "I don't wanna marry, just wanna be your man." Often his relationships ended abruptly. "He was kinda high-tempered, flighty," says Hayes McMullen. "If those women made him mad, he'd jus' fight, and, you know, knock 'em out with that old guitar. I knew one of his wives, named Lizzie, and she said one day he just walked on off with his guitar and never came back. She hadn't done nothin' to him. He hadn't done nothin' to her. Well, after that, she would talk a lot about how mean he was. But she kept his picture right there on her mantel. She kept it till the day she died." Lizzie would probably have said it was Charley Patton who had a heart like railroad steel.

THERE ARE NO INDICATIONS that Patton rambled any farther beyond the Delta than western Tennessee, eastern Arkansas, and northeastern Louisiana. But within his world, he was constantly on the move, so much so that various reports have him living in several places at once. Around 1924, when he was still ensconced at Dockery's, he struck up a long-lasting relationship with a woman who lived in Merigold, ten miles north of Cleveland on Highway 61. He spent enough time in the town to make the acquaintance of Sheriff Tom Day, Day's successor, Tom Rushen, and a black bootlegger named Holloway, all of whom eventually figured in the witty "Tom Rushen Blues," recorded at Patton's first session in 1929.

There's trouble in the Merigold jailhouse. Day's ambitious deputy, Tom Rushen, is running against him for sheriff. Into this tense situation stumbles Papa Charley, who has apparently fallen into a drunken stupor in some public place and been hauled in by Rushen. In the past Patton wouldn't have minded very much, since Sheriff Day was a regular customer of the bootlegger Holloway and would provide his prisoner with moonshine, perhaps in exchange for a song or two. But now Day is running scared, and Patton has to endure a stretch in jail without his boozey-booze. Despite its generally circumspect wording, the recorded version of "Tom Rushen Blues" is an incisive little gem. It dissects some complex social relationships that cut across racial lines. Musically, it's an unusually effective performance, with plaintive slide guitar echoing the lyrics, an authentically whiskey-soaked vocal, and the cheerful, unexpected confession in the last line.

Laid down last night, hopin' I would have my peace
I laid down last night, hopin' I would have my peace
But when I woke up, Tom Rushen was shakin' me

When you get in trouble, it's no use to screamin' and cryin'
When you gets in trouble, it's no use to screamin' and cryin'
Tom Rushen will take you back to the prison house flyin'

It was late one night, Holloway was gone to bed
It was late one night, Holloway was gone to bed
But Mr. Day brought whiskey taken from under Holloway's head

Awww it's boozey-booze now, Lord, to cure these blues
It takes boozey-booze Lord to cure these blues
But each day seem like years in the jailhouse where there is no booze

I got up this mornin', Tom Day was standin' 'round
I got up this mornin', Tom Day was standin' 'round
If he lose his office now he's runnin' from town to town

Let me tell you folkses just how he treated me
I'm gonna tell you folkses just how he treated me
Aw he caught me yellin', I was drunk as I could be

Residents of Merigold have reported Patton living there between 1924 and 1930, and several musicians encountered him at
Dockery's during this period; he probably lived in a variety of
places with a variety of women, or no place at all. If the tangled
itinerary of his "High Water Everywhere" is to be believed, he was
all up and down the Delta during the winter and spring of 1927,
when the region was buffeted by tornadoes, rocked by earth-
quakes, drenched with the heaviest rains anyone could remember, and finally all but washed away by the rampaging Mississippi,
which overflowed its banks and inundated the lowlands.

Then, as now, the alluvial plain on either side of the river was
protected from floods by a system of earthworks called levees. The
trouble with levees is that they force a river to stay within its
channel, and when an unusually large mass of water is moving
down that channel, the pressure on the levees grows more and
more intense. In 1927 the levee system was still relatively new,
and although high water was expected, the U.S. Army Corps of
Engineers assured the people of the lower Mississippi valley that
the levees would hold. As Pete Daniel points out in his book on the
flood, *Deep'n As It Come*, this overconfidence was to some extent a

byproduct of the optimism of the times. Nineteen twenty-seven was the year Lindbergh flew the Atlantic, the year of the first talking motion picture, the year of Babe Ruth; the coming Depression was not yet in sight. The Army Engineers continued to issue comforting statements as late as mid-April, when hired laborers, predominantly black, were working day and night in the pouring rain to shore up the levees with sandbags while the water licked at their feet. In river towns like Greenville, people stood nervously on street corners looking up at the groaning levees and watching riverboats sail by high above them on the crest of the flood.

On April 21 the river broke through the levee at Mound Landing, Mississippi, twenty miles north of Greenville. The earth shook for miles around, and a wall of muddy water twenty feet high burst out over the cotton fields with a bloodcurdling roar. But once the water had dug a crevasse where the section of levee collapsed, it went about its advance in a less spectacular, more chillingly methodical manner, oozing over the land at a clip of approximately fourteen miles a day. In his book, Daniel quotes the account of a Delta planter, as recorded by a citizen of Greenville: "Standing on the veranda of his handsome home, he saw the flood approach in the form of a tan-colored wall seven feet high, and with a roar as of a mighty wind." By April 23, Helena, Greenwood, Holly Ridge, Indianola, Leland, and scores of smaller towns were under water. At its widest extent, the flood formed a lake almost a hundred miles across. Trees, telephone poles, Indian mounds, the upper floors of multistory buildings, and the tops of some of the levees provided the only immediate refuge.

Disaster followed disaster; it must have seemed that the end of the world was at hand. On May 6 a tornado demolished part of Tunica, Mississippi, in the upper Delta. On May 9 another twister either leveled or heavily damaged every business block in Pine Bluff, Arkansas. Earth tremors rocked Memphis and the northern Delta. In partially flooded Little Rock, Arkansas, a mob wrested a black man accused of attacking two white women away from the police; they hanged him, shot him repeatedly, dragged his body through the streets, and finally burned him near the black part of town, in front of a crowd that included thousands of women and children. The state called in troops to prevent further violence.

Many blacks in rural areas apparently refused to believe the whites' repeated flood warnings until the water actually bore down on them. They climbed into trees or up telephone poles or huddled on top of Indian mounds until they were picked up by rescue boats and taken to refugee camps that had been hastily set up on the flat tops of the levees. At Greenville, an organized committee of white citizens put up a tent city which soon was providing shelter and Red Cross food and relief supplies for ten thousand blacks. But while most of the town's white men had sent their women and children away to stay with relatives or friends, the blacks—men, women, and children—remained crowded into the tents for more than two months, and when the water began to recede, they grew restless. The whites who were directing relief efforts ordered them to stay in the camp until the homes that had been flooded could be cleaned and disinfected, and until it was no longer necessary to feed them at a central location. But soon large numbers of refugees began leaving the camp and spending their days in town, and it became more and more difficult for the whites to round up volunteers to unload food supplies. Apparently, a number of the blacks had felt from the beginning that even though the food was free, those who worked unloading it should be paid.

William Alexander Percy, a plantation owner who was serving as county chairman for flood relief, finally asked the National Guard to recruit a black work team by force. In the course of the "recruiting" a trigger-happy Guardsman shot and killed a recalcitrant black, and the town, still partly flooded, was plunged into a racial crisis. The blacks stood firm, and after a period of extraordinary tension, the Red Cross revised its regulations so that workers unloading relief supplies could be paid. But there was lingering bitterness on both sides. The blacks were convinced that the whites had tried to dupe them in a time of emergency. The whites were convinced that the blacks had failed to help themselves and were as lazy and shiftless as they were popularly made out to be.

The blues Charley Patton recorded as "High Water Everywhere" doesn't mention the tent cities or the shooting in Greenville, and it fails to capitalize on the apocalyptic overtones of the flood and its attendant disasters, which surely must have impressed a man who had tried his hand at preaching. But there is a sense of fear and confusion in "High Water Everywhere," and in the second part of the performance, which finds Patton groaning like an evangelist as he describes the plight of the flood victims, there is compassion. It's possible that verses critical of the whites' relief effort did not get recorded, but it seems more likely that Patton sang about fear, confusion, and compassion simply because those were the emotions he felt at the time. Certainly he knew about the events in Greenville. Everyone in the Delta knew about them, and they made banner headlines in both black and white newspapers across the country. But in the recorded version of "High Water Everywhere," as in "Tom Rushen Blues," Patton found public events truly meaningful only insofar as they impinged on his private world—his perceptions, his feelings.

This is one of the fundamental distinctions between blues and the black music that came before it. Those earlier songs about possums and train engineers and desperadoes deal in archetypes. The singer-narrator remains relatively cool and uninvolved. In blues, there is no narration as such, and while one finds signs and symbols and proverbial homilies aplenty, there is nothing as abstract as an archetype. The singer is so involved that in many cases his involvement becomes both the subject and substance of the work. Such unflinching subjectivity may seem callous and self-involved, but in the context of its time and place it was positively heroic. Only a man who understands his worth and believes in his freedom sings as if nothing else matters.

The backwater done 'round Sumner, drove me down the line
Backwater done rose at Sumner, drove poor Charley down the line
Lord, I tell the world, the water done jumped through this town

The . . . the whole round country, Lord, river has overflowed
Lord, the whole round country, man, is overflowed
    (*Spoken:* You know I can't stay here, I'm goin' where it's high, boy)
I would go to the hill country, but they got me barred

Now looka here now Leland, river was risin' high
Looka here boys around Leland tell me, river was raisin' high
    (*Spoken:* Boy, it's risin' over there, hear?)
I'm gonna move over to Greenville 'fore I tell you good-bye

Look here, the water now lordy, done broke, rose most everywhere
The water at Greenville (*Spoken:* and Leland) mowin' down rows everywhere
     (*Spoken:* Boy, you can't never stay here)

I would go down to Rosedale, but they tell me it's water there
Now the water now, mama, done took Charley's town
Well, they tell me the water done took Charley's town
     (*Spoken:* Boy, I'm goin' to Vicksburg)
Well, I'm goin' to Vicksburg for that high of mine

I am goin' out of that water where lands don't never flow
Well, I'm going over the hill where water, oh it don't never flow
     (*Spoken:* Boy, Sharkey County an' everything was down in Stovall)
Bolivar County was inchin' over that Tallahatchie sho'

Lord the water done rushed all, down old Jackson road
Lord the water done raise-ed, over the Jackson road
     (*Spoken:* Boy, it starched my clothes)
I'm goin' back to the hilly country, won't be worried no more

                 (Part Two)

Backwater at Blytheville, doctor weren't around
Backwater at Blytheville, done took Joiner town
It was fifty families (*Spoken:* and children) suffer to sink and drown

The water was risin' up at my friend's door
The water was risin' up in my friend's door
The man said to his womenfolk, Lord, we'd better dro'

The water was risin', got up in my bed
Lord, the water it rollin', got up to my bed
I thought I would take a trip, Lord, out on a big ice sled

Oh I hear, Lord Lord, water upon my door
     (*Spoken:* You know what I mean?)
I hear the ice boat, Lord, went sinkin' down
I couldn't get no closer, Marion City gone down

So high the water was risin', I been sinkin' down
Then the water was risin', at places all around
     (*Spoken:* Boy, they's all around)
It was fifty men and children, come to sink and drown

Oh, Lord, oh lordy, women and grown men down
Ohhh, women an' children sinkin' down
   (*Spoken:* Lord have mercy)
I couldn't see nobody home and wasn't no one to be found

DURING THE SUMMER OF 1929 Patton was in Jackson, Mississippi, where a white music store owner, Henry C. Spier, arranged to send him up to Richmond, Indiana, to record. Patton spent most of Friday, June 14, in Gennett Records' Richmond studio, a barnlike frame building just a few feet from a railroad track. The building also housed a pressing plant, and the freshly pressed records could be conveniently dispatched by rail, but recording had to stop whenever a train approached. Nevertheless, Patton recorded fourteen tunes that day, including "Pony Blues," "Pea Vine Blues," and "Tom Rushen Blues." He was probably well lubricated—most companies gave "race" and hillbilly artists liquor to loosen them up—but his performances were flawless. Paramount, the company that had underwritten the session, issued a disc coupling "Pony Blues" and "Banty Rooster Blues" almost immediately, and it became, for a "race recording" distributed almost exclusively among Southern blacks, a substantial hit, probably selling in the tens of thousands.

Patton was back at Dockery's in time for the fall harvest, having left his Merigold woman as he had left so many others. But he was spending more and more time in the upper Delta. Sometime during this period he met Henry "Son" Sims, a black fiddler who lived in the vicinity of Clarksdale. When he was contacted by Paramount to make further recordings, he took Sims with him up to the company's new studio in Grafton, Wisconsin. They were a good match. Sims sawed roughly at his instrument, which sounds like it may have been homemade, producing incisively rhythmic lead lines and an unsentimental, astringent timbre. It was probably shortly after these late November–early December sessions with Sims that Patton, rambling through the northern Delta town of Lula, met the woman he was to live with, sometimes harmoniously and sometimes not, for the rest of his life. Her name was Bertha Lee, and she cooked for a white family in the vicinity.

Patton set up housekeeping with Bertha Lee on a plantation near Lula, a hamlet with a population of around four hundred. The new residence gave him access to a wider and somewhat more cosmopolitan world than the one he had known during his years at Dockery's, for Lula was only a few miles by gravel road from the ferry landing at Dundee, and just across the Mississippi from Dundee, commanding a bluff that rises dramatically from the river's muddy banks, was Helena, Arkansas. By 1930 Helena was the Delta's liveliest blues center. As the only river port of any consequence between Memphis and Vicksburg, it boasted a bustling economy. There were always plenty of riverboats tied up by the Helena levee, and the crewmen and stevedores who worked there loading and unloading cotton and other goods were mostly black. With their pay in their pockets and women and entertainment on their minds, they should have been an ideal audience for a celebrated blues singer, and Patton was a celebrity. During 1930, the first year he lived with Bertha Lee in Lula, Paramount issued thirteen of his records and advertised them lavishly in black newspapers across the country. No other blues singer had as many sides released that year.

Nevertheless, Patton doesn't seem to have spent a lot of time in Helena. The blues scene there was fiercely competitive, and many of the cafés and joints featured pianists. They tended to be a more urbane lot than their guitar-playing counterparts; their clothes and their manner were stylish and flashy, and their music was loud and percussive. Patton, already well past forty, would have sounded more than a little old-fashioned by comparison. Many of the younger blues guitarists were beginning to borrow rhythmic ideas from the pianists, especially walking basses and the stomping boogie-woogie beat. Patton's playing was hard-driving, but it didn't have the pummeling regularity many of the pianists favored; it was more freely polyrhythmic. His audience was a country audience, and he seems to have continued to play mostly in the country and the little towns of the upper Delta.

Often he played with Willie Brown, who by this time was living a few miles from Lula in Robinsonville. Their favorite hangout was the Joe Kirby plantation, located near Claxton on Highway 61, where most of the area's moonshine was manufactured. The Kirby plantation boasted another attraction, a spunky little pianist

named Louise Johnson who often performed in a barrelhouse run
by Liny Armstrong. Louise's playing was rocking and muscular.
She'd evidently listened to other pianists on records, but her work
retained some of the flavor of her native Delta. Sometimes she
even duplicated Patton's characteristic bass runs. She also sang,
in a lusty voice that belied her small frame, some very naughty
blues, one of which celebrated in fairly graphic detail the joys of
having sex standing up. "I'm goin' to show all you women," she
bragged, "honey, how to cock it on the wall." Brown met her first
and eventually introduced her to Patton, who was impressed
and began romancing her, presumably while Bertha was busy
cooking.

Eddie "Son" House, a failed preacher, convicted murderer,
solid if rudimentary guitarist, and extraordinary blues singer,
wandered into the Lula area sometime in late 1929 or early 1930
and made the acquaintance of Patton and Bertha Lee. During the
next few months Son and Charley played together frequently, and
House, a careful observer of human nature, watched the way Patton operated with some amusement. "Man, he was tight with
money," House told interviewers Nick Perls and Steve Calt in
1966. "He wouldn't even give Bertha no money much. . . . He
wouldn't even buy food half the time 'cause she's the cook, and
he'd wait on her to come from the white folks' kitchen and bring
him his food. That's the way he ate, out the white folks' kitchen.
He didn't spend anything much. Charley sure was choicy about
that."

House was born in 1902 near the Coahoma County village of
Lyon. As a young teenager, he was a hard worker in the cotton
fields and a passionate churchgoer. He preached his first sermon
at the age of fifteen, and by the time he was twenty, he was pastor
of a small Baptist church in the country just south of Lyon. His
downfall was a woman in her early thirties. After a sizzling affair,
they ran off to her home territory, northern Louisiana, where they
farmed for a while. But House had had his fill of hard manual
labor before he began preaching, and by 1926 he was back in the
vicinity of Lyon, alone. There he drank, rambled, halfheartedly attempted to resume his preaching career, and took up the guitar
under the tutelage of an otherwise obscure thirty-five-year-old
musician named James McCoy.

House learned from McCoy two blues that were to become Delta staples. He recorded them with several different titles and sets of lyrics, but his original recordings, made in 1930, were called "My Black Mama" and "Preachin' the Blues." The former, which included the unforgettable lines "My black mama's face shine like the sun / Lipstick and powder sure won't help her none," furnished the basis for Robert Johnson's celebrated "Walkin' Blues" and for Muddy Waters' "Country Blues," the first song he recorded for the Library of Congress, and "Feel Like Going Home." "Preachin' the Blues" employed some floating verses, like almost every other Delta blues, but it was unusually personal. It vividly described the tussle between the church and the blue devils for House's soul, a tussle the church kept losing.

Oh, I'm gon' get me religion, I'm gon' join the Baptist church
Oh, I'm gon' get me religion, I'm gon' join the Baptist church
I'm gon' be a Baptist preacher and I sure won't have to work

Oh, I'm gon' preach these blues now, and I want everybody to shout
Mmmmm-hmmmmm, and I want everybody to shout
I'm gon' do like a prisoner, I'm gon' roll my time on out

Oh, in my room, I bowed down to pray
Oh, in my room, I bowed down to pray
Say the blues come 'long and they drove my spirit away

Oh, and I had religion, Lord, this very day
Oh, I had religion, Lord, this very day
But the womens and whiskey, well they would not let me pray

Oh, I wish I had me a heaven of my own (*Spoken:* Great God Amighty!)
He-e-e-ey, heaven of my own
Then I'd give all my women a long, long happy home

Yeah I love my baby, just like I love myself
O-o-o-oh, just like I love myself
Well if she don't have me, she won't have nobody else

Hey I'm gon' fold my arms, I'm gon' kneel down in prayer
Oh, I fold my arms, gon' kneel down in prayer
When I get up I'm gon' see if my preachin' suit a man's ear

Now I met the blues this mornin' walkin' just like a man
O-o-o-oh, walkin' just like a man
I said good mornin' blues, now give me your right hand

Now it ain't nothin' now, baby, Lord, that's gon' worry my mind
O-o-o-oh, Lord, that's gon' worry my mind
Oh, I'm satisfied, I got the longest line

Oh, I got to stay on the job, I ain't got no time to lose
He-e-e-ey, I ain't got no time to lose
I swear to God I've got to preach these gospel blues
    (*Spoken:* Great God Amighty!)

Oh, I'm gon' preach these blues and choose my seat and sit down
Oh, I'm gon' preach these blues now and choose my seat and sit down
When the spirit comes, sisters, I want you to jump straight up and down

    Blues musicians were well aware that their singing was comparable to preaching, both in style and in the effect it could have on an audience. "Preachin' the Blues" made the connections explicit in a manner that must have seemed scandalously outspoken to many who heard it. Much was made of Ray Charles's mixing of blues themes and gospel music in the 1950s, but House was preaching the "gospel blues" in the late twenties. The song assumed its final shape after 1927 when Son fell under the spell of another Delta bluesman with a preaching background and strong church leanings, Rubin Lacy, and began emulating his slide guitar style. By 1930, House had fashioned a remarkably pure and original style of his own out of his church roots, the influence of men like McCoy, Lacy, and Charley Patton, and his limited guitar technique. His instrument became a congregation, responding to his gravelly exhortation with clipped, percussive bass rhythms and the ecstatic whine of the slider in the treble. There was nothing fancy about House's music, except perhaps for the rich embroideries that occasionally found their way into his singing, but it was a stark, gripping, kinetic music that demanded to be danced to and would have left few listeners unmoved.
    Practically every man who lived in the Delta in those days carried a gun, and sometimes there was trouble. In 1928 House shot and killed a man at a drunken house party near Lyon, and al-

though he pleaded self-defense, he was sent to the state penal farm at Parchman. He'd always been rebellious—he once told an interviewer how he spent afternoons in a Clarksdale movie theater when he was a teenager, watching westerns and quietly but fervently hoping the outlaws would win—and the experience at Parchman, where he had to work at the sort of manual labor he'd tried to avoid by preaching and singing the blues, made him even more restive. But he was obliging and polite when, after around two years, a judge in Clarksdale reexamined his case and gave him his freedom. The judge also suggested that House leave the vicinity of Clarksdale as expeditiously as possible, a suggestion that he was quick to act on.

Judges in the Delta could dispose of cases involving blacks pretty much as they saw fit. During the twenties, the Clarksdale *Press Register* reported on encounters between blacks and the law in a regular column called "Good Mawnin' Judge." A sample entry from 1927: "Mary Manning, negress, charged with possession of whiskey, was fined $110.00. The court stated that on account of blindness he did not assess her with days in the county jail as it was Mary's first offense. Judge Franklin and police officers stated that they had heard of Blind Tigers, but this was the first time they had ever seen one."

Son fled the area where he'd spent almost all his life, heading north, and on his way through Lula, he encountered Charley Patton. Since the older man liked his music and the nearby Kirby plantation offered plenty of work for a bluesman and plenty of potent moonshine, he decided to stick around. A few months later, in May 1930, a Paramount representative named Art Laibley stopped at Lula on his way to Texas and arranged with Patton for another recording session in Wisconsin. The company had asked Patton to direct talent their way when he recorded the previous summer, and he had brought them the fiddler Henry Sims, who accompanied several of Charley's vocals and recorded four selections of his own. This time Patton recommended Willie Brown, Louise Johnson, and Son House. Laibley entrusted Charley with a hundred dollars to cover expenses on the trip and arranged for a somewhat reluctant driver, singer Wheeler Ford of the Delta Big Four gospel quartet, to transport this lively crew to Grafton.

Just north of Memphis, Ford stopped his Buick by unanimous request so that his passengers, who were crammed in with the three Stella guitars belonging to Patton, Brown, and House, could buy some moonshine. While the teetotal driver sat grimly at the wheel ("I don't claim to be no chauffeur," goes the appropriate blues line, "but I holds it in the road"), everyone else proceeded to whoop it up. Patton and Louise, sitting in the front seat, began arguing, and Louise demanded that Ford stop the car again so that she could get in the back. "That's when it went to happen," House recalled. "Charley, he's mad. He's sitting in the front. Right along . . . I commence to leaning over talking trash to her. I say, 'I really kinda like you, gal.' And we take another big swallow. So when we got to Grafton, Charley didn't know that I had done made her, see. So they have a little hotel there in Grafton, where the recorders stay at. And we's all out getting the grips and every- thing, and so the man come over what attend to the place and giv- ing everybody their keys to the different rooms. So I come up, and they's telling me 'bout 'the man done been here and give us all the keys.' I said, 'Where did he go, 'cause he ain't give me no key,' and so Louise say, 'Yes he did.' I say, 'No he didn't.' Say, 'I got me and your key.' I say, 'Oh, oh, that's it then.' And that's the way it hap- pened. . . . Me and her stayed in our little room."

Everyone went to the recording session together the next day. Even though Patton, Brown, and House had been playing to- gether regularly, it was decided that they should each perform solo, with Brown backing Patton on two of his four selections. Louise cut four boisterous piano blues, including a cleaned-up but still lascivious "On the Wall," with Patton, Brown, and House shouting merrily in the background. In all it was a sparkling ses- sion, with Patton and Brown sounding particularly forceful on their two duets, "Moon Going Down" and "Bird Nest Bound," set to similar guitar accompaniments. In "Moon Going Down," Pat- ton sang about both the upper Delta (Clarksdale, Helena) and his old stomping grounds, Sunflower County. There was some of his familiar boasting, especially in the third verse, a vivid visual image of a favorite whorehouse, but the overall mood was wistful and maybe a little desperate. The last two verses, with their railroad- related images of light, darkness, motion, and loneliness, have the disquieting immediacy of a dream—not a bad dream exactly, but the kind of dream that leaves one with a sharp, unaccountable sense of loss.

Aw that moon is goin' down, baby, Clarksdale sun to shine
Aw that moon's goin' down, baby, Clarksdale 'bout to shine
Rosetta Henry told me, Lord, I don't want you hangin' 'round

Oh well where were you now, baby, Clarksdale mill burned down?
Oh well where were you now, babe, Clarksdale mill burned down?
    (*Spoken:* Boy, you know where I was)
I was way down Sunflower with my face all fulla frowns

There's a house over yonder, painted all over green
There's a house over yonder, painted all over green
    (*Spoken:* Boy, you know I know it's there)
Some of the finest young women, Lord, man most ever seen

Lord, I think I heard that Helena whistle, Helena whistle, Helena whistle
    blow
Lord, I think I heard that Helena whistle blow
    (*Spoken:* Well, I hear it blowin' now)
Lord, I ain't gonna stop walkin' till I get in my rider's door

Lord, the smokestack is black and the bell it shine like, bell it shine like,
    bell it shine like gold
Ahhh the smokestack is black and the bell it shine like gold
    (*Spoken:* Shuckin' you, boy, you know it looks good to me)
Lord, I ain't gonna walk here, tarry 'round no more

Oh yeah evil was at midnight when I hear the local blow
I was evil at midnight when I heard the local blow
    (*Spoken:* Boy, I'm gettin' lonesome —Patton
            Same here, buddy —Brown)
I got to see my rider, when she's gettin' on board

It's impossible to tell whether having been spurned by Louise Johnson, a woman a good twenty years Patton's junior, had affected him, whether he was thinking of Bertha Lee, whether he was feeling older and unwell (for the signs of the heart ailment that would kill him four years later must have been apparent by this time), or whether he was simply mellowing. In any event, his second duet with Brown, "Bird Nest Bound," was the first of Patton's recorded blues to express longing for a resting place, a retreat, a home. It had probably been a long time since Patton felt at home anywhere, if he ever did. One senses genuine regret in the third, fourth, and fifth verses; their images of hopelessness, ambivalence, and the end of another relationship seem to negate the more positive appeal of verses one and two. But then, in a reversal that is without parallel in Patton's recordings, he offers the woman he's addressing a firm, almost otherworldly assurance. Where is the "safe sweet home" he visualizes, and what kind of car will make the trip? Was he thinking of Wheeler Ford's Buick or of a celestial chariot? However one chooses to interpret this final image, "Bird Nest Bound" is plaintive and dazzling.

Come on, mama, out to the edge of town
Come on, mama, go to the edge of town
I know where there's a bird nest, built down on the ground

If I was a bird, mama. . . . (*the two guitars finish the line*)
If I was a bird, mama, I would find a nest in the heart of town
    (*Spoken:* Lord, you know I'd build it in the heart of town)
So when the town get lonesome, I'd be bird nest bound

Hard luck is at your front door, blues are in your room
Hard luck is at your front door, blues are in your room
Callin' at your back door, what is gonna become of you

Some time I say I need you, then again I don't
Some time I say I need you, then again I don't
    (*Spoken:* You know it's true, baby)
Some time I think I'll quit you, then again I won't

Oh I remember one mornin', standin' in my baby's door
    (*Spoken:* Sure, boy, I was standin' there)
Oh I remember one mornin', standin' in my baby's door
    (*Spoken:* Boy, you know what she told me?)
Looka here, Papa Charley, I don't want you no more

Safe sweet home, sweet home, baby, through that shinin' star
Safe sweet home now, through, ahhh, that shinin' star
    (*Spoken:* Lord, you know I'm just stayin' there)
You don't need no tellin', mama, take you in my car

After the 1930 recording session, Patton returned to Lula and to Bertha Lee. Shortly thereafter, he took her back south with him, and they settled in Cleveland, which was no longer the rough little outpost it had been when Will Dockery was carving out his empire. The population was approaching three thousand, and cotton money had brought prosperity; many of the whites lived on pleasant tree-shaded streets in white frame cottages of Greek Revival design. The black section was less appealing, but a little of Cleveland's wealth trickled down to the underprivileged, and on weekends several thousand blacks would swarm into town from the nearby plantations to shop, gossip, see and be seen. Saturday was their day, as surely as Sunday was the Lord's. The whites would finish their business early that morning and retreat to their homes, except for the merchants and salespeople, who staunchly manned their counters while a few white policemen and deputies attempted to keep order. It was a fruitful situation for a blues singer as locally renowned as Patton. He would play on the streets, at the railroad station, or perhaps in a store or café on a Saturday afternoon and work at a country dance later that night.

Sometime during this period someone attempted to slit Patton's throat. Cleveland gossips blamed Bertha Lee; their many violent arguments were a matter of public record. But a niece of Charley's told researcher David Evans that a man (probably a jealous man) attacked him with a long, wicked knife when he was singing one night in Merigold. It wasn't an uncommon sort of occurrence. Leadbelly had his throat cut in a Texas juke joint and survived, but with an ugly scar that ran almost from ear to ear. Patton was scarred, too, and after this cutting scrape his voice seemed to grow more gravelly. But that was the least of his problems. He'd been chain smoking and drinking heavily for years, and he knew his health was beginning to go. He complained of pain whenever he slept on his back, and although he ate ravenously, he wasn't able to put on weight. In drunken fits he would rail against Bertha, or whoever he was with, complaining that his women were starving him. By 1933, when he moved with Bertha Lee to the hamlet of Holly Ridge, he was suffering severe and continual exhaustion and chronic shortness of breath.

In January 1934, W. R. Calaway of the American Record Company began looking for Patton. The Depression, which had hit the recording industry hard during the early thirties, was abating, and someone, perhaps Calaway himself, remembered Patton's popularity in 1929–30. After trying Jackson, where Henry Spier refused to help him, Calaway eventually located Charley and Bertha in Belzoni, a town on the Yazoo River in the lower Delta. Unfortunately, they were both in jail, having become embroiled in a violent scrap at a house party or juke joint. Calaway bailed them out and took them with him to New York City.

If New York impressed Patton, he gave no indication of it in the songs he recorded. In all likelihood, he was so ill that the three days of recording passed in a haze. For the most part, his guitar playing was listless, with little of the old spark; his vocals were heavy and, at times, positively lugubrious. Bertha Lee sang strongly, like a countrified Bessie Smith, on two blues, one of which covered the Memphis Minnie hit "Bumble Bee." Her other selection, "Mind Reader Blues," ostensibly a boast of extrasensory powers, indicated that after four years of living with Charley Patton she didn't really need clairvoyance to guess what was on his mind.

> Baby I can see just what's on your mind
> Baby I can see just what's on your mind
> You got a long black woman with her gold teeth in her face
>
> I take a long look right smack down in your mind
> I took a long look right smack down in your mind
> And I see more women, all up and down the line
>
> Now don't kid your mama, you ain't foolin' nobody but yourself
> Now don't kid your mama, you ain't foolin' nobody but yourself
> And what I see on your mind, you will not have no friends
>
> I remember days when I was living in Lula town
> I remember days when I was living in Lula town
> My man did so many wrong things that I had to leave the town
>
> Down by the riverside my man is got a transfer boat
> Down by the riverside my man is got a transfer boat
> And last time I seed him, with a gal way up the road
>
> Well I'm worried now and I won't be worried long
> Well I'm worried now and I won't be worried long
> Well I'm worried now and I won't be worried long

Charley accompanied "Mind Reader Blues" with some of the most unimaginative guitar playing of his recording career. In his own blues, he seemed to clearly anticipate what was coming. "Poor Me," a sentimental country ballad, repeated twice the lines "Don't the moon look pretty shinin' down through the tree / I can see Bertha Lee, Lord, but she can't see me." In "34 Blues," he anticipated 1935 with a plea: "And it may bring sorrow, and it may bring tears / Oh Lord, oh Lord, let me see a brand new year." He also recorded six religious songs, as many as he had cut at all his previous sessions combined. They were a morbid lot. "I've Got a Mother Up in Kingdom," "Oh Lord I'm in Your Hands," and "Oh Death" were three of the titles.

Patton and Bertha Lee returned from New York early in February, and Charley died on April 28. The death certificate blames a mitral valve disorder. The trouble probably began years earlier, with a childhood case of rheumatic fever or, more likely, with the contraction of syphilis when he was a young man. He had consulted a doctor, probably for the first time in his life, between April 17 and April 20. Delta blacks rarely went to local doctors, all of whom were white, and Son House once opined that if Patton had wanted to consult a specialist, he would have sought out a hoodoo doctor or root man.

Patton's niece told David Evans that Charley lay on his deathbed for a week and spent most of it preaching, returning obsessively to his favorite sermon. He had recorded a version of this text, which was drawn from several different chapters of Revelations, at his second session in 1929:

Well, friends, I want to tell you, they tell me when He come down, his hair gonna be like lamb's wool and his eyes like flames of fire, and every man gonna know He's the son of the true living God. Round his shoulders going to be a rainbow, and his feet like fine brass. And my friends, I wanted you to know again, He said that He going to have a river water that's flowing through the garden, 'clared the preacher. And he's gonna have a tree before the twelve manners of food, and the leaves gonna be healing damnation, and the big rock that you can sit behind, the wind can't blow at you no more, and you gonna count the four and twenty elders that you can sit down and talk with and that you can talk about your trouble that you come . . . world that you just come from.

The images of hair like lamb's wool and feet like fine brass are from Revelation 1:14–15; 1:17–18 states, "And when I saw him, I fell at his feet as dead. And he laid his right hand on me, saying unto me, Fear not; I am the first and the last; I am he that liveth, and was dead; and, behold, I am alive for evermore, Amen; and have the keys of hell and of death."

According to his death certificate, Patton expired in a house at 350 Heathman Street in Indianola, a town some twenty miles south of Dockery's. The document doesn't mention Bertha Lee; the only informant gave the name Willie Calvin, a name that meant nothing to Son House or any of Patton's other surviving cohorts. Bluesman Honeyboy Edwards says he learned of Patton's death shortly after it occurred, at a plantation store just south of Indianola. He was told that Charley had been living with Bertha Lee in a rented room above the store and playing for Saturday night parties at an Uncle Sherman's house. Did he leave Bertha Lee at the very last, rent a room, and die alone or with members of his family? Or did Bertha Lee (who insisted in an interview she gave Bernard Klatzko a few years before her own death that Patton expired in her arms with the words, "Honey, from now on you're going to have it tough") decline to get involved in the postmortem, perhaps because she and Charley had never been legally married? The death went unreported in the local and national press, and we will probably never know.

WHILE CHARLEY PATTON CONTEMPLATED his imminent departure for a safe, sweet home, where he would finally find shelter from the cruel wind that had blown him so precipitously through the world, a man named James Coyner was leaving Indiana and returning home to his mother, who was farming a small plot of land about a mile from Cleveland, Mississippi, and needed his help. It was unusual for a black to own land in the Delta, let alone a black woman; Coyner had come from ambitious stock. It was perhaps even more unusual for a Delta black to read Schopenhauer and William James, as Coyner did. He'd had plenty of time to ponder their concepts of fate and free will since 1926 or

'27, when he began serving a three-to-ten-year sentence at the Indiana State Prison near Michigan City for stealing the body of a white woman from a graveyard.

The area around Cleveland and Dockery's had changed since Coyner's youth and Charley Patton's heyday. For one thing, the burning off and clearing of large tracts of land had largely been completed, and with the end of the frontier spirit that had accompanied intensive development came a palpable constriction of horizons, of possibilities. As towns like Cleveland grew from precarious crossroads settlements into communities with a life and purpose of their own, they attracted more and more poor whites from the hills who brought to the Delta's paternalistic social structure an atmosphere of barely repressed violence, a burning need to acquire money and power, and an outspoken racism that neatly suited their purposes. They went to work in stores that some of them eventually bought, they started other businesses and brought their kinfolk and friends in to help run them, and before too many years had passed, they controlled most of the newer Delta towns economically and politically. The balance of power was shifting, and the planter class, never numerically strong, could only watch it shift. Meanwhile, blacks could hardly fail to notice that incidents of harassment, incarceration on trumped-up charges, and lynching were on the increase. The Delta, already tense, coiled tighter and tighter.

Somehow the tension that erupted always seemed to carry sexual overtones. A white woman in a town or on a small farm would allege that she'd been raped by a black, and a likely suspect—perhaps an actual rapist, perhaps a local troublemaker, perhaps someone fated to be in the wrong place at the wrong time—could always be found. When the planters were the Delta's absolute masters, they usually tried to prevent lynchings, but once a mob from a town like Cleveland or Clarksdale got its hands on a rape suspect, there was little a planter or even a group of planters could do, especially when the town police were the mob's overt or tacit accomplices.

James Coyner felt the Delta's racial and sexual tensions thundering within himself, and in the essays of Schopenhauer and James he believed he'd found the justification to act. One night in late December, while his mother slept, he concealed a pistol, a knife, and a blunt instrument under his coat and made his way to a small house on the outskirts of Cleveland where a white man, his pregnant wife, and their young son lay sleeping. He shot the man in the back of the head, bashed the boy's skull in, battered the woman's head against the bedroom wall until her brains splattered over the pillowcase, cut slices of flesh from her legs and thighs, and ripped the unborn child from her womb.

Within a few days, white women in Cleveland began receiving anonymous obscene letters. At the same time, federal officials investigating a rash of similar letters that were being received by women in Indianapolis noticed that all the letters bore a Cleveland, Mississippi, postmark. Coyner, who subscribed to an Indianapolis newspaper, was easily apprehended when he visited the Cleveland post office to collect his mail. Since federal investigators were involved, there was no chance for a lynch mob to form. Coyner was spirited away to the state capital in Jackson before anyone in Cleveland knew of his capture. His prison record in Indiana quickly came to light and a few days later, he confessed. But he still had to be returned to Cleveland for his trial.

Both the sheriff of Bolivar County and the district attorney formally asked Governor Conner to send in the National Guard. It was a suicidal decision politically, since every poor white who wanted to lynch Coyner was also a potential voter and the blacks were effectively disenfranchised. But the sheriff was not running for reelection, and anyway, everyone knew that bringing Coyner back to Cleveland without the militia would guarantee a quick lynching, and perhaps a full-scale race war. So six hundred National Guardsmen, recruited from counties that were a good distance away, were mobilized and sent in. The Cleveland courthouse was surrounded by barbed wire, machine-gun nests were set up behind sandbags, and the nearby streets were cleared. More troops set up positions on the roofs of adjacent buildings and on the courthouse lawn, and Coyner was driven from the train station to the jail and then to the courthouse surrounded by rows of Guardsmen with fixed bayonets.

During times of high racial tension, rural blacks stayed away from Cleveland, and town blacks stayed indoors. But the news of the Guard's arrival spread like wildfire, and on the morning of the trial, the streets were as thick with blacks as if it had been a Saturday afternoon. Poor whites were there in abundance, too, and the two groups eyed each other silently while the Guardsmen kept their weapons at the ready and their eyes open. Inside the courthouse, the sheriff produced near-pandemonium by producing from a small box squares of the murdered woman's skin; they had been tanned like leather. Coyner, who had been lecturing his guards on Schopenhauer and James throughout the trip up from Jackson and was now sitting quietly and calmly, betraying not a trace of emotion, was sentenced to be hanged on March 5 in Jackson.

David L. Cohn, whose book *Where I Was Born and Raised* contains the most detailed and vivid description of the trial, interviewed some of the poor whites who were milling in sullen knots beyond the barbed wire barricades. "I wish they'd lemme have him," said a man in an Army overcoat left over from the World War. "I'd cut out his black balls and throw 'em to the hogs." Another man pointed at the Guardsmen and said contemptuously, "Niggers are a-braggin' on ever' plantation in the county that the government's protectin' 'em, and we gonna have to kill a lot of the black bastards to knock some sense into their kinky heads." The blacks seemed surprisingly lighthearted, almost festive. A few were selling cold drinks to the crowd and the Guardsmen. Many of them assumed that President Roosevelt had dispatched the troops in order to prevent local whites from massacring them wholesale. Why shouldn't they celebrate? Washington hadn't sent them such an unmistakable sign that the President was concerned about their welfare since the day Lincoln set them free. Later, after the troops left and James Coyner was quietly executed and life went on as usual, they began to remember that Washington was very far away.

PART
II

CHAPTER 3
Mojo Hand

Muddy Waters' juke house was in full swing. The home-made whiskey was selling briskly, fish were frying in the kitchen, and under the flickering light of coal oil lamps, knots of men were throwing dice, squinting intently to make out the numbers that came up. Muddy was playing the blues, with his childhood friend Scott or the grizzled fiddler and guitarist Son Sims helping out from time to time. When the hour grew late, he pulled out a metal kazoo, shoved it in a wire neck rack, and sang jazzy, trumpetlike phrases into it while bearing down on the rhythm. "At night," he remembers, "in the country, you'd be surprised how that music carries. The sound be empty out there. You could hear my guitar way before you get to the house, and you could hear the peoples hollerin' and screamin'."

The stranger stopped just inside the door and coolly took in the action. He was elegantly dressed and carried himself proudly; even among Muddy's diverse customers, whose clothing ranged from dusty overalls to Saturday-night finery, he stood out. When he tried his hand at the dice and the cards, the news of his arrival rippled through the crowded room. Calmly, imperturbably, he won game after game. "He been down to New Orleans," Muddy heard somebody say. "Got himself a mojo, a gamblin' hand."

Muddy had seen plenty of mojo hands. They were little red flannel bags that smelled of oils and perfumes; some were pierced by a needle or two. You bought them from a "doctor," a specialist in charms and magic. "We all believed in mojo hands," Muddy says. "You get you a mojo, and if you're gamblin', it'll take care of that; you win. If you're after the girls, you can work that on the woman you want and win. Black people really believed in this hoodoo, and the black people in Louisiana was a little more up into that thing than the peoples in the Delta part, as far as makin' things that would work."

Muddy put his guitar away and eased across the room to watch the stranger roll the dice. Pretty soon he was taking his turn, and his friend Scott was drawn into the action too. It didn't take the stranger long to practically clean them out. People were crowding around the circle of lamplight there on the board floor, shaking their heads and muttering darkly. The stranger took time out for a drink, and Muddy and Scott had a hushed conference in the corner. They'd always heard that pepper and salt would "kill" a gambling hand; here was their chance to find out.

They disappeared into Muddy's kitchen and came back with handfuls of ground chili peppers and salt. The stranger was back in the game. By this time news of his presence had spread around the plantation, and every man who considered himself a gambler was waiting to test his luck. Muddy watched, expressionless. The lamplight hit his high cheekbones and cast Fu Manchu shadows up over his slitted eyes. While the stranger kept one eye on Muddy and the other on the game, Scott circled casually around the action, until he was close enough to slip a pinch of chili pepper into the pocket of the stranger's jacket. After a suitable interval, Muddy strolled around the growing crowd and casually dropped salt on the floor all around the stranger, making sure to lightly dust his shoulders as well. Then he signaled Scott with a quick glance, and the two of them got back into the game.

Sitting in his kitchen in the suburbs of Chicago more than forty years later, rolling an inch or so of champagne around in his long-stemmed goblet, and shooting knowing grins at his man Bo, Muddy laughed deeply. "We gambled all that night," he said, "and after we put the pepper on him and salted him down, he got unlucky. We won the shoes off his feet! We thought we'd killed his mojo. So the next day I goes into Clarksdale and goes to see the doctor. He was about the age I am now, and he was a long, tall guy with real light silver-gray hair, no bald on his head. He looked weird, and he had weird ting-a-lings hanging up there in his place. He did some real fine writin' on a little piece of paper, rolled it up reeeeal tight, sealed it in an envelope, put some perfume on the envelope, and told me I wasn't supposed to open it. I paid three dollars for it, I believe. And it was two or three years before I won another quarter!" Bo squealed and wheezed with laughter.

"Imagine," Muddy added, "I thought we had done killed the man's mojo, and instead of me goin' and buyin' me some food or some clothes, I bought me a mojo with my little money! After two or three years, man, I got mad. I got broke once in a crap game, and I decided I'm gonna open it and see what's in it. And it was just some little writin'—'you win, you win, you win, I win, you win, I win.' I had it read to me." He looked down at the table for a few seconds, thinking to himself. "It's just a con game on people's heads, you know, gettin' the fools. And these mojo doctors was drivin' big cars, owned big homes, 'cause the peoples was brainwashed. My grandmother and father, their mother and father, was so brainwashed, they thought people could point their finger at you and make snakes and frogs jump out of you, or make you bark like a dog. They said if they get some of your hair from a certain spot right on the top of your head, and bury it or put it in runnin' water, that could give you a headache. Now that could be possible. And I think down in Louisiana, they could've had a few things that would do somethin'. But if such a thing as a mojo had've been good, you'd've had to go down to Louisiana to find one. Where we were, in the Delta, they couldn't do nothin', I don't think. And there is no way I can shake my finger at you and make you bark like a dog, or make frogs and snakes jump out of you." Muddy laughed heartily. "Bull*shit*," he added emphatically. "No way."

"But you know, when you're writin' them songs that are coming from down that way, you can't leave out somethin' about that mojo thing. Because this is what black people really believed in at that time. We played so many times, 'I'm goin' down to Louisiana / Get me a mojo hand,' and I tried to make it a picture so you could see it, just like you're lookin' at it. When I was singin' it, I didn't believe in it no way. But even today, when you play the old blues like me, you can't get from around that. I'd get so many requests, I could play 'Goin' to Louisiana' every night if I would do it."

"Louisiana Blues" was Muddy's first nationwide hit. He recorded it for the Chess label on October 23, 1950, with Little Walter's harmonica providing spare, evocative echoes to his powerful singing and slide guitar while bassist Big Crawford and drummer Elgin Evans laid down a loping double-time. It entered the *Billboard* rhythm and blues chart (which had been called the "Race Records" chart until 1949 and was a weekly tabulation of the records blacks were buying) during the first week of 1951 and attained a top position of number ten. In several of his subsequent rhythm and blues hits, Muddy offered elaborations on the hoodoo theme. "I got a black cat bone / I got a mojo too / I got the John the Conqueroo / I'm gonna mess with you," he sang, unforgettably, in "I'm Your Hoochie Coochie Man," a song written for him by Willie Dixon that reached number eight on the r&b chart in 1954.

But "Louisiana Blues," the first really successful recording of the new, heavily amplified Delta blues and the song that established the imperial, commanding persona Muddy would project on virtually all his subsequent hit records, was special. It had the *power*—a force that Muddy's hardcore fans, most of whom were from or of the Delta, could not ignore. The power was in the tune, a variation on the venerable Delta standard "Rolling and Tumbling." It was in the supercharged whine of Muddy's electric slide guitar, which introduced "Louisiana Blues" with a quavering, voicelike phrase built around the tonic and a flattened seventh and then kicked into the rhythm and the first verse with a chilling, deeply bluesy falling fifth. It was in the clarity, presence, and intensity of the recorded sound, which seemed to fairly leap out of the grooves of the blue-labeled 78-rpm disc.

I'm goin' down to Louisiana
Baby behind the sun
I'm goin' down to Louisiana
Honey behind the sun
Well y'know I just found out
My trouble's just begun

I'm goin' down to New Orleans
Get me a mojo hand
I'm goin' down to New Orleans, umm-hmmm
Get me a mojo hand
     (*Walter, shouting:* Aw, take me witcha, man, when you go!)
I'm gonna show all you good-lookin' women
Just how to treat your man

Whether Muddy believed in the power of the mojo hand or not (and even today he seems ambivalent), "Louisiana Blues" had a power all its own—the power of the Delta's deepest music unleashed full force by the power of electricity. It was irresistible, but then Muddy had always been that.

MUDDY WAS BORN MCKINLEY MORGANFIELD on April 4, 1915, in Rolling Fork, Mississippi, which is in the southernmost part of the Delta on Highway 61, about halfway between Vicksburg and Greenville. His father, Ollie Morganfield, farmed and played some guitar, but Muddy never had a chance to learn from him because his parents separated and his maternal grandmother took him to live with her in the countryside nearby when he was six months old. Three years later she carried him north to Coahoma County, where she set up housekeeping on the Stovall plantation. Theirs was one more journey in the south-to-north movement that had brought the Patton family to Dockery's plantation in 1897 and deposited Tommy Johnson in the same area around 1912–14. But by the time Muddy and his grandmother settled on Stovall's, the promise of industrial jobs was drawing more and more blacks from the upper Delta farther north to Chicago. Charley Patton's mentor, Harry Sloan, left Dockery's for Chicago, never to be heard of again, around 1918, within a year or so of young Muddy's arrival.

Like the countryside in the vicinity of Dockery's, Coahoma County was still partly wilderness in those days. Bears and panthers lurked in the remaining uncut forests along with deer, rabbits, squirrels, coons, and other game. But the Stovall plantation was hardly a pioneer outpost. Much of the land had been cleared and cultivated by the Choctaws long before they ceded it to the United States government in 1830, in the Treaty of Dancing Rabbit Creek. Colonel William Howard Stovall, who owned and operated the plantation when Muddy lived there, arrived in the area from Memphis around the end of World War I and took over from his mother—the land had been passed down through the women of the family since the 1840s, and somehow they'd managed to hold onto it through the Civil War and Reconstruction. It was rich cotton land, close to the Mississippi and, except for a few patches of woods and the cypress-shaded bottoms that provided natural drainage, flat as a tabletop.

"The peoples lived scattered way apart," Muddy remembers. "Our little house was way back in the country. We had one house close to us, and then the next one would've been a mile. If you got sick, you could holler and wouldn't nobody hear you. We had our own horses, mules, cows, goats, and chickens, and I watered 'em from the time I was a kid. Had to pump the water, and that pump would put blisters in my hand. Even for one cow, you gotta pump a lot of water. She'd take two draws out of one of those big tubs, swallow twice, and that'd be it."

Even before he got to Stovall's plantation, McKinley had been rechristened Muddy. "When I got big enough to crawl around, I would play in the mud and try to eat it," he says. "My grandma started that Muddy thing, and after we were up there near Clarksdale, the kids started the Waters." By that time he was a budding musician. "When I was around three years old, I was already beatin' on bucket tops and tin cans. Anything with a sound I would try to play it. I'd take my stick and beat on the ground tryin' to get a new sound and be hummin' my little baby song along with it. My first instrument, which a lady give me, was an old squeeze box, old accordion. I must've been five. I never did learn to play anything on it, and one of the older boys pulled it apart. The next thing I had in my hand was a Jew's harp. I learned pretty good on that thing, and then when I was about seven, I started playing with what they call the French harp at home, the harmonica. That's when they started in with the Waters, and that was even what my family started to call me: 'Go on, ol' Muddy Waters.' I didn't like that. It made me mad, but that's the way it goes on me, you know.

"Now when I was nine, I was gettin' a *sound* out of the French harp. When I was thirteen, I was very, very good. I was playin' it with my friend Scott at fish fries, picnics, and things. I should never have given it up! But then when I was seventeen, I put the harp down and switched to the guitar. The first one I got, I sold the last horse we had. Made about fifteen dollars for him, gave my grandmother seven dollars and fifty cents, I kept seven-fifty and paid about two-fifty for that guitar. It was a Stella. The peoples ordered them from Sears and Roebuck in Chicago. I got about three guitars from Sears and Roebuck before I came up this way."

Now that they were a two-guitar team, Muddy and Scott found more work. "We could make more sound with the two guitars," he explains. "But it was so long before I even made a dollar! Coming up through my childhood life, I tried to stay with the music, but we didn't get no pay for it—fifty cents, seventy-five cents. You couldn't stay there with it if you ain't got it deep down in your soul."

Though he never tried his hand at preaching like Son House, Muddy did go to church. "Can't you hear it in my voice?" he asks. "I'd go every Sunday. Plenty of people would stay up all night and listen to the blues and go home, get all ready, and go to church. Back then there was just three things I wanted to be—a heck of a preacher, a heck of a ball player, or a heck of a musician. I *always* felt like I could beat plowin' mules, choppin' cotton, and drawin' water. I did all that, and I never did like none of it. Sometimes they'd want us to work Saturday, but they'd look for me, and I'd be *gone,* playin' in some little town or in some juke joint."

Between helping out around his grandmother's house along with a shifting cast of siblings and other young people, laboring in the cotton fields, and playing his harmonica and then his guitar around the immediate area, Muddy had little time for schooling. The subject came up near the beginning of our conversations when I asked about his friend Scott's last name. Various writers have transcribed Muddy's pronunciation of it as Bowhanna, Bowhandle, and Bohannon. I asked how it was spelled, and Muddy and Bo tossed it back and forth, trying various finely shaded pronunciations, trying to remember exactly what the name had *sounded* like. Eventually they settled on something close to the fairly common surname Bohannon. "I had bad schooling," Muddy explained. "Went to about the second or third grade, and what I learned to do, I was doing *that* really wrong."

He laughed softly when he said that and glanced down appreciatively at the champagne in his glass. Near-illiteracy had been a handicap, but he was living better than most of the Delta people who'd moved north, and there was no compelling reason to regret circumstances buried deep in the past. Besides, his lack of schooling had also been a source of strength. Like almost anyone who grows up without the benefit of book learning, Muddy discovered at an early age that he had to use his eyes and ears. He has learned to read fairly adequately by this time, but he still sizes up whoever he's talking to in quick takes from behind those lazy-looking eyelids, noting the most fleeting changes in facial expression while listening carefully for telltale shifts in vocal pitch and emphasis. This built-in radar saved Muddy's life more than once in the rough-and-tumble of Deep South and Northern ghetto joints and taverns, but it's more than survival equipment. Without it, Muddy probably wouldn't be the great and subtle vocalist he is.

Singing the blues—and this is particularly true of the Delta's deep blues—involves very precise manipulations of vocal timbre, very subtle variations in timing and inflection, very fine gradations in pitch. When Muddy sings, he screws up the side of his face and then relaxes it, opens and contracts his throat, shakes his jowls, constantly readjusts the shape (and thus the resonating capacity) of his mouth cavity, all in order to get different, precisely calibrated vocal sounds, from the purest falsetto to deep, quivering moans to a grainy, vibrato-heavy rasp. It's possible to catch more urbane blues singers like Kansas City's Joe Turner or Memphis's Bobby "Blue" Bland using some of the same tricks. Like Muddy, Turner and Bland perfected their art when they were functional illiterates.

Muddy's timing is a kind of standing joke (a joke always tempered with respect and, in some cases, with bafflement) among musicians who have played with him. "I'm a delay singer," he says. "I don't sing on the beat. I sing behind it, and people have to delay to play with me. They got to hang around, wait, see what's going to happen next." But his mastery of the fine points of intonation is the true glory of his singing. Those infinitessimally flattened thirds, majestic falling fifths, and glancing slides between tones all *mean* something, just as the slightest shift in the pitch level of a person's speech means something when someone who hears as acutely as Muddy does is listening. Exactly how flat he sings a note will depend on where in the melody line that note falls (a purely musical value) and on the emotional weight of the feelings the line is meant to convey. As in the singing of the Akan of Ghana, the flatter the pitch, the more intense the feeling. One recognizes in this artful pitch play an unmistakable reflection of the African preoccupation with music as language and, more specifically, of the pitch-tone languages so many Africans spoke when they first arrived in the Americas.

Muddy uses his slider to execute comparable subtleties on the guitar. Listen to his solo on "Honey Bee," which is on several of the Chess Muddy Waters album compilations. A musician trained in, say, the classical music of India, which puts a premium on the ability to hear and execute fine microtonal shadings, would recognize in the astonishing precision and emotional richness of the variously flattened thirds and fifths sprinkled through the solo something very close to his own tradition. Literacy, which trains one to focus on the linear continuity of words and phrases rather than on their intonational subtleties, tends to obliterate such minutely detailed and essentially nonlinear modes of expression. Perhaps this explains why many of the young, city-bred blacks who have taken up the blues in recent years have had almost as much trouble playing music as subtle as Muddy's as the legions of blues-smitten whites.

Muddy doesn't think in terms of microtones, of course, but when he's asked about "notes that would fall between the cracks on the piano," he nods his head emphatically. "Yeah, yeah," he says, "but these days there's just no hope of getting my bands to play any of that part of it—no way. When I play on the stage with my band, I have to get in there with my guitar and try to bring the sound down to *me*. But no sooner than I quit playing, it goes back to another, different sound. My blues looks so simple, so easy to do, but it's not. They say my blues is the hardest blues in the world to play."

He learned with his ears, then, and by watching mature masters like Charley Patton and Son House. The basis for his music came from the Delta's common stock, the legacy of Henry Sloan,

Tommy Johnson, Patton, House, and dozens of other musicians, known and unknown. "It just came down from nation to nation, you know, from the top of the old blues thing that all the black people were into," he says.

One of the first Delta standards Muddy learned was "Walkin' Blues." "That was the theme in Mississippi," he says. "Most every guitar player played that." He later transformed "Walkin' Blues" into the first blues he recorded for the Library of Congress ("Country Blues") and one of the first he recorded for Chess records in Chicago ("I Feel Like Going Home"). Another early favorite was "Catfish Blues," a brooding, minor-hued drone piece that seems to have originated around Bentonia in southern Mississippi and was first recorded by Tommy McClennan and Robert Petway, two musicians who were popular around the Delta town of Greenwood, in 1941. From "Catfish" came Muddy's 1950 Chess recording "Rollin' Stone," which gave "the world's greatest rock and roll band" and the world's most successful rock newspaper their names, and "Still a Fool," probably the most impassioned and *electric* performance of his recording career. And he learned "Rollin' and Tumblin'," which he recorded several times in more or less traditional versions before he reworked it into "Louisiana Blues." In addition to mastering these specific tunes, he absorbed a certain way of doing things, a "sound." "Every country had its own music," he says, "and I got the Delta sound. There's so many musicians, they can sing and play the guitar so good, but they can't get that sound to save their life. They didn't learn that way. That's the problem. They learned another way, and they just can't get it."

But Muddy wasn't a rustic, isolated "folk artist" who only learned from the local tradition in which he was immersed. "The lady that lived across the field from us had a phonograph when I was a little bitty boy," he says. "She used to let us go over there all the time, and I played it night and day. Then we had one at my grandma's house later on." By the time he began playing guitar, he'd been listening to records by popular blues artists like Blind Lemon Jefferson, Memphis Minnie, Leroy Carr, Lonnie Johnson, and Tampa Red, not to mention local favorites Charley Patton and the Mississippi Sheiks, for more than five years. And after he married (at the age of eighteen), moved out of his grandmother's house, and opened his own juke house, he put in a new jukebox that played the latest blues hits.

THE FIRST BLUES heard outside the rural South was performed and disseminated by black vaudeville entertainers, like Ma Rainey, who stumbled on the music in the course of their travels. Subsequently, W. C. Handy and other "legitimate" musicians began publishing blues compositions, many of which were derived or stolen outright from folk sources. Handy's tunes, especially "Memphis Blues" and "St. Louis Blues," were similar to the popular ragtime pieces of the day. Each had several themes, only a few of which were recognizably related to authentic blues either musically or lyrically. Once such compositions became widely popular through sheet music sales, it wasn't long before they found their way onto discs.

Phonograph records had existed since 1897, when the National Gramophone Company introduced them as an alternative to the recorded cylinders invented by Thomas Edison in 1877. A few black artists who hoped to appeal to a white audience were recorded during the late 1890s and early 1900s—vocal ensembles singing formal arrangements of spirituals, or "Negro novelty" performers like George W. Johnson, whose biggest hit was "The Whistling Coon." But apparently the idea of making recordings by and for blacks hadn't occurred to anyone in a position to do anything about it when the so-called blues craze hit around 1914–15, so Handy's "blues" and the blues of other popular tunesmiths, black and white, were recorded by whites, many of them specialists in Negro dialect material.

Such recordings are rarely heard today, but some of them probably reflected contemporary black folk styles with at least a modicum of accuracy. One of the few examples available on lp (on the album Let's Get Loose: Folk and Popular Blues Styles from the Beginnings to the Early 1940's, issued by New World Records) is "Nigger Blues," copyrighted by a white minstrel entertainer from Dallas in 1913 and recorded in 1916 by a Washington lawyer and businessman, George O'Connor. The dialect is grotesquely transparent, and O'Connor further betrays his racial identity by singing perfectly articulated major thirds, without a hint of "blue" pitch treatments. But the verses were already traditional among blacks. One would later figure in a memorable recording by the Delta bluesman Robert Johnson.

You can call the blues, you can call the blues any old thing you please
You can call the blues any old thing you please
But the blues ain't nothing but the doggone heart disease

Jazz recording began in 1917 in much the same way—with a white group, the Original Dixieland Jass Band, recording in a style they'd learned from blacks. Then, in 1920, the New York–based black vaudeville singer Mamie Smith made several recordings with jazz band accompaniment, including "Crazy Blues." The number was more a vaudeville tune than a blues, and the singer's urbane style was accurately reflected by her label billing— "Mamie Smith, contralto." But "Crazy Blues" was closer to the main currents of black popular music than anything that had been on records before, and it sold tens of thousands of copies, alerting recording executives to a vast untapped market. More blues recordings followed. Almost all of them were by women who sang on stages with accompaniment by schooled pianists or jazz bands, though a few of these performers, including Ma Rainey and the exceptionally popular Bessie Smith, sang extravagantly blue thirds, affected rough, grainy vocal timbres, and won loyal followings in the rural South. Gradually, authentic down-home blues singers found their way onto records, beginning with the southeastern blues-ragtime guitarist Sylvester Weaver in 1923, continuing with black minstrel show entertainers like Daddy Stovepipe and Papa Charlie Jackson in 1924, and culminating in 1925 with the first Paramount recording sessions by Blind Lemon Jefferson.

Sammy Price, a black pianist who'd studied formally with Booker T. Washington's daughter and was working in a Dallas music store in the mid-twenties, wrote to Paramount's recording director to recommend Jefferson. Price was still performing widely in 1979 and had fond memories of the blind, guitar-playing bluesman he'd heard as a child. "Blind Lemon was using the term 'booger rooger' and playing in that boogie-woogie rhythm as far back as, oh, 1917–18, when I heard him in Waco," the pianist recalled one night, between sets in a Greenwich Village nightclub. "A little later, in Dallas, he used to spend every day walking from one end of town to the other, playing and singing on the street and in various taverns for tips."

On his records, Jefferson would often start off playing a rocking rhythm, only to stop playing at the end of a vocal line, hammer on the strings in imitation of what he'd just sung, and then plunge back in with a snappy, syncopated figure. He was a loose, improvisational, sometimes anarchic guitarist, and his jazzy single-string work bore fruit in the 1940s in the pioneering electric blues of T-Bone Walker, who grew up in Dallas and used to occasionally accompany Jefferson on those walks across town.

Jefferson's singing combined sprightly phrasing with an ever-present hint of lonesome melancholy, and he seemed to know and be able to remember an astonishing number of blues verses and themes. Some of his records—"That Black Snake Moan," "Match Box Blues," "See That My Grave's Kept Clean"—made such a lasting impression on Southern bluesmen that they were copied more or less exactly for decades; a surprising number of verses and entire Jefferson pieces were still turning up on down-home blues discs in the 1950s. But the almost immediate success of Jefferson's records also had to do with Paramount's innovative mail-order service, which penetrated into rural communities without local record dealers. In September 1926 the Paramount company struck pay dirt again with Arthur Phelps, a personable singer and phenomenal blues and ragtime guitarist from Florida (or possibly the Georgia Sea Islands) who was also blind and recorded as Blind Blake.

In June and again in November of that year, the Okeh company made the first recordings of Mississippi Delta blues. The artist, Freddie Spruell, who recorded as Papa Freddie and Mr. Freddie, was already living in Chicago and made his records there. Almost nothing else is known about him, but he may well have been one of the thousands of Delta blacks who took the Illinois Central north during World War I. Whatever his exact origins were, the records he made in the 1920s, especially "Low Down Mississippi Bottom Man" (1928) and several versions of the same piece with different words, offer convincing evidence that he either spent

time on or near Dockery's or learned from someone who had. The
piece is unlike anything recorded by any other blues artist up to
that time and seems to be Spruell's version of a Dockery's favorite
that Patton and Tommy Johnson both recorded, the former as
"Moon Going Down" and under several other titles, the latter as
"Big Fat Mama." Spruell cut "Low Down Mississippi Bottom
Man" in or around July 1928; Tommy Johnson recorded "Big Fat
Mama" in Memphis in August of the same year; Patton made his
very first recordings in June 1929; and the Delta bluesman Kid
Bailey (with Willie Brown on second guitar) recorded "Mississippi Bottom Blues," his own version of the theme, in September
1929. Since Tommy Johnson's relatives have confirmed that
Tommy was already playing "Big Fat Mama" when he returned
from his first visit to the Delta, around 1914–16, it seems likely
that Spruell, whose other recorded pieces have a similar if more
elusive Delta flavor, learned it there himself. His lyrics offer further evidence:

> In the low lands of Mississippi, that's where I was born
> In the low lands of Mississippi, that's where I was born
> Way down in the sunny South, amongst the cotton and corn
>
> Honey, down in the Delta, that's where I long to be
> Way down in the Delta, that's where I long to be
> Where the Delta bottom women are sure goin' crazy over me
>
> I'm lookin' for a woman who's lookin' for a low-down man
> I'm lookin' for a woman who's lookin' for a low-down man
> Ain't nobody in town get more low-down than I can
>
> I likes low-down music, I likes to barrelhouse and get drunk too
> I likes low-down music, I likes to barrelhouse and get drunk too
> I'm just a low-down man, always feelin' low-down, that's true

Spruell never sold impressive quantities of records and made a
total of only ten sides before slipping back into obscurity, but the
success of Blind Lemon Jefferson and Blind Blake led the record
companies of the day to begin a serious search for down-home
blues talent. Since few of the company artist-and-repertoire men
who supervised recording sessions had a very clear idea of what

would sell to rural blacks—a few A&R men were educated Northern blacks, but most were white—a broad spectrum of music was preserved on discs. For however widely blues had spread at the turn of the century, when it seems to have been known principally and perhaps only in Mississippi and Texas, by 1926 it was performed throughout the Southern states as well as in cities like Chicago and St. Louis that had large black populations with rural origins.

Following the example of the pioneering A&R man Ralph Peer, who took remote recording equipment designed by a former associate of Thomas Edison's south to Atlanta in June 1923, some of the larger companies, including Columbia, Vocalion, and Victor, began sending field units south. First they would find a suitable location, usually a hotel suite or ballroom or an empty warehouse or industrial loft, in a city like Atlanta, Dallas, Fort Worth, Memphis, Charlotte, or Jackson, Mississippi. Then they would arrange to have their presence announced in local newspapers and, where possible, over the radio, and audition all the aspiring musicians who showed up. Other companies engaged Southern record and phonograph dealers to audition musicians, who were then sent north to record. Both methods yielded profitable results, and quickly.

In 1927 a medicine show entertainer named Jim Jackson who was born in Hernando, in the north-central Mississippi hills, and made his headquarters in Memphis, traveled to Chicago to record for Vocalion. His first release, "Jim Jackson's Kansas City Blues," racked up astonishing sales, leading some latter-day record collectors, who found copies of it everywhere they canvassed for old 78-rpm discs, to call it the first blues million-seller. Others have questioned this figure, but the record was immensely popular and the song became a standard among Mississippi and Memphis bluesmen. Muddy Waters' friend Robert Nighthawk and a white hobo and songster from Arkansas, Harmonica Frank Floyd, recorded versions of "Kansas City Blues" as late as 1951. (Jackson's song should not be confused with the blues that begins "I'm goin' to Kansas City, Kansas City here I come," which was written by two white teenagers, Jerry Leiber and Mike Stoller, in 1952.)

In 1928 pianist Leroy Carr and guitarist Scrapper Blackwell recorded "How Long—How Long Blues," another best-seller, at a radio station in Indianapolis. Theirs was a more urban, sophisticated sound, with Carr singing softly and plaintively over his rolling piano rhythm while Blackwell punctuated with aggressive, single-string lead guitar fills and punching bass riffs. That same year, Tampa Red (born Hudson Whittaker in Lee County, Georgia) and Georgia Tom (born Thomas A. Dorsey in Carroll County, Georgia) recorded a bantering double-entendre ragtime tune called "It's Tight Like That" in Chicago and scored another race hit. Both songs, and the progressive styles of both piano-guitar duos, survived into the postwar years. "How Long—How Long" is a blues band staple even today, and the first recorded collaboration between Muddy Waters and Little Walter, in 1948, produced "I Want My Baby," one of countless "Tight Like That" derivatives.

Other early blues successes included Lonnie Johnson, an accomplished and versatile guitarist from New Orleans whose discs ranged from self-accompanied blues to impressive jazz solos with the Duke Ellington orchestra; Blind Willie McTell, the crying singer and twelve-string guitar virtuoso, who first cut his enduring "Statesboro Blues" (a rock hit for the Youngbloods and the Allman Brothers Band) when a Victor recording unit visited Atlanta in 1927–28; the Mississippi Sheiks, whose "Sitting on Top of the World," recorded in Shreveport, Louisiana, in 1930 became a Delta and Chicago blues standard and a 1957 r&b hit for Howlin' Wolf; the tough, creative guitarist and singer Memphis Minnie, who was born in Algiers, Louisiana, grew up in Memphis, and recorded her celebrated "Bumble Bee" in New York and again in Memphis in 1929 and 1930; and of course Charley Patton, whose 1929 recording of "Pony Blues" sold well all over the South.

Stylistically, the early blues recording stars were a mixed lot. There was a world of difference between Jim Jackson, whose style and repertoire smacked of nineteenth century minstrelsy, and the very modern Carr and Blackwell, whose recordings prefigured the city blues that would flower in the late thirties. The good-time picking of Blind Blake was mush flashier and more melodic than the harsh, deep Delta blues of Charley Patton. Bessie Smith and other jazz-accompanied blueswomen retained their popularity as well. Muddy Waters listened to them all. One might suppose that because they came into his life through a new and almost magical medium they would have turned his head completely, leading him to forget his local roots and emulate styles that were nationally popular. But that didn't happen, not to Muddy and not to the other Delta musicians of the period. They studied new blues records carefully, learned the songs, borrowed guitar riffs and other touches that appealed to them, but somehow when they repeated what they'd learned, the music came out Delta blues. The first two songs Muddy mastered on the guitar came from records, which, unlike live performances, could be repeated over and over at the student's discretion. The records were Carr's "How Long—How Long Blues" and the Sheiks' "Sitting on Top of the World." But instead of imitating the city slickness of the former and the country string-band lilt of the latter, Muddy played both of them with a bottleneck, in the stinging, heavily rhythmic Delta style of local influences like Son House. Similarly, he tampered with Memphis Minnie's "Bumble Bee" until he'd made it into his own "Honey Bee," which later became one of his classic recordings for Chess.

THE MAN WHOSE RECORDS Muddy learned the most from was Robert Johnson. Robert was only four years older, spent most of his childhood in or near the upper Delta hamlet of Robinsonville, borrowed the themes for several of his most gripping blues from Son House, and didn't make his first recordings until 1936, when Muddy was already an accomplished guitarist. But the virtuosity and force of Johnson's music simply overwhelmed Muddy, who actually saw him only once: "It was in Friar's Point, and this guy had a lot of people standin' around him. He coulda been Robert, they *said* it was Robert. I stopped and peeked over, and then I left. Because he was a *dangerous* man. I got to see his picture a little while back, and since I've seen it, I think I really heard him."

There's more than a trace of lingering awe in this description, which Muddy has repeated more or less verbatim to several interviewers. Robert Johnson wasn't *physically* menacing: he was slender, small-boned, brown-skinned, and handsome enough, with his delicate features and wavy hair, to attract legions of female admirers, but he started more fights than he finished. He was considered dangerous because he was in league with the Devil. "Hello, Satan, I believe it's time to go," he sang in his "Me and the Devil Blues" with a kind of grim relish that convinced his listeners he was ready.

Johnson was born in Hazelhurst, Mississippi, down below the Delta south of Jackson and Crystal Springs, on May 8, 1911. His mother, Julia, had been married to Charles Dodds, a relatively well-to-do black furniture craftsman and landowner, but several years before Robert was born, Dodds injured a member of a prominent white family in a fight and fled to Memphis with a lynch mob at his heels. Robert's father was a man named Noah Johnson, about whom almost nothing is known, and his earliest years were spent with his mother in Delta labor camps and on various plantations. Julia and Robert tried living with Charles Dodds in Memphis for a few years, but he'd taken a mistress and the experiment didn't work out. Robert stayed on in the city for another year or two. Around 1918 Dodds sent him to live in Robinsonville, where Julia and Robert's new stepfather, Dusty Willis, looked after him until he was eighteen.

With three different fathers before he was seven, a series of sudden uprootings, and a succession of name changes, Robert had a confused and confusing childhood. In Memphis he'd taken the name Spencer, Charles Dodds's assumed name, but when he was in his teens, his mother told him about his real father, and he began referring to himself as Robert Johnson. By that time he was interested in music, having, like Muddy, progressed from the Jew's harp to the harmonica to the guitar. One of the first songs he learned to pick was Muddy's early favorite, "How Long—How Long Blues" by Leroy Carr. The tune must have seemed to be the epitome of world-weary sophistication to a black teenager growing up in the Delta in 1928: "How long, how long has that evenin' train been gone? / How long, how long, baby, how long?"

At the same time, Robert began hanging around with Robinsonville resident Willie Brown, who demonstrated some of the fingering and chording techniques for which he was so widely respected. Charley Patton would visit Brown from time to time, and Robert would follow the two of them to picnics, juke houses, and country stores, carefully studying both their solo work and their practiced interplay. It was during this period, in February 1929, to be exact, that he met and married sixteen-year-old Virginia Travis. The couple moved in with Robert's half-sister and her husband on the Klein plantation near Robinsonville, and apparently the man who would later compose and sing "Me and the Devil Blues" and "Hellhound on My Trail" was an attentive husband. But in April 1930, Virginia died in childbirth, along with their child. Coming on the heels of Robert's unstable early years and his adolescent crises of identity (to some people, he was still Robert Dodds or Robert Spencer), this must have been a crushing blow.

A few months later Son House arrived in Robinsonville and began playing with Willie Brown and Charley Patton (who'd become a more frequent visitor since meeting the pretty young pianist Louise Johnson). House became Robert's favorite musician, both for his simple, clean slide guitar playing and for the almost frightening intensity of his music, an intensity not even Patton could match. But before long, Johnson, who was still a novice and often an object of ridicule when House, Patton, and Brown were drunk and feeling mean, abruptly left the area. He returned some time later—a few months according to some accounts, but in fact probably more like a year—singing and playing with the dazzling technique and almost supernatural electricity that were so evident on his first recordings in 1936. Years later, several of Johnson's relatives told blues researcher Mack McCormick that Robert had sold his soul to the Devil and claimed they knew the exact backcountry crossroads where the deal was made. "The Devil came there," said one, "and gave Robert his talent and told him he had eight more years to live on earth." Robert probably encouraged the rumor, as Tommy Johnson had years earlier.

The facts, insofar as they've been pieced together by McCormick and other diligent blues researchers, are that after Johnson left Robinsonville he returned to the vicinity of Hazelhurst, which he must have only dimly remembered from his earliest childhood, and married an older woman. She worked to support him while he developed his guitar playing under the tutelage of a musician named Ike Zinneman, who was from Alabama and claimed to have learned to play by visiting graveyards at midnight. Hazelhurst is close to Crystal Springs, and Tommy Johnson, who was living there again after his years in the Delta, may well have crossed Robert's path. Certainly Robert would have *heard* of Tommy Johnson, his huge rabbit's foot charm, and his supposed covenant with Satan, for Tommy was the most popular and influential bluesman in the area and was still enjoying widespread esteem because of his recordings of 1928 and 1930. According to information turned up by researcher David Evans, the two men may even have been distantly related. Oddly, though, little of Tommy's music seems to have rubbed off on the younger man; perhaps Robert considered it old-fashioned. It's difficult to judge how much impact Ike Zinneman had since he never recorded, but certain songs Robert later recorded that sound more like melodious East Coast blues than like the harder, harsher music of the Delta may have come from him—"From Four Till Late," for example, and "Last Fair Deal Gone Down."

When Robert returned to the Delta after his stay in Hazelhurst, Son House, Willie Brown, and other former associates were amazed by the progress he'd made, and no wonder. House and Brown listened to the popular race records like everyone else and weren't above borrowing from them, but their styles and repertoires had been shaped mostly by local influences and weren't particularly susceptible to innovation. Robert Johnson had absorbed their tradition and broadened it enormously by incorporating musical influences from a variety of sources—Ike Zinneman's flowing East Coast style, Leroy Carr's distinctive melodies and chordal figures, the aggressive single-string picking of Scrapper Blackwell and Lonnie Johnson. All these influences except for Zinneman came from phonograph records, and during the next few years, while Robert was cementing his reputation as the most formidable young bluesman in the Delta, he borrowed heavily from recordings by three more musicians—Kokomo Arnold, Peetie Wheatstraw, and Skip James.

Arnold, a slide guitarist from Georgia who settled in Chicago in 1929, enjoyed a nationwide race hit in 1934 with his "Old Original Kokomo Blues," a relative of a 1928 "Kokomo Blues" by guitarist Scrapper Blackwell. Robert fashioned his celebrated "Sweet Home Chicago" from Arnold's piece by radically reworking the guitar accompaniment and revising the lyrics. The Arnold record's flip side, "Milk Cow Blues," later an early regional hit for Elvis Presley, must have impressed Robert as well, for he combined it with some lyrics from Son House's "My Black Mama" to make his "Milkcow's Calf Blues." And hearing Arnold sing "I believe, I believe I'll dust my broom" on his next record, "Sagefield Woman Blues," must have inspired Johnson to invent his celebrated signature piece, "Dust My Broom." Even Robert's "Dust My Broom" guitar riff, a dramatic full-octave slide that somehow has never grown stale despite countless reworkings (Elmore James in the fifties, Fleetwood Mac in the sixties, George Thorogood in the seventies), seems to have been adapted from the more fluid, less aggressive, but still recognizable bottleneck guitar fills on "Sagefield Woman."

Arnold made his living as a bootlegger and considered recording blues hits a sideline, but this fact wasn't advertised, and Robert probably never knew much about him other than his music. But William Bunch probably worked harder at projecting an image than any other blues artist of the period, and it was an image Robert Johnson took a fancy to. Bunch billed himself as Peetie Wheatstraw, the Devil's Son-in-Law, the High Sheriff from Hell. He recorded more than 160 blues between 1930 and 1941 and was one of the most popular and widely imitated bluesmen of the period, but little is known about him. He was born in 1902 in Ripley, Tennessee, a farming community north of Memphis, and apparently he grew up in the Arkansas Delta. But his musical career and biography begin, for all practical purposes, when he arrived in St. Louis, probably around 1929–1930. The city itself, and violent, wide-open East St. Louis across the Mississippi River in Illinois, were well known among traveling bluesmen, especially pianists. Roosevelt Sykes, Walter Davis, Lee Green, and Sunnyland Slim, all accomplished ivory ticklers and all products of the Mississippi-Arkansas Delta, were either St. Louis residents or frequent visitors in the early thirties, but Bunch, who played both piano and guitar, quickly established himself as their peer. His rocking, two-fisted barrelhouse piano work was simple, effective, and instantly recognizable. His most distinctive calling card, though, was an utterly unique vocal style—frayed timbre, mush-mouthed delivery, and a falsetto cry, "Ooh, well, well," that he tended to insert at the end of almost every verse.

Wheatstraw's blues were set in a fairly limited musical mold that grew more and more predictable with each passing year, but his lyrics were another matter. In his "Peetie Wheatstraw Stomps," he advertised his sexual prowess and bragged of his close association with the Devil. His slower blues dealt graphically with sex ("Well, the first woman I had, she made me get on my knees / And had the nerve to ask me, ooh, well, well, if I liked limburger cheese"), fits of suicidal depression ("I'm going down to the Mississippi, I believe I'll take me a long, lonesome dive / Do you think that if I commit murder, well, God, will I ever get back alive?"), hints of sudden violence ("I did more for you than you understand / You can tell by the bullet holes, mama, now here in my hand"), and suffering that was caused by women, the Depression economy, and vivid but unnameable mental maladies.

Robert Johnson may have been inspired by the injunction at the end of Wheatstraw's "Six Weeks Old Blues" ("When I die, ooh, well, please bury my body low / So, now, that my old evil spirit, mama, now, won't hang around your door") to compose the chilling lines that conclude his "Me and the Devil Blues": "You may bury my body down by the highway side / So my old evil spirit can catch a Greyhound bus and ride." But the comparison makes a telling case for Johnson's genius, for while Wheatstraw's image is a fairly straightforward rendering of a prevalent black folk belief, Johnson seizes on the Greyhound buses that were beginning to crisscross the Delta's growing network of two-lane highways for a contemporary, strikingly specific image. Similarly, Johnson altered Wheatstraw's formulaic "Ooh, well, well," which later figured in several recordings by Muddy Waters, to suit his own expressive purposes. Robert's sudden jumps into the falsetto were usually much more elaborate and recalled Mississippi field hollers, and, when he did use the stereotyped "Ooh, well, well," it was strategically placed for maximum effect.

Skip James may have influenced Johnson directly. He was from Bentonia, Mississippi, on the southern perimeter of the Delta between Jackson and Yazoo City, and during the thirties he traveled widely. But it's more likely that James's Paramount recordings, made in 1931, found their way onto Robert's phonograph. Robert's "30-20 Blues" was a more or less direct copy of James's "22-20 Bues"; and James's "Devil Got My Woman," a blues that was widely known around Bentonia by the early thirties as "It Must Have Been the Devil," furnished the melody, the guitar part, and probably the poetic impetus for Robert's "Hellhound on My Trail." A verse from "Devil Got My Woman" also turned up in

Robert's "Come on in My Kitchen." It isn't surprising that James's music, which was typical of a very localized "school" of guitar bluesmen centered around Bentonia, profoundly impressed Johnson. As David Evans has written, the Bentonia style "is distinctive for its high melismatic singing and complex melodies, its minor-keyed, intricately picked guitar parts, and haunting, brooding lyrics dealing with such themes as loneliness, death, and the supernatural. Altogether it is one of the eeriest, loneliest, and deepest blues sounds ever recorded."

It's tempting to ascribe Johnson's rapid evolution to his broad listening tastes, but no list of influences can explain what happened to his music and his personality during that year or so in Hazelhurst and the next few years he spent rambling around the Delta. According to Robert Lockwood, Johnson was already playing guitar in a revolutionary manner when he returned from Hazelhurst. He made the instrument sound uncannily like a full band, furnishing a heavy beat with his feet, chording innovative shuffle rhythms, and picking out a high, treble-string lead with his slider, all at the same time. Fellow guitarists would watch him with unabashed, open-mouthed wonder. They were watching the Delta's first modern bluesman at work, and the experience must have induced more than a few cases of future shock. As for his personality, Robert had been gripped by an extreme, obsessive wanderlust. Soon after he was back in the Delta, he left his second wife, who returned to Hazelhurst and died a few years later. He boomeranged from woman to woman, town to town, trusting no one and taking on few musical associates, acting for all the world like there really was a hellhound on his trail.

ONE MUSICIAN WHO DID STICK with Robert Johnson for a time was Johnny Shines, a spunky, solidly built young contemporary of Muddy's who was born on April 26, 1915, on the outskirts of Memphis and learned his guitar rudiments in the Arkansas Delta from Chester Burnett—the Howlin' Wolf. Johnny says he was introduced to Robert in Helena, Arkansas, by a pianist known only as M&O, after the Mobile and Ohio Railroad that ran from St. Louis down through the Delta and into southern Mississippi.

Helena in the mid-thirties was the blues capital of the Delta. Among the musicians who were in and out of town frequently were the harmonica virtuoso Rice Miller, guitarists Robert Lee McCoy (later known as Robert Nighthawk), Howlin' Wolf, Elmore James, and Honeyboy Edwards, and pianists Memphis Slim and Roosevelt Sykes. But to Shines, Robert Johnson was the one, "the greatest guitar player I'd ever heard. The things he was doing was things that I'd never heard nobody else do." Despite Robert's standoffishness—"He was kind of long-armed," Shines notes—the two began traveling together, hitching rides, hopping freight trains, perpetually on the move from somewhere to somewhere else. "Robert was a guy, you could wake him up any time and he was ready to *go,*" Shines says. "Say, for instance, you had come from Memphis to Helena, and we'd play there all night probably and lay down to sleep the next morning and hear a train. You say, 'Robert, I hear a train. Let's catch it.' He wouldn't exchange no words with you. He's just ready to go. We'd go right back to Memphis if that's where the train's going. It didn't make him no difference. Just so he was going."

There were plenty of places *to* go. The worst effects of the Depression were beginning to wear off, and while jukeboxes, or "vendors" as they were called by Delta blacks, were already popular in some of the town cafés and highway joints, for the most part they supplemented live music rather than supplanting it. It was one of the best periods for guitar-playing bluesmen, who could carry their instruments with them and perform almost anywhere.

Houston Stackhouse, for example, remembers hearing Robert Nighthawk and the Mississippi Sheiks playing in two drugstores in Hollandale around 1930: "The Black Cat Drugstore was down on the low end, that's kinda colored place, like where they hung out. They had a little old piano player there at that time. I can't think of his name, but anyhow, William Warren, he was a good guitar picker, and Robert was blowin' the harp. Then Bo and Lonnie [Chatmon] and them, they'd play at the next drugstore, on Saturday evenings and things like that. White people owned it, but they had colored people in there playin'." Floyd Jones, from the Arkansas Delta, gave his first public performance at a baseball game in Parkin, Arkansas. "Howlin' Wolf gave me the first guitar

I played," he remembers, "in the spring of 1933. I made my first professional play at a ball game, fourth day of July, 1933. I was sixteen years old on the twenty-first of July. Anyway, I played at this ball game, and they had a dance that night over in the school building. At the time, we was working for sixty cents a day, farmin' and so on, and that particular day and night, I made seventeen dollars."

Honeyboy Edwards, who is a few months younger than Muddy and Johnny Shines and was born between Cleveland and Leland, Mississippi, out in the country not far from Highway 61, recalls some of the other ways musicians made a few dollars. "Here's how it would go," he says. "On Saturday, somebody like me or Robert Johnson would go into one of these little towns, play for nickels and dimes. Some little towns, you'd have to go and see the mayor or the judge and ask him if you could play on the streets. Some of 'em would say, 'No, crowds on the streets, somebody might get hurt.' And sometimes, you know, you could be playin' and have such a big crowd it would block the whole street. Then the police would come around, and I would go on to another town where I could play at. But most of the time, they would let you play. Then sometimes the man who owned a country store would give us something like a couple of dollars to play on Saturday afternoon. We'd sit in the back of the store on some oat sacks or corn sacks and play while they sold groceries and whiskey and beer up front, and the people would come in and listen to us and pitch in. In the afternoon or maybe in the evenin', we'd go to the movie theater and play before or between the movies. Then people would start leavin' town. About eight or nine o'clock at night they'd go out in the country where they could make all the noise they wanted, drink that corn, dance all night long. The people that was givin' a dance, they would put coal oil in a bottle, put a wick in it, and hang it up in a tree. We'd follow that light going to the dance. Maybe the man giving the dance would see you in town that afternoon and hire you to come out and play there that night. Wasn't too much money, but we'd play, eat, drink, have a good time. They would cook fish, sell fish sandwiches and white whiskey. Some outside gambling on a old table, bad lights, way out in the country, you know. We'd play inside, sit down in a chair and relax.

"Sometimes they'd give a big picnic out in the country, dig a deep hole in the ground, put charcoal down in that hole, put an iron grate across it, and lay a whole hog on that grate. They'd let that hog steam, mop it with that hot barbecue sauce, and keep it turnin' all night long. In the mornin' it would be so tender, you could take a fork and just cut the meat right off the bone. They'd have whole barrels of lemonade sitting out there, some guy got four or five gallons of corn whiskey. Sometimes they'd get a wagon, two mules, three or four men, and rent a piano in town, haul it out there, have a platform built with a brush arbor over it, have piano and guitar playin' under there.

"There wasn't that many blues players, you know. We would walk through the country with our guitars on our shoulders, stop at people's houses, play a little music, walk on. We might decide to go on, say, to Memphis. We could hitchhike, transfer from truck to truck, or if we couldn't catch one of them, we'd go to the train yard, 'cause the railroad was all through that part of the country then. We'd wait till the train was pullin' out and jump in the second blind, or else get a reefer—that's the car they put the ice in, for fruit and stuff, so it's something like a deep freezer. We'd get down in an empty reefer, pull the door down over us, and the handle was inside the car, see, so couldn't nobody get to us. Then when we were ready to come out, we'd just knock the handle up and come out. I'd walk around the blind side of the train and come out on the passenger side, just like I got off the passenger car, go out and catch a cab to where I'm goin'. In Memphis, you could play in front of the big hotels, sometimes in the lobbies. And in the evening, you could always go down to Handy Park, there off Beale Street. People would be getting off from work, and they'd stop off at the park, get them a drink and listen to the blues, because some of the fellows would always be there playin'. From there, we might hop a freight, go to St. Louis or Chicago. Or we might hear about where a job was payin' off—a highway crew, a railroad job, a levee camp there along the river, or some place in the country where a lot of people were workin' on a farm. You could go there and play, and everybody would hand you some money. I didn't have a special place then. Anywhere was home. Where I do good, I stay. When it gets bad and dull, I'm gone. I knowed a lot of places and had enough to go to to make it. Man, we played for a lot of peoples."

Honeyboy was a rambler, but he didn't ramble as widely as Robert Johnson, who probably knew most of the places Honeyboy went but also found audiences in black working-class taverns and on street corners in Michigan, Illinois, Indiana, New Jersey, New York City, Buffalo, and even Ontario, Canada. Like Honeyboy, Houston Stackhouse, and most other itinerant bluesmen who preferred living by their wits to staying in one place and farming, he would play whatever he thought an audience, black or white, wanted to hear, including "My Blue Heaven," "Yes, Sir, That's My Baby," hillbilly numbers, cowboy songs from the movies—whatever was popular. When he hit a run of bad luck, he was good at improvising. "We was staying in West Memphis at a place called John Hunt's," Johnny Shines told interviewer Pete Welding, "and this place burnt down and burnt our guitars up. I didn't know that Robert knew anything about harmonica at all, but he come up with this old harmonica. We were out on Highway 61, and he started blowing this harmonica and slapping his hands—patting his hands, blowing and singing—and in a few minutes, the whole highway was almost blocked off with cars, people pitching us nickels, dimes, quarters. He'd sing, I would sing. And when we got to Steels, Missouri, we bought ourselves little guitars. We had enough money to buy guitars with! And truthfully speaking, we didn't have no money when we started out."

No matter how rough the weather or hard the journey, Robert always seemed to look sharp—sharp enough to charm a crowd and attract a woman. "We'd be on the road for days and days," Shines told another interviewer, Alan Greenberg, "no money and sometimes not much food, let alone a decent place to spend the night, playing on dusty streets or inside dirty places of the sort you played in those times, and as I'd catch my breath and see myself looking like a *dog*, there'd be Robert, all clean as can be, looking like he's just stepping out of church." Sometimes they'd go to sleep, and Johnny would wake up to find Robert gone. He'd have to guess which way he went, and sometimes they'd meet again, days later, and resume their travels as before. At other times Robert would have a little too much to drink and began lavishing his attentions on somebody's wife or girl friend. Then there would be trouble and, guitars in hand, the pair would make a quick getaway.

Muddy Waters heard about such adventures from the wandering bluesmen he encountered around Coahoma County, but he never really lived that way himself. "I rambled all the time," he maintains, "and that's why I made that song 'Rollin' Stone.' I was just like that, like a rollin' stone. But I didn't ramble that *far*. I remember when Robert Nighthawk came through in the late thirties and said he was goin' to Chicago and make a record, I thought he was just jivin'. He says, 'You come along. You might get on with me. We'll do a record.' I thought, 'Oh, man, this cat ain't goin' to Chicago.' I thought goin' to Chicago was like goin' out of the world. Finally he split, and the next time I heard, he had a record out. But you know, I was in love with my grandmother. She was gettin' old, and I didn't want to push out and leave her." For the most part, Muddy stayed put, visiting various haunts close to Clarksdale when the mood struck him but playing in his country barrelhouse most weekends. He changed with the times, learning some of the current blues hits, but mostly he played basic Delta blues.

Compared to Robert Johnson, who was four years his senior, Muddy was a conservative, almost a throwback. Robert was perpetually inquisitive about all kinds of music and would probably have perfected an electric, jazz-influenced brand of modern blues had he lived into the 1940s. Muddy stayed with the old, richly ornamented, pentatonic blues melodies that still sounded much like field hollers and the spine-chilling bottleneck guitar figures and chopping bass runs he'd synthesized from local sources, primarily Son House and Charley Patton. The blues records he'd listened to earlier had influenced his repertoire much more than his style, and the Robert Johnson records that particularly impressed him when they began appearing early in 1937 were the ones that were most firmly rooted in the blues he already knew.

BY THE TIME ROBERT JOHNSON RECORDED his first session in a hotel room in San Antonio, Texas, on November 23, 1936, it had been almost three years since Charlie Patton made his last records. The heyday of remote recordings by field units had come to an abrupt end some years earlier, in 1930, when the full force of the Depression began to be felt. Memphis, strategically located at the top of the Delta, had been visited by nine different field units between 1927 and 1930, and several of them had stayed for weeks, recording prolifically. Their work is responsible for much of what we know about Delta blues in the 1920s. They recorded a number of Delta singer-guitarists, including Tommy Johnson, Booker T. Washington "Bukka" White, the team of Kid Bailey and Willie Brown, and Rubin Lacy. Lacy sang slow blues in a deep, heavy preacher's voice, with groans and hoarse, tortured melodic decorations, and was an important influence on both the churchy singing and incisive bottleneck playing of Son House. They captured blues accordionist Walter Rhodes (whose "The Crowing Rooster" became a Delta favorite and who reportedly died after being struck by lightning) and his accompanists, the guitar-playing brothers Pet and Can. Can was Richard Harney, an exceptional technician whose busy, dense finger-picking style was far removed from the more heavily rhythmic playing of the Patton-House school and who was regarded by many musicians as the best guitarist in the Delta.

Meanwhile, other musicians from the Delta region were recording as far afield as Atlanta, Georgia (where Hambone Willie Newbern made the first recording of the Delta standard "Roll and Tumble Blues," or "Rolling and Tumbling," in 1929), and Richmond, Indiana (where Crying Sam Collins's bottleneck guitar, referred to as a "git-fiddle" on the record labels, seemed to literally weep). But no more field units came to Memphis between 1930 and 1939, and then there was only one relatively brief visit until after World War II. During most of this period few field units recorded anywhere.

Delta pianists, who like blues pianists everywhere were a relatively urbane breed, made their recordings and their reputations in cities like St. Louis, Chicago, and even New York. But the men who played guitars and sang deep blues continued to perform mostly in the country and in little Delta towns, and, for the most part, the A&R men from record companies in Chicago and New York lost interest in them. After all, hard-core Delta blues had never been overwhelmingly popular. Paramount must have profited from Charley Patton's recordings, especially "High Water Everywhere" and "Pony Blues," but even these records sold almost exclusively in the Deep South, and no other blues musician from Patton's Delta circle recorded a comparable hit.

Later, between 1937 and 1941, Tommy McClennan and Robert Petway from Greenwood, Bukka White, and Helena's Robert Nighthawk, who was then known as Robert Lee McCoy, would have substantial if not spectacular sales on discs. Joe Williams, who grew up in eastern Mississippi but absorbed much of Patton's Delta style, recorded successfully in Chicago beginning in the mid-thirties. But records by Delta or Delta-influenced guitar bluesmen never sold as well as discs by Blind Lemon Jefferson, Blind Blake, Jim Jackson, Leroy Carr, Tampa Red, Memphis Minnie, Kokomo Arnold, or Peetie Wheatstraw. And by the mid-thirties, most recorded blues had taken a sophisticated turn. Popular blues performers like Wheatstraw, Arnold, Tampa Red, and Big Bill Broonzy (a native of Mississippi, but a cosmopolitan musician influenced primarily by Blind Blake and Lonnie Johnson) were recording in Chicago with bass, drums, and jazz trumpeters and clarinetists, in a city style that foreshadowed the rhythm-and-blues of the post–World War II years. So Robert Johnson's first recording session was something of an anomaly. The American Record Company wouldn't have bothered to send him all the way to San Antonio, where they were recording jazz, that peculiar hillbilly-jazz hybrid known as western swing, and other modern, up-to-date music, if ARC field representative Ernie Oertle hadn't found his talent extraordinary.

Johnson initiated his first session by going to Jackson, Mississippi to see Patton's old mentor, H. C. Speir, who'd been acting as a talent scout for ARC. Speir recommended him to Oertle, and a date was arranged. By the time Robert got to San Antonio, he'd been hard at work polishing his songs for months, perhaps in some cases for years, discarding and adding verses until he had tight, compact pieces just long enough to fit onto 78 records. In this respect, his approach to blues composition was similar to that of most of the blues recording stars of the thirties, who worked at fashioning tight, thematically coherent lyrics. It was distinctly unlike the approach of Charley Patton, Son House, and the Muddy Waters of the Library of Congress recordings, who still considered themselves primarily live entertainers and whose songs tended to be fairly loose assemblages of traditional and original verses that could be stretched out, often to the detriment of their thematic continuity, according to how much people wanted to hear and how long they wanted to dance. Robert Johnson could perform that way too, of course, and often did, but by 1936 he thought of himself as something more than a juke joint entertainer. He was self-consciously an artist.

Out of that first day's recording session came "Terraplane Blues," a sexy automobile blues ("I'm gonna get deep down in this connection, keep on tanglin' with these wires / And when I mash down on your little starter, then your spark plug will give me fire") that became an immediate Delta favorite when it was released as his first single with the ominous "Kind Hearted Woman Blues" ("She studies evil all the time") on the flip side. At the same session, Johnson recorded three tunes that were to become standards of postwar electric blues: "I Believe I'll Dust My Broom," "Sweet Home Chicago," and "Ramblin' on My Mind." A few days later, on Friday, November 27, he cut another session which included "Preachin' Blues" (his version of Son House's "Preachin' the Blues"), "Walkin' Blues" (the Delta anthem), "If I Had Possession over Judgment Day" (his version of "Rolling and Tumbling"), and "Cross Road Blues." As the English blues writer Bob Groom has noted, at these recording sessions Johnson "was truly standing at a crossroads in blues history, looking back to the country blues of men like Son House and Willie Brown and forward to the Chicago blues of the forties and fifties."

Each of Johnson's blues recordings is packed with detail, both musical and verbal, and almost all of them crackle with intensity. "Cross Road Blues," which Eric Clapton and his rock group Cream revived more than thirty years later, is a good example of both the density and power of Johnson's music. The guitar rhythm is deliberate and driving, but Johnson repeatedly interrupts it to hammer and bend a single string, so forcefully that the instrument momentarily sounds like an electric guitar. Examined more closely, the guitar accompaniment is a complex, carefully constructed, mercurially shifting succession of two-beat and three-beat figures, and an equally complex, equally mercurial alternation of driving bass riffs and high, bottlenecked lead lines.

The singing is tense, as if Johnson was forcing wind through a throat constricted by fear.

The fear in "Cross Road Blues" is actually a complex of fears, some rational and immediate, some more metaphysical. The most literal reading of the tune is as a description of an actual experience. Johnson finds himself alone at a country crossroads, attempting to flag a ride as the sun sets. He has ample reason to be afraid. He's in a part of the country where he isn't known. If a white law officer or a passing redneck discovers him there, he could be jailed, or worse. But that isn't all Johnson's afraid of. In blues lore, the crossroads is the place where aspiring musicians strike their deal with the Devil, and Robert claimed to have struck such a deal. No wonder he sang in the song's first verse that he "fell down on my knees / Asked the Lord above, Have mercy, save poor Bob if you please." No wonder he called on his "friend Willie Brown" for help and cried out, twice in the first of two recorded takes, that he was "sinkin' down." Anyone who's ever stopped at a deserted Delta crossroads in the dead of night knows what a spooky experience it can be. Everything's empty and black—black bottomland stretching away for miles in every direction, cloudy black sky above—and unnervingly quiet. A friend who grew up in the Delta once told me of running out of gas late at night, walking several miles until he came to a deserted crossroads, hearing a far-off splashing, probably some animal crossing a creek or slough, and suddenly being seized with an unreasonable panic. He actually believed, before he got a grip on himself, that some sort of hideous swamp monster was lumbering toward him. Robert Johnson, alone in similar circumstances, might have imagined he was hearing the approach of Papa Legba, the Black Man. "Don't the Delta look lonesome when that evenin' sun go down?" sang an Arkansas bluesman named William Brown on a 1942 Library of Congress recording, adding in a spoken aside, "just 'bout good an' dark." It is one of the lonesomest places on earth.

And yet, a crossroads is also a landmark, a haven. In a region as perfectly flat as the Delta, it's one of the few features of the landscape that really stands out. Driving south toward Clarksdale in 1979, I noticed at the junction where Highway 49 crosses Highway 61, running off west toward Lula and Helena and east toward

Sledge and the central hills, a combination gas station/restaurant called the Crossroader. When I got to Clarksdale, I bought gas at the Crossroads Service Station, Highway 61 at DeSoto Street. Curious, I looked in a local telephone directory and found a Crossroad Laundry and Cleaners, Crossroad Sporting Goods, Crossroads Branch Bank of Clarksdale, and Cross Roads Wrecker Service. The familiarity and ubiquity of the crossroads in Delta iconography lends an added immediacy to Johnson's tale of terror.

There's a school of thought that sees voodoo symbolism in almost every line Robert Johnson ever sang, and this point of view has rightly been ridiculed by blues scholars. But it's undeniable that Johnson was fascinated with and probably obsessed by supernatural imagery. This fascination seems understandable enough, since blues was widely believed to be the Devil's music, and some of Johnson's satanic references were simply macho posturing. But when other bluesmen, Peetie Wheatstraw for example, claimed familiarity with the Devil, they did so in boasting songs. Wheatstraw never recorded anything as chilling and apparently dead serious as "Hellhound on My Trail" or "Me and the Devil Blues," which Johnson cut on Saturday, June 19, 1937, in an otherwise deserted Dallas warehouse that was serving as a makeshift studio. This was his last session, and in retrospect it was rife with omens. The first song he sang that day began "I got stones in my passway and my road seem dark as night / I have pains in my heart, they have taken my appetite." In "From Four until Late," he offered the philosophical observation that "a man is like a prisoner, and he's never satisfied." "Hellhound on My Trail" is pure, icy cold paranoia, and "Me and the Devil Blues," which begins with Satan knocking on Johnson's door, ends with "You may bury my body down by the highway side / So my old evil spirit can catch a Greyhound bus and ride." Johnson also recorded several boasting pieces, including "Stop Breakin' Down Blues" (revived by the Rolling Stones on their *Exile on Main Street* album) and a tune full of local references, "Travelling Riverside Blues," which talks about "rockin' " and barrelhousing in Vicksburg, Rosedale, and Friar's Point, "on the riverside." "Honeymoon Blues" is unique, a straightforward declaration of love for someone named Betty Mae. But the session ended with "Love in Vain," one of the most perfect and troubling lyrics in all blues, and the restless, disjointed "Milkcow's Calf Blues."

ROBERT JOHNSON has been called "the most influential of all bluesmen," but despite the relative success of "Terraplane Blues," his subsequent recordings sold disappointingly, and a number of his finest performances went unreleased until white rock and folk musicians began recording his songs in the 1960s. As we've seen, the Johnson records that influenced Muddy Waters were the ones in a more or less traditional Delta mold. "Walkin' Blues" and "Preachin' Blues" were derived directly from Son House, and "Terraplane Blues," with its implied boogie feel, sudden falsetto howls, and lightning-fast bottleneck runs, has a pronounced Delta flavor. These are the songs Muddy mentions when Johnson's name is brought up. Elmore James, who sometimes played with Johnson in the Delta, was the man who made "Dust My Broom" into a postwar blues standard and inspired most later rock versions of the tune. "If I Had Possession over Judgment Day," Johnson's version of "Rolling and Tumbling," wasn't even issued until the sixties. Muddy and his sidekick, Baby Face Leroy, established "Rollin' and Tumblin' " as a Chicago blues standard. Kokomo Arnold's "Old Original Kokomo Blues" far outsold Johnson's later derivation, "Sweet Home Chicago" (although Johnson's lyrics made the song a natural for Chicago bluesmen, and it's his version that survived in the repertoires of performers like Magic Sam, Robert Lockwood, and Junior Parker). The version of Johnson's "Stop Breaking Down" sung by most postwar Chicago blues artists is a version with somewhat different lyrics recorded by John Lee "Sonny Boy" Williamson in 1945. It's really through disciples like Muddy and Elmore James, and through the recordings of his songs made by Eric Clapton, the Rolling Stones, Taj Mahal, and other rock and folk performers in the sixties and seventies, that Johnson exercised his widest and most lasting influence.

One wonders how many of these younger performers were actually attracted by Johnson's music and how many were drawn by his legend—the death under mysterious circumstances, the pact with the Devil. Eric Clapton, whose "Crossroads" with Cream is the only later version to include the line about Willie Brown and achieves an intensity and power of its own, must have thought long and hard about the Johnson legend. After an extended bout with heroin addiction, he reemerged in the early seventies playing in a more restrained, less bluesy style. In 1974, *Rolling Stone* interviewer Steve Turner asked him if the change in his music reflected a change in attitude, and instead of answering the question directly, he told Turner a story. "Once with the Dominos [a post-Cream Clapton group], we dropped some acid in San Francisco," he said, "and apart from the fact that the guitar was made of rubber, every bad lick I had, every naughty lick, blues lick . . . whatever you want to call it, turned the audience into all these devils in sort of red coats and things. And then I'd play a sweet one, and they all turned into angels. I prefer playing to angels, personally."

When Robert Johnson was recording in Texas, he wasn't playing for the angels, but he knew he was playing for posterity. Most blues musicians have taken pride in their recordings, but Johnson was a special case. In his "Phonograph Blues," which wasn't released until the sixties, he developed a phonographic/sexual metaphor that was without precedent in recorded blues. Researcher Mack McCormick, who has located and interviewed several of Johnson's children, says that shortly before he died, Robert visited all of them, leaving each a copy of one of his records. Honeyboy Edwards, whose cousin Willie Mae was a girl friend of Robert's in 1937, recalls running into him in the spring of that year, on Johnson Street in Greenwood: "He was standing there playing on the street, and this lady walked up to him and said, 'Can you play "Terraplane Blues"?' 'Cause that record had just come out, but she didn't know who she was talkin' to. He said [and here Edwards assumed a tone of dignified, inviolable cool], 'Miss, that's my number.' Like *that*. She said, 'I don't believe you.' He said, 'Give me fifteen cents and I'll play it.' And he *played* that 'Terraplane,' man, he wore it out."

In August 1938, Robert was hired to play at a country house party near Greenwood. According to Edwards and others who were in the area at the time, he drank too much, flirted with his employer's wife, and was given poisoned whiskey. A friend took him home, where he lay near death for several days before expiring on August 16. The death certificate, unearthed by blues researcher Gayle Dean Wardlow, states that there was "no doctor" in attendance, and the death was presumed due to natural causes. Robert's mother was notified and came with one of his brothers-in-law to claim the body, which was buried in the graveyard of the Zion Church near Morgan City, Mississippi, just off Highway 7. From there, it would have been easy enough for Johnson's spirit to catch a Greyhound bus and ride.

A few months later, Don Law, the man who'd supervised Robert's last recording session in Dallas, was surprised to get a call from the New York record producer, critic, and impresario John Hammond, the man who had launched the skyrocketing careers of Count Basie, Billie Holiday, and Benny Goodman. Hammond was organizing a Spirituals to Swing concert, the first presentation of black American music ever to be held in Carnegie Hall, and he'd been impressed enough with some Robert Johnson records he'd heard to ask Law whether Johnson could be found. When locating him proved impossible, Hammond settled for Big Bill Broonzy, who'd been making jazzy recordings with full band accompaniment in Chicago but was obligingly folksy for the occasion.

One of the sensations of the concert, which was held on December 23, 1938, was an appearance by three blues pianists, Chicagoans Meade Lux Lewis and Albert Ammons and Kansas City's Pete Johnson, who played driving music with a boogie-woogie beat and also backed the forceful Kansas City blues shouter Joe Turner. They were booked for an extended engagement at Café Society Downtown following the concert, and their popularity in New York helped launch a national boogie-woogie craze that lasted into the early fifties, infecting popular singers (the Andrews Sisters did "Boogie Woogie Bugle Boy"), swing bands (Tommy Dorsey had a hit with "T. D.'s Boogie Woogie"), hillbilly acts (the Delmore Brothers recorded "Hillbilly Boogie"), and of course blues musicians, who had been playing or implying boogie rhythms for decades.

(West African words such as the Hausa "buga" and Mandingo "bug," both of which mean "to beat" as in "to beat a drum," may represent the linguistic roots of the word "boogie," though the words "bogy," "booger," and possibly "boogie" have long been common in English slang, and have in fact been used to refer to blacks, or to dark apparitions like the bogy man. Blind Lemon Jefferson was using the term "booger rooger," apparently slang referring to a particularly wild party, at least as early as 1917–18, and the New Orleans pianist and songwriter Clarence Williams remembered hearing Texas pianist George W. Thomas play a tune with a boogie-woogie bass part [later published as "New Orleans Hop Scop Blues"] in Houston in 1911. The first recording with the term "boogie-woogie" in the title was "Pine Top's Boogie Woogie," made by the Alabama-born pianist Clarence "Pinetop" Smith in 1928. It was a hard-rocking dance record and a race hit and spawned numerous imitations, including an early fifties recording by Delta pianist Joe Willie "Pinetop" Perkins, later a mainstay of the Muddy Waters band.)

Blues researchers have encountered persistent rumors that Robert Johnson was playing an electric guitar and intermittently leading a small band that included a drummer in the months just before his death. If he'd lived to perform at Carnegie Hall, on a program that included the first concert appearance by the Count Basie band as well as the boogie-woogie pianists, he almost certainly would have been inspired to tighten up his implied boogie rhythms and perform and record with band backing. In the process he probably would have created what we now know as Chicago blues. And what if white American and European jazz fans, for whom the Spirituals to Swing concert was a truly epochal event, had begun buying his records? He might have been able to introduce unvarnished deep blues to an international audience before the onset of World War II. At the very least, he should have become the first Delta bluesman to decisively break out of the music's regional straitjacket and win a broad following among American blacks. But of course the man who finally accomplished all these things was Muddy Waters, and it took him another twenty years to do it.

CHAPTER 4
Chicago Pep

When Muddy Waters left the Delta, in May of 1943, he was still a young man, just turned twenty-eight. But he'd seen the Delta change, and change dramatically, in his lifetime. He rarely heard or saw an automobile when he was a child growing up on Stovall's plantation, and when he did run across one it was often stuck or broken down, for the roads were treacherous, rutted dirt tracks that turned to mud in the Delta's sudden downpours. When the W.P.A. and other federal agencies began putting men to work during the worst years of the Depression, one of Mississippi's first priorities was paved roads, and by 1943 highways crisscrossed the state. Electric lights, found only in the towns when Muddy was growing up, were spreading to the country. There were still plenty of blues musicians playing in the area, but jukeboxes were becoming the rage, not just in downtown taverns but in country stores and even in little juke joints like Muddy's.

Important as these changes were, they were only beginning to alter the texture of day-to-day life. Most blacks were still sharecroppers and lived in shotgun shacks much like the ones their parents had been born in. There were more automobiles, but on Saturdays plenty of black families still rode into town in horse-drawn wagons. After working all week long in the cotton fields, folks still packed into house parties and juke joints on Friday and

Saturday nights to dance and party to the blues. Amplified guitars and harmonicas were being introduced, and more and more bluesmen were working with bands that included drummers; the music was getting louder. But melodies, lyrics, guitar parts, even entire songs that had been in vogue when Charley Patton was a young man, more than thirty years earlier, were still common currency.

Phonograph records had been bringing the songs and styles of black and white performers from all over America into Delta shacks and juke joints for more than twenty years, and the Delta had produced musicians who liked these new styles and decided to emulate them—as dance band players, jazz musicians, ballad singers. But the blues that people played and listened to in the country was as isolated from the American mainstream as it had been in Patton's time, perhaps more so. After all, Patton had played deep blues, white hillbilly songs, nineteenth century ballads, and other varieties of black and white country dance music with equal facility; Son House and Muddy Waters could play blues and spirituals and not much else. There was no pressing need for them to learn to play white popular music, as there had been in Patton's time. Black musicians who preferred entertaining whites could now be found in many Delta towns and on most of the larger plantations. They were specialists, unlike the jack-of-all-trades songster-bluesmen of Patton's generation. Most of the younger bluesmen now played mostly or only for blacks. This was one more symptom of the general tendency for whites and blacks in the Delta to draw further and further apart and regard each other with increasing mistrust.

With the aid of hindsight, it's possible to discern a gradual, evolutionary process of change operating in Delta blues during its first few decades. But compared to the rapidity with which jazz changed during the same period of time, Delta blues was practically standing still. Jazz was still developing out of a mix of folk, popular, and European classical influences around the same time blues started to emerge as a clearly definable genre. In 1900, when Patton was learning to play blues from Henry Sloan, jazz was a loose, collective music, still largely unknown outside New Orleans and other Southern cities, played by groups that typically included brass, a clarinet, banjo, guitar, string bass or tuba, and sometimes a piano and/or a set of drums. By 1925 Louis Armstrong, Sidney Bechet, and a few other musicians were radically altering the music's format to make room for improvised solos and establishing exacting standards of virtuosity. By 1935 the New Orleans–style jazz group was considered old hat, and big bands, with sections of brass and saxophones that played written arrangements and a typical rhythm section of piano, string bass, and drums, were in fashion. By 1943, the music of the "swing bands," as Benny Goodman and other white musicians who appropriated the big-band format called them, was beginning to sound dated to younger black jazz musicians in Kansas City and New York, and probably elsewhere. The bebop or modern-jazz movement, spearheaded by Charlie Parker and Dizzy Gillespie, was transforming jazz from a danceable, entertainment-oriented idiom into an art music performed for seated audiences in listening rooms and concert halls.

Jazz bands had been popular with black listeners across the country since the early 1920s, especially when they featured singers. In the Delta, black jazz bands often performed for whites, and for blacks in the larger towns. As the big-band style began to pass out of fashion in the forties, partly due to the impact of modernism and partly because World War II made it difficult to keep large bands together, the black popular audience began picking up on a new sort of music that would eventually be called rhythm-and-blues. Its pioneers included the jazz vibraphonist Lionel Hampton, whose stomping big-band blues "Flying Home," complete with a choked, screaming tenor saxophone workout, was a big "race" hit in 1942, and Louis Jordan, a jazz saxophonist who began recording light blues and novelty songs in the early forties with his small jump combo the Tympany Five. Hampton and Jordan both combined the popular boogie-woogie rhythm, a grittier version of swing-era saxophone styles as exemplified by Coleman Hawkins and Ben Webster, and playfully humorous lyrics or verbal asides that were frequently laced with jive talk.

There was still an audience for blues records, but during the thirties and early forties the blues market had become increasingly monopolized by a group of Chicago-based artists. When Muddy got to Chicago, most of the big names in blues recorded either for Columbia or for Victor's celebrated Bluebird label, and both companies depended upon a white record producer, talent scout, and publishing magnate named Lester Melrose for their blues product. Melrose's artists had down-home backgrounds: Tampa Red, a top-selling blues star since the late twenties, was from Georgia; John Lee "Sonny Boy" Williamson, who was largely responsible for transforming the harmonica from an accompanying instrument into a major solo voice, was from Jackson, Tennessee, just north of Memphis; Washboard Sam was from Arkansas; Big Bill Broonzy was a Mississippian by birth. But in the interests of holding onto their increasingly urbanized audience and pleasing Melrose, who was interested both in record sales and in lucrative publishing royalties, they recorded several kinds of material, including jazz and novelty numbers, and began to favor band backing. During the mid-thirties the bands tended to be small— guitar and piano, sometimes a clarinet, a washboard, a string bass. But by the time Muddy arrived in Chicago, the "Bluebird Beat," as it has been called, was frequently carried by bass and drums. The music was a mixture of older black blues and vaudeville styles and material with the newer swing rhythms. Some of the records even featured popular black jazzmen—Peetie Wheatstraw's Chicago sessions of 1940–41 gave solo space to trumpeter Jonah Jones and tenor saxophonist Chu Berry and were kicked along by Big Sid Catlett, swing drummer supreme.

Muddy's own sister had told him, "They don't listen to that kind of old blues you're doin' now, don't nobody listen to that, not in Chicago." Some Bluebird releases of the period included harmonica accompaniments by Muddy's old friend Robert Nighthawk, who also made solo discs, and the Greenwood-based Tommy McClennan became a Bluebird artist in 1939. But most of the new blues records Muddy heard on Delta jukeboxes can only have convinced him that his sister was telling the truth. So even though he had always considered himself a special person, a musician, and not just another field hand, when he arrived in Chicago music was practically the last thing on his mind. The first thing was a job. "Man, it was the war time. There was jobs all over," he remembers. "My train got in on a Saturday morning. I took that taxi and went and found my sister and her husband, Dan

Jones, and Saturday evenin' I had that job in the paper container factory. And on Monday morning the paper from the draft board came."

As an experienced tractor driver on a plantation owned by a well-connected man, Muddy had been effectively exempt from the draft. After all, cotton for uniforms and bandages was a wartime necessity. "I went by the draft board in Coahoma before I left," Muddy says, "and told them that I had to go to Chicago because my angel died. I put my lie in. I told them I'd be gone for a few days, and if they need me, here's the address to send the papers to—3656 Calumet. I think that guy, the overseer, Mr. Fulton, the one I had the problem with, might have got on the phone, 'cause on Monday morning the paper was there. So I go over to the board, to Thirty-eighth and South Park, where there was one of my friends, Danny O'Neal, taking the papers there. He said, 'Go on. We'll handle it from here.' So they drafted me, but I never did make the grade. I had kind of bad eyes, and I had bad schooling. Some of the other guys down there tried to help me with the papers, and they laughed at me scratching. So when I got through, they stopped the line, and I know what my paper said. It said, 'Reject.' I said, 'What do I do now?' 'Oh, you go home, man.' I said, 'Uh-hunnnh!' " The memory brings a satisfied chuckle, for while Muddy was no political radical, and certainly no pacifist, he was well aware that going to war would mean risking life and limb for a country owned and operated by and for whites. "They said I could go on down to the mess hall and eat. Man, I ate lunch there, and they had *good* food, but I didn't want *nothing* to eat there. I got dressed and hit that door wide open and got on a streetcar and went home."

Muddy had been a country boy all his life, but he kept his mouth shut and his eyes open and adjusted to Chicago without much trouble. The environment wasn't wholly alien. He started playing his blues at house parties as soon as he arrived, first at the Joneses' and soon in the apartments of other recently trans-planted Mississippians. He'd built up quite a reputation as a blues singer during his years in Mississippi—Willie Dixon remembers people talking about him in Chicago as early as the mid-thirties—so the news of his arrival spread through the community. "After about two or three weeks," he says, "I found out I had a bunch of cousins here. Well, really, *they* found out *I* was here, and they come and got me and brought me from the South Side over to the West Side to stay with them. I was there about two or three months, and then I got myself a four-room apartment." Now he was set—his own place, with his woman Annie Mae installed, a regular paycheck, and work playing house parties almost every night. Practically everywhere he went, people fresh up from Mississippi, or people who'd been in Chicago for a while but remembered seeing him play years before, would recognize him and yell out, "Hey! Muddy Waters!"

THE FIRST BLACK CHICAGOAN was also the first Chicagoan—Jean Baptiste Pointe du Saible, a trader from Santo Domingo who built a cabin near the mouth of the Chicago River around 1790. During the 1840s, when Chicago was a town of around four thousand people, fugitive slaves and Northern free blacks began settling there; by 1860 they were almost a thousand strong. Some of the more prominent black citizens were active in the antislavery movement, and Chicago developed a reputation throughout the generally conservative Midwest as a "nigger-loving town." Between 1880 and 1900 around fifty thousand Jews arrived in Chicago from Eastern Europe, and while the black population grew more slowly, by 1915 there were over fifty thousand blacks. The older settlers moved to contain these new arrivals, and by the outbreak of World War I, there were distinctly demarcated Jewish and black ghettos. The blacks were crowded into a narrow South Side "black belt" and a smaller but growing enclave on the West Side, with Jewish and other ethnic neighborhoods acting as buffers between blacks and the white residential and business districts. Most of the blacks—more than 80 percent according to the census of 1900—were migrants, and the majority of these had come from the upper South: Kentucky, Missouri, northern Tennessee. Seventeen percent were identified as natives of the Deep South, an area that included Virginia, Georgia, and other southeastern states as well as Mississippi, Arkansas, and Louisiana.

These figures help explain the varied regional origins of the earliest Chicago blues stars—Tampa Red from Georgia, Papa Charlie Jackson from Louisiana, Blind Blake from Florida, and so on.

When the United States entered World War I, Chicago was the world's busiest railroad terminal, with more than four hundred trains arriving every day; an important Great Lakes port; and a major center for meat packing, printing, steel, and other heavy industries. Jobs in these industries had been one of the city's principal attractions for Eastern European immigrants, but they were integrated into the work force only after considerable labor unrest, and many of them eked out livings in the ghetto as best they could—selling from pushcarts, delivering merchandise with a horse and wagon. Before World War I, industrial jobs remained closed to blacks, who could only hope to work as porters, janitors, or servants, or, in a few cases, as help in up-and-coming Jewish businesses. But the draft, the rapid expansion of heavy industry to meet the demands of the war machine, and the sudden cutoff of European immigration conspired to create an acute labor shortage, and by 1920, despite opposition from the unions, threats, taunts, constant tension, and bloody race riots in 1917 and 1919, blacks were working at steel mills and foundries, in the stockyards and meat-packing houses, and in plants that manufactured locomotives, farm equipment, paper products, and other commodities. And there were many more blacks; at least fifty thousand had arrived since 1916.

Most of these new migrants were from the Deep South. Two great rail lines, the Illinois Central and the Gulf, Mobile and Ohio (M&O), ran directly into Chicago from Alabama, Louisiana, and Mississippi. Many Northern cities experienced enormous influxes of Southern blacks, especially Detroit and Cleveland, but in the Southern countryside, Chicago was much more celebrated. The Chicago *Defender*, which was founded in 1905 and rapidly became the most popular black newspaper in the country, actively encouraged the migration, running headlines such as "More Positions Open Than Men for Them," editorializing at length on the contrast between freedom and economic independence in the North and lynchings and servitude in the South, and even setting a date—May 15, 1917—for the Great Northern Drive. The *Defender* found its way into many a Delta cropper's shack, and wasn't the only Chicago publication to do so. Rural blacks depended heavily on Sears Roebuck and Montgomery Ward, whose lavishly illustrated catalogues and reasonably priced merchandise—including many bluesmen's first guitars—came from Chicago.

At the same time, the Delta and other cotton-producing areas were reeling from a succession of natural disasters. The boll weevil, an insect parasite that first entered the United States from Mexico in 1892 and is the subject of some of the earliest blues lyrics, ravaged cotton crops throughout Mississippi in 1915–16. During the same period, heavy flooding ruined thousands of acres. Southern blacks who'd depended on sharecropping for subsistence found themselves facing an uncertain future just when the Northern labor shortage was reaching its peak.

In 1917–18 some of the larger Chicago firms sent agents south to attract black workers with free railroad passes and promises of guaranteed employment. The employment often turned out to be backbreaking labor, and blacks soon learned that they were last hired and first fired. The housing available to them was run-down and overcrowded; Chicago had not yet replaced many of its old frame houses with brick and stone tenement buildings. The South Side black belt was a strip of one- and two-story frame dwellings, many of them unpainted and lacking the most rudimentary sanitary and heating facilities, set end to end, row on row, with wooden sidewalks and rutted streets that were always badly in need of repair. Several rail lines ran through the South Side, and in many cases the back porches of ghetto buildings were built right up to the grading, so that the houses rattled and shook with every passing train. Garbage collection was spotty, and a number of buildings lacked electricity. And the ghetto kept decaying and getting more overcrowded, for Chicago's whites were holding the line against black expansion into other areas by any means at their disposal, including bombings. The city's black population increased 148 percent between 1910 and 1920, according to the official census figures, but the size of the black belt hardly increased at all.

The migration waxed and waned between the two world wars, slowing drastically at the height of the Depression, but it never stopped. David L. Cohn reported in his book *Where I Was Born and Raised* that "within a period of ninety days during the twenties, twelve thousand Negroes left the cottonfields of Mississippi, and an average of two hundred were leaving Memphis every night." Delta whites began to wonder how they were going to raise their cotton if all their cheap labor moved north. Planters and other civic-minded whites began giving picnics for local blacks, with free cold drinks and food and speeches on "the advantages of the Delta as a home for Negroes." Labor agents from the North were forced to apply for licenses at exorbitant rates or were beaten or run out of town. But the exodus continued. The 1940 census for Mississippi revealed that whites outnumbered blacks statewide for the first time in a hundred years. Between 1940 and 1950 the state lost one fourth of its remaining black population. During the same period, the black population of Chicago increased by 77 percent. The city now boasted more residents born in Mississippi than any city outside Mississippi, including Memphis and St. Louis.

Toward the end of World War II, W. K. Anderson, of the 16,000-acre King & Anderson plantation near Clarksdale, decided to try to find out why so many of his tenants were leaving for the North. He sent two of his white overseers to Chicago to contact former King & Anderson sharecroppers and persuade them to come back, and with the help of a Chicago minister the overseers were able to arrange a meeting in the apartment of a laundry worker who had grown up on the plantation. As word of the meeting spread, it took on the air of a festive occasion. People who had known each other on King & Anderson crowded into the apartment, bringing liquor, chicken, and other comestibles. One of the overseers, a Mr. Russell, gave an informal talk detailing all that the plantation management was doing to make King & Anderson a more attractive place to live and work—installing electricity in tenant housing, replacing the shacks of former years with row houses located next to paved roads, rendering itemized debit and credit statements to each tenant automatically at specific times of the year.

Then it was the blacks' turn. They asserted that they were being overcharged for commodities and underpaid for their cotton crops despite the detailed accounts, and they complained about being mistreated by overseers and by lawmen in nearby towns. A man stood up and gave an impromptu speech of his own, which Anderson reported to David Cohn as follows:

> Up here we have a little more freedom. If we get off from work, buy us a bottle of whiskey, and take a drink, nobody objects. If we get a little too much, as all of us do sometimes, the police take us to jail. Next morning they let us out without having beat us over the head or making us pay a fine. We think we get better protection from the law up here. Going into towns down home, the law would get us, beat us up, handle us rough. We don't get that treatment here.

It must have been an eloquent speech. When the overseers asked if anyone was interested in returning to King & Anderson, nobody volunteered.

Anderson also sent his two overseers to St. Louis, where they got a similar response. Then he contacted a number of the elected officials and business leaders of Clarksdale and told them he wanted to sit down and have a serious talk. The eventual result was a request to the town's recognized black leaders for a list of grievances or causes for the migration. There was a town meeting at which the list was presented.*

1. Better Economic Conditions.
   (a) Low wages in Clarksdale versus high wages elsewhere.
   (b) Unsatisfactory crop settlements and abuses by plantation managers.
   (c) Discrimination in employment and inequalities in wages for the same work.

2. Constant Intimidations.
   (a) Wanton killings of Negroes without recourse.
   (b) Intimidations on public conveyances.
   (c) Law officers forcing women to work who are not vagrants.
   (d) Unfavorable newspaper publicity and scurrilous references to Negro soldiers.
   (e) Maltreatment of Negro soldiers while home on furlough.

3. Lack of Educational Opportunities.
   (a) Poor school buildings.
   (b) Short school terms.
   (c) Low salaries paid Negro teachers.

     (d) Lack of high school facilities.
     (e) Lack of recreational facilities.
4. Activities of Loan Sharks.
     (a) Excessive rates of interest charged.
     (b) Refusal to give receipts.
     (c) Threatening borrowers with bodily harm.
5. Lack of Sanitary Facilities.
     (a) Failure to collect garbage in Negro areas.
     (b) Lack of sidewalks and drainage in most Negro residential sections.
     (c) Lack of hospitals for Negroes.

Steps were taken. Promises were made. Pictures were taken and hands were shaken. But the discontent was much too widespread and deep-seated, and the lure of Chicago and other urban centers was much too strong. Older Delta blacks might cherish fond memories of the countryside where they'd spent their childhood and youth and, perhaps, of the white paternalism that was rapidly eroding as political and economic power passed from planters to townspeople. Younger blacks had fewer memories to hold them back. As they left, they were replaced by machines—tractors to do the work of dozens of field hands with mules, and more and more sophisticated planting and harvesting equipment, much of it manufactured in Chicago.

So on they came, rolling up the Illinois Central and M&O lines, young men out on their own for the first time, determined women clutching children, whole families dressed formally in their Sunday best. They packed into the "colored" passenger cars so tightly that many who barely made the train had to endure the journey (twelve hours from Memphis) standing up. When they first stepped out into the huge, crowded, impossibly noisy Central Station, after hurtling through what seemed to be miles of ramshackle, densely packed ghetto, many of them must have at least thought about turning right around and going back home, especially if it was winter and the freezing wind ("the hawk," as locals called it) was whipping in off Lake Michigan. Muddy was lucky enough to arrive in the springtime, after the winter's blizzards

* From *Where I Was Born and Raised* by David L. Cohn, Boston: Houghton Mifflin, 1948.

and before the onslaught of the sweltering summer. He already knew by word of mouth that when the weather was nice, a new arrival could be sure of running into old friends and hearing plenty of down-home blues in one central location. Officially it was known as the Maxwell Street Market, but to the blacks, it was Jewtown.

ONCE MUDDY HAD SETTLED into his four-room apartment at 1851 West Thirteenth Street, he was living a relatively short distance from the mile-long stretch of Maxwell Street that operated on weekends as a teeming bazaar. Maxwell was a long, wide (sixty feet), straight east-west thoroughfare bounded by brick and frame buildings, none taller than three stories. Jewish peddlers with pushcarts had started to congregate there some time after the Chicago fire of 1871, and soon a few enterprising souls began putting up wooden stalls at the curbside, paying for the privilege, no doubt, with a tip to the merchant who owned the storefront behind the stall and another tip to the cop on the beat. In 1912 the Chicago City Council officially recognized the Maxwell Street Market, a strip about a mile from Lake Michigan, and before long there were more or less permanent wooden stands lining the street. Most of the stores had awnings that stretched out to the curbs, so the sidewalks were effectively turned into long, shaded tunnels. The stores, the stands, and the pushcart trade remained overwhelmingly Jewish-operated even after Jewish immigrants began moving out of the neighborhood and blacks began moving in. By the mid-forties the area was mixed residentially, with some lingering Jewish, Mexican, and gypsy enclaves, but it was mostly black.

On a sunny Sunday afternoon one could buy just about anything on Maxwell Street. There were spice stands, used appliances, horse-drawn wagons loaded with country produce, cheap dresses, used socks with the holes carefully folded inside, gypsy fortune-telling parlors, furtive men with watches up and down their arms and legs, even more furtive men connecting for heroin and morphine in the shadows behind the stands, blankets loaded with merchandise of every description spread out on the sidewalks, and an almost limitless variety of individual scams. Ira Berkow, who worked on the street as a child and years later wrote *Maxwell Street,* a fascinating memoir, recalls a legless snake oil salesman whose horse wrote numerals, from one to four, on a blackboard according to how many times the man snapped his whip. He also remembers the frequent violence that earned the street the sobriquet "Bloody Maxwell," center of the roughest police precinct in all Chicago. There were frequent chases, with policemen pursuing thieves and junkies on mad dashes through back alleys or across rooftops. Nobody wanted to end up in the precinct house, which was on Maxwell three blocks west of Halstead. It had its own lockup in the basement, a dingy chamber of horrors where the prisoners urinated and defecated into troughs that ran past the cells and huge rats slept on the hot water pipes near the ceiling, their tails hanging down and flicking languidly.

All along Maxwell Street—on the curbs, on busy corners, in the entrances to alleyways, in the rubble of vacant lots—blues musicians wailed away on guitars, harmonicas, and battered drum sets. Amplification had already made its appearance by 1940. Enterprising guitarists would buy long cords for their amplifiers from one of the cut-rate electrical stores on the street and plug into sockets in convenient stores or ground-floor apartments. Over the hubbub of the bartering and hawking that arose from the market, one could hear the cutting whine of bottleneck guitars, and under it throbbed the bass patterns of "Rollin' and Tumblin' " and "Dust My Broom." The musicians were playing only for tips, but it was possible to make money. Hound Dog Taylor, who grew up near Greenwood, Mississippi, and had learned to play Robert Johnson and Elmore James licks with a bottleneck by the time he arrived in Chicago in 1940, reported to Berkow, "You used to get out on Maxwell Street on a Sunday morning and pick you out a good spot, babe. Dammit, we'd make more money than I ever looked at. Sometimes a hundred dollars, a hundred twenty dollars. Put you out a tub, you know, and put a pasteboard in there, like a newspaper? . . . When somebody throw a quarter or a nickel in there, can't nobody hear it. Otherwise, somebody come by, take the tub and cut out. . . . I'm telling you, Jewtown was jumpin' like a champ, jumpin' like mad on Sunday morning."

Muddy enjoyed visiting Maxwell Street, and he played there on occasion, but he looks back on the experience with evident disdain. "A lot of peoples was down there trying to make a quarter," he told Berkow, "but I didn't like to have to play outside in all the weathers, and I didn't like to pass the hat around and all that bullshit." Nevertheless, in the early forties, right up to the time Muddy arrived, Maxwell Street and informal house parties were the principal sources of musical employment for blues musicians just in from the South. The nightclubs that featured blues artists were dominated by the clique that had risen to prominence through Lester Melrose's connections with Bluebird and Columbia—John Lee "Sonny Boy" Williamson, Big Bill Broonzy, Memphis Minnie, Tampa Red, and their friends. Robert Nighthawk stayed in Chicago off and on and recorded fairly prolifically for Melrose after 1937, but he was an inveterate drifter and kept returning south. Tommy McClennan, Robert Petway, and Arthur "Big Boy" Crudup, the only other Delta musicians on the Melrose roster, would come to Chicago, rehearse at Tampa Red's house, which doubled as the Melrose rehearsal studio, make their recordings, and return home almost immediately. Apparently not all the black blues fans in Chicago appreciated these singers' country ways; in *Chicago Breakdown*, Mike Rowe tells of McClennan being bodily ejected from a Chicago house party, with his guitar broken over his head, for singing emphatically about "niggers."

But as World War II neared its end, more and more of Chicago's blues fans were Mississippi natives who liked their music rural and raw. The key artist in this transition, and probably the most admired Chicago-based bluesman of the period, was John Lee Williamson, who had arrived in the city in 1937 and made his first recordings for Bluebird that May accompanied by two Delta guitarists, Robert Nighthawk and Joe Williams. The session, held at Victor's studio in Aurora, Illinois, was an important one. Nighthawk, then known as Robert Lee McCoy, cut "Prowlin' Nighthawk," the blues that gave him his name. Williamson, who sang in a personally plaintive style that was somewhat reminiscent of his early western Tennessee cronies Sleepy John Estes and Yank Rachell, recorded "Good Morning Little Schoolgirl," which was a hit and almost immediately became a blues standard, destined to be copied and recopied by rhythm and blues and rock and roll groups. More importantly, with these first recordings Williamson firmly established the harmonica as a versatile solo instrument. Bluesmen had been playing the harp for a long time, of course, but Williamson featured it in sensitively phrased instrumental choruses and played it right into the recording microphone, switching between voice and harp so rapidly that the two sounds seemed to merge into one. His early music was still firmly country-rooted, especially when Nighthawk and Williams were filling in behind him with a mesh of thumping bass patterns and chorded cross-rhythms. But he soon began recording with larger groups, and in May 1940, at a session that produced "I Been Dealing with the Devil," "My Little Machine," and other classics, he first used a drummer. From then on his music developed an increasingly urban rhythmic thrust, while his singing and harmonica playing remained both distinctive and down-home.

As the urbane, rocking, jazz-based music of artists like Louis Jordan and Lionel Hampton gained in popularity, bluesmen and the more commercially minded jazz musicians began favoring a heavy, insistent beat. The new r&b, or jump blues, appealed to black listeners who no longer wished to identify themselves with life down home, and the field offered attractive financial opportunities for skilled jazzmen willing to "play for the people," as Louis Jordan put it. By 1945, a number of Chicago clubs that had been booking Melrose-approved blues artists were switching over to city r&b, and the established blues stars found themselves being squeezed out of many of the smaller joints by musicians fresh from the country who were willing to work for much less. If Sonny Boy's increasingly heavy rhythmic emphasis was in some sense a reaction to the challenge of r&b, his reaction to the increasing domination of the local blues market by Delta-style artists was equally direct: he began hiring some of the best of them.

Eddie Boyd, a pianist who was born on the Frank Moore plantation in Coahoma County and was a childhood friend of Muddy's, arrived in Chicago around 1941 and quickly graduated from marginal tavern work with country bluesmen like Johnny Shines (another 1941 arrival) to a series of engagements with Sonny Boy, in groups that also included guitar, bass and drums. A recording ban had been imposed by the American Federation of Musicians in 1942, in a futile attempt to prevent the burgeoning jukebox business from putting live musicians out of work. It lasted until 1944 and probably kept Boyd from recording with Williamson earlier; in 1945 he went into the studio with Sonny Boy for a session that produced the popular "Elevator Woman" ("Everybody tells me you must be the elevatingest woman in town"). Williamson enjoyed his whiskey and had trouble keeping permanent groups together, a fact that worked to the advantage of some of the younger Delta musicians. Muddy worked with him sporadically, and so did guitarist Johnny Young (who grew up in Muddy's birthplace, Rolling Fork) and the pianist who was to play a central role in the transformation of Chicago blues into amplified Delta blues, Sunnyland Slim.

ONE HUMID NIGHT IN MAY 1978, I drove to Morgen's Liquors, at Sixty-first and Calumet on the South Side, to hear Sunnyland play. Morgen's was in the shadow of an El stop, and when one walked in it seemed to be a perfectly ordinary ghetto liquor store. But behind a curtain in the back, where you'd expect to find a stockroom, there was a long, crowded, dimly lit bar, and in back of that, behind a heavy door, was a plain, square music room, with cheap plywood wall paneling, bare bulbs, and a few paper streamers. Slim, long, lanky, and weathered, was sitting on the tiny bandstand behind a battered red Wurlitzer electric piano, flanked by guitarist Louis Myers, from Byhalia, Mississippi, and a much younger rhythm section. He flexed his arms, grimaced, and downed a shot of booze—he was stabbed in both arms in a 1968 South Side robbery and says he has trouble limbering up—and then Myers counted off a crisp shuffle rhythm and stepped to the microphone. "Woke up this mornin', lookin' 'round for my shoes / You know I had them mean old walkin' blues." It was "the theme," as Muddy calls it, the Delta anthem, and the crowd, all black except for my friend and me, was a middle-aged Mississippi crowd. The beat was different—a trace of funk from the bassist, snappy fills from the drummer—but Louis and Sunnyland were playing "Walkin' Blues" pretty much the way they played it in the thirties.

Slim sounded magnificent, rapping out tone clusters in the treble and walking the basses with all the authority of someone who's been playing the blues for sixty-odd years. "I don't like to play in these kind of places no more," he said during a break, pushing his face up close to be heard over the buzz of conversation and the B. B. King record on the jukebox. "I'll be seventy-two soon. I just been out to California, playin' in Europe. . . . I'm just down here helping Louis out on his gig." Muddy's name came up. "Me and Muddy started out together at the same time," he said. "I brought him in to play guitar for me when I got the call to make a record, 1947. We did a couple of my numbers, and then the man asked me, 'Say, what about your boy there? Can he sing?' Talkin' about Muddy, you know. And I said, 'Like a bird!' "

Slim was born Albert Luandrew on September 5, 1907, on a farm near Vance, Mississippi, twenty or thirty miles southeast of Clarksdale. "It was my grandfather's farm," he says. "Old master was his daddy. At that particular time, white man got pretty much what he wanted. If he seen a woman and want her, he could make it hard, 'cause the blacks was slaves to people then. Anyway, my grandfather split rails, made crossties when the railroads come in, and bought that land—wasn't but seventy-five cents an acre then. He bought another place there near Lambert, and a place in Marks. There where I grew up, we farmed. Plenty of acres of fruit, plenty of pumpkins, nothin' to buy, really, but black pepper and salt and sugar and flour, mules and horses. But wasn't much money, either. It snowed a little in the wintertime, and we didn't have no boots. We had to put sacks around our feet to go out to work. When I was about six, my mother, she got her feet in some water or snow, and she died of double pneumonia.

"Then this new white man, he started puttin' up fences, fenced all the niggers into their land so they couldn't come out, plowed up the road comin' into town. So we moved over there near Lambert, and my daddy, who was a preacher, he remarried. My stepmother, she didn't have no children, and after my daddy married her, she never did create no children. And she treat me so bad till when I was ten or eleven years old, she hurt my head whippin' me with a cane and I ran off. I was big for my age, and I went down to Crenshaw, made a good day pickin' cotton. They come and got me the next mornin', carried me on back home with 'em, but when I was thirteen or fourteen, I left out of there for good."

As the child of landowning, churchgoing folk, Sunnyland had

little early exposure to the blues. Some of his first memories of music are memories of church services, and the instrument that attracted his attention was a pump organ. "Wasn't too much piano playing there in the country," he says, "but my stepmother's Uncle Jimmy had a piano, and every time I could get her to let me, I'd go there. He'd show me a little bit. My cousin in Marks had a good piano, so I was able to go and play that a little. I learned 'Tramp, Tramp, Tramp, the Boys Are Marching,' that was popular then, and 'If I Could Hear My Mother Pray.' Then when I got around twelve or thirteen, I'd go over to see this old lady that went to my daddy's church. I'd cut her kindling, and she'd let me play her organ. I wrote out on a shoebox where I put my fingers at so I could take that home and practice with it."

When he ran away for the last time, Sunnyland found work carrying water for a railroad gang. He worked as a cook, he drove an automobile for a doctor in Lambert, and soon he landed a job playing Wednesday and Saturday nights at a juke joint in the country outside town, a joint that had a piano but hadn't been able to attract a more experienced player. Actually, Sunnyland says, he wasn't bad by the time he was fifteen. He'd been hearing blues here and there, especially after he left home and started working for the railroad, and "they had a boogie kinda thing, fast music, in church. So already, I could play the blues in maybe three keys. I started at fifty cents a night workin' for this fellow, and he would fry fish and hamburgers, have a crap game. I didn't know too much about the dice, but I learned to play pretty good cards. I used to watch them hustlers, and I picked up a few little tricks. This was in '22, and by the end of the year I got hired to play for a motion picture show. Then a fella came out from one of the big farms, got a big place out where there's a lot of quarter houses. I played for him. He gave me two dollars and fifty cents. Then I heard about these places where they cut logs and had piano players. And I was gettin' to be exciting good."

In 1923 Sunnyland ran into Little Brother Montgomery, one of the seminal Deep South blues pianists of the twenties and thirties. Montgomery was from Kentwood, Louisiana, a sawmill town where his father ran a barrelhouse. When he was very young (he was born a year and a half before Sunnyland, on April 18, 1906), he heard pianists with fanciful professional names like Rip Top and Papa Lord God play the blues for his father, and while he soon began absorbing other piano music, including ragtime and early jazz stylings from New Orleans, he concentrated on blues. Like Sunnyland, he ran away from home early—he says he was eleven—and perfected his art by playing long hours for low pay, mostly in the rough-and-tumble Saturday night joints that always clustered around sawmills and lumber camps. Around 1919–20, he found himself in Ferriday, Louisiana, which is just across the Mississippi River from Natchez and would later attain a certain notoriety as the birthplace of rock and roll's piano-pumping wild man, Jerry Lee Lewis. There he met two pianists who worked the joints in Louisiana and Mississippi, Dehlco Robert and Long Tall Friday, and together the three of them worked on more and more elaborate variations of a blues strain that was already popular in the Delta and eventually became best known as "Rollin' and Tumblin'." When they were finished, they had created "The Forty Fours," which Montgomery says is "the hardest barrelhouse blues of any blues in history to play because you have to keep two different times going in each hand."

Montgomery and his friends were already playing pieces with boogie-woogie-style bass patterns, which may well have been created in the logging and turpentine camps and oil boomtowns of Texas, Louisiana, and Mississippi around the turn of the century. They knew these eight-to-the-bar patterns as "Dudlow Joes." "They used to call boogie piano Dudlow Joes in Mississippi," the Vicksburg-born blues bassist Willie Dixon told Karl Gert zur Heide, author of *Deep South Piano*. "I didn't hear it called boogie till long after. If a guy played boogie piano, they'd say he was a Dudlow player. Later on guitars played boogie, too." And later still, there was another change in terminology. "It was in the thirties," says Sunnyland, "that people started talkin' about rockin', like 'rock this house.' But they been playin' that, with the shuffle in it to make it move, since at least 1923 or '24. All them Mississippi people that you never heard of, they been rockin' all their fuckin' life."

"The Forty Fours" wasn't a boogie or a rocker. It was a medium-slow blues with an extravagant, ascending bass line that seemed to operate in an altogether different rhythmic sphere than the familiar downward-tumbling melody. The piece impressed everyone who heard it. It became the ultimate test piece on which Louisiana and Mississippi pianists would gauge each other's mettle. Montgomery has always resented the fact that Lee Green, a pianist from southern Mississippi who learned it from him and from Long Tall Friday, and Roosevelt Sykes, from Helena, Arkansas, both recorded their versions of the theme in 1929, a year before Little Brother cut his own, definitive version, "Vicksburg Blues."

Sunnyland was traveling with a pimp-gambler friend and a car full of whores the night he met Montgomery. They had been jailed overnight in some small Mississippi town, the whores had left under their own power, and then the car broke down on a gravel road outside Canton, Mississippi. As luck would have it, there was a large sawmill nearby, with an impressive, two-story wooden barrelhouse where a hot Saturday night was in progress. Before long, Sunnyland and his friend were heavily involved in a popular card game, Georgia Skin, but there was accomplished piano blues, with occasional ragtime and jazz thrown in, coming from upstairs, and eventually Sunnyland left the game and went up to investigate. Montgomery, who was still, like Sunnyland, a teenager, was loaded on corn whiskey, but he was playing and shouting lustily there in the makeshift parlor, where roaring drunk sawmill hands with ready cash picked out whores to take into the adjoining rooms.

Sunnyland began talking with Brother, expressing admiration for his playing, and Montgomery, whose voice was starting to go, asked him if he could sing. They worked as a team until four or five in the morning, Sunnyland singing in his high but powerful voice while Montgomery played just about every blues he knew. Finally Little Brother stumbled away from the piano stool and collapsed in a corner. The house madam offered Sunnyland some bread and molasses and a cup of coffee, and after he'd eaten, he felt emboldened to try out the piano himself. He sat down and started playing his own version of "Rollin' and Tumblin'," which he'd learned in the Delta, and Montgomery sat bolt upright. "He got up and staggered over," Sunnyland recalls with a chuckle, "and asked me, 'Why in the hell didn't you tell me you could *play?*' 'Cause they'd had him playin' there for hours and hours. Then we both laughed, and we been buddies ever since." Sunnyland learned bass patterns and got other ideas from Montgomery, but in those days he learned from just about every pianist he met. It would be eight years before Montgomery's recordings began spreading his influence and established him as the master of "The Forty Fours." "Meantime," Sunnyland continues, "my friend was downstairs all night skinnin' and makin' himself some money. So we got the car fixed, and our next stop was Memphis."

When country guitarists arrived in Memphis in the twenties, they usually found their way to a little park just off Beale Street (now Handy Park) where they could play and pass the hat. But the pianists, many of whom, like Sunnyland, came from more upwardly mobile family backgrounds, had entrée into different circles. Beale Street was the Midsouth's black main street in those days, and while the large vaudeville theaters tended to employ only nationally known stars like Bessie Smith or the comedy team Butterbeans and Suzy (and maintained pit bands that could either read from sheet music or play improvised jazz), there were plenty of cafés and gambling dens on and around Beale. Generally these places were oblivious to the charms of guitar blues. Their patrons, city slickers and country boys with ambition, would have considered Charley Patton or Son House primitive and déclassé. But pianists, if they dressed flashily and cultivated a worldly air, were welcome.

"Memphis used to be a barrelhouse town," Sunnyland remembers exuberantly. "All the best-dressin' fellows in the world came from Memphis. All the sportin' players came from Memphis. It was the greatest town in the world for pimps and hustlers. That's where a whole lot of people got killed, you know." During the heyday of Beale Street, Memphians committed more murders per capita than the citizens of any other city in the southern United States—89.9 murders for every 100,000 citizens according to a 1916 report by the Prudential Insurance Company. Waves of reformist sentiment were sweeping the town even before 1911, when E. H. Crump was elected mayor and began his three-and-a-half-decade reign as the city's political boss. But the cleanup proceeded gradually. In the late twenties and early thirties, Beale Street and the rougher black neighborhoods of south Memphis, some of which were spreading out toward the Mississippi line, still offered abundant employment opportunities for a blues pianist and card shark of Sunnyland's caliber. Sometimes he played on the outskirts of town and in the country with Walter Horton, a teenage harmonica wizard from northern Mississippi who was to become one of the premier Chicago blues soloists after World War II, and Little Buddy Doyle, a blind dwarf who picked guitar and sang in the streets when he wasn't in a stupor from moonshine, jimson weed, and other intoxicants. "My mind in such a condition till I hardly know the days of the week," Doyle sang in "Bad in Mind Blues," which he recorded, with Horton on harp, in Memphis in 1939.

Sunnyland also worked in West Memphis, Arkansas. "When Mr. Crump cut all that out, everybody starts to get out to West Memphis, and West Memphis had a barrel of blues all the time," he says. "Everywhere you go in West Memphis, there was a gambling joint and honky-tonks. I used to play all them places. It used to be so muddy in the streets you had to carry hip boots to get around." And he rambled up and down the Mississippi, stopping in the towns that were wide open. "Caruthersville [Missouri] was the jumpingest town in the world. Women could hustle and do what they want to do and have protection, you know what I mean? At the sea walls, right 'side the Mississippi River. All them river towns where the boats come in was good." There were also levee camps along the river where the men who labored maintaining the earthworks or sandbagging against the rising current during flood season were usually ready for some entertainment at night. Out in the Deep South's uncut forests, there were lumber and turpentine camps—makeshift towns of unpainted shacks. Sunnyland didn't just play in these camps. He learned to do electrical wiring and fit pipe struts, and sometimes, when money was tight, he would work all week and then play all weekend. But his mind was on his music, which never strayed very far from the basic blues themes he learned in the Delta.

During the early years of his career he was still known as Albert Luandrew. It was in the thirties that he acquired the nickname Sunnyland Slim. At the time, railroads were both the lifeline of the nation and an institution with considerable mythic significance. Southern blacks tended to ascribe personal characteristics to certain trains. "The Sunnyland train," Slim explains, "was a fast train, run right out of Memphis to St. Louis on the Frisco. I started singing about it because, man, it killed peoples. They would be coming to town along those gravel roads, farmers in their wagons gettin' supplies for their families, and people would just get caught comin' across the tracks. The Sunnyland train killed my aunt's husband down there, comin' fast through that brush." In the flat tableland of the Delta, railroad tracks cut right through the fields. If you don't know the area well, you can be riding or driving along a back road and come right up to the tracks without realizing they're there. When trains come through, you can see them from afar. They look sleek and menacing, like snakes, gliding, without any visible means of locomotion, "through that brush." So tall, skinny Albert Luandrew became Sunnyland Slim—a man who traveled far and fast and could be dangerous.

By the early forties, Sunnyland had made the acquaintance of an extraordinary number of blues musicians, including the pianists Roosevelt Sykes and Peter Chatman (Memphis Slim, who moved to Chicago and began recording for Bluebird in 1940), the guitarists Robert Johnson and Honeyboy Edwards, and the harmonica players John Lee "Sonny Boy" Williamson, Rice Miller (who began calling himself Sonny Boy Williamson some time in the forties, after John Lee was a popular Bluebird recording artist), and Little Walter Jacobs (who was very little then, a child runaway hustling for spare change and sleeping on pool tables). Except for Robert Johnson, all these musicians, and many, many more, made the move to Chicago sooner or later. Sunnyland made his move around 1942 or 1943, and with his outgoing disposition and taking-care-of-business attitude, he was soon well known among both the established blues stars and the newer arrivals. He renewed his acquaintance with John Lee Williamson, and he began working with Peter Cleighton, who, as Dr. Clayton, enjoyed a brief run of popularity as a Bluebird recording artist before his wife and two children were run over by a train and he drank himself to death. Cleighton died in 1946, and by that time Sunnyland was chummy with the long-established Tampa Red, whose house he rented when Tampa decided to move to a better neighborhood.

SUNNYLAND MET MUDDY WATERS at the Flame Club on Chicago's South Side sometime in the mid-forties. It was Muddy's first really decent musical job, fifty-two dollars a week as guitar accompanist to his old friend Eddie Boyd. He was still holding down a day job as well. His musical engagements in Chicago up to that point had included house parties with guitarists Jimmy Rogers and Lee Brown, occasional out-of-town gigs with John Lee Williamson (who was drinking more and more and seems to have appreciated the fact that Muddy owned a car and was willing to drive to nearby towns like Gary and back to Chicago overnight), and a few informal tavern engagements, in West Side joints that paid five dollars a night, if that, with Rogers on harmonica and Blue Smitty (Claude Smith, from Marianna, in the Arkansas Delta) on second guitar. During the course of these jobs Muddy picked up, largely from Smitty, a rudimentary but adequate knowledge of guitar styles that were at the time considered "modern." When he came to Chicago, he was limited to Delta-style bottleneck playing, while Smitty's more urban style has been described by Mike Rowe as "an awkward compendium of such diverse influences as [Big Boy] Crudup, Yank Rachell, and [the jazz guitarist] Charlie Christian." It was a single-string lead guitar style, a more basic version of the kind of melodic runs and fill-ins a jazz guitarist might play behind a singer.

The sophisticated jump blues of performers like Louis Jordan and smooth blues ballads, as sung by Charles Brown, Nat "King" Cole, and other California-based artists, were the latest trends in black popular music, and these were the sounds Eddie Boyd was purveying at the Flame Club. Despite the coaching he'd had from Smitty, Muddy just didn't fit in. "Eddie wanted me to play like Johnny Moore," he says, referring to the fluent, jazzy guitarist who picked tastefully behind Charles Brown. "He wanted it to be a sweet kind of blues." But then Sonny Boy Williamson offered Boyd a better-paying job playing for steel mill workers in Gary, and he left the Blue Flame; Sunnyland Slim replaced him. With Sunnyland and Muddy playing strong Delta bass patterns, Blue Smitty filling in modern-style leads, and all three singing, they had a jumping little combo. But Smitty kept sweet-talking various women and disappearing into a nearby hotel when he was supposed to be on the bandstand, and one evening he drank too much and made the mistake of picking a fight with Sunnyland. As a result, the band lost their job, and their next gig at the Cotton Club as well.

By that time Sunnyland had had enough of Smitty, but he liked Muddy. They were both from the Delta, both old enough to be serious and professional about their music (Muddy was in his early thirties, Sunnyland almost forty), both proud, dignified men who showed up for work well dressed and sober—even if they didn't always stay that way all night. "I got drunk and got in a fight once on that job with Eddie Boyd," Muddy admits. "I was foolin' around with one of them little ole girls. She made good money and was paying the note on a car, and she started it all. I throwed all the whiskey bottles they had on the table, and when I got through, I went behind the bar and started throwing *them* whiskey bottles. They put me in jail overnight. But mostly, you know, I didn't do that. I wanted to be nationally known, and I worked on it." Sunnyland stayed in touch.

In September 1946, Lester Melrose arranged a session for Columbia Records featuring three unknown blues vocalists. Sunnyland, who was asked to play piano on the session, made sure one of them was Muddy. (The other two, Homer Harris and James "Beale Street" Clark, rapidly dropped from sight.) Muddy and Harris played guitars, Sunnyland filled in the sound with his rolling upper register tremolos, and an unidentified bassist and drummer carried the rhythm. Muddy tried his best to sound modern. He picked simple single-string lead figures and heavy boogie basses on his three vocal selections, and his bottleneck was nowhere in evidence. His singing was strong but restrained. The result was a set of recordings that were slick and shallow compared to what Muddy could do but too down-home, it seems, for Columbia. The company released nothing from the session, and Lester Melrose, the kingpin of Chicago blues recording for more than a decade, let the city's next and eventually its biggest blues star slip through his fingers.

By this time Muddy was working days at "the best job I ever had in my life," driving a delivery truck for a company that manufactured venetian blinds. "After I learned all the calls in the city," he says, "I'd take my load out at eight-thirty, and by one in the afternoon I'd be back at my house—in the bed. Around four-thirty I'd get up and carry the mail to the post office—boom!—I'm through. I had to sleep 'cause I was playing five nights a week."

Sometime in 1947 Sunnyland arranged to record a session for Aristocrat, a company that had been started earlier that year by two Polish-born Jews, Leonard and Phil Chess, along with a woman named Evelyn. The Chess brothers, who arrived in the United States in 1928, had worked hard; by 1947 they owned several bars and clubs on the South Side, including the Macomba, where popular jazz and rhythm and blues artists performed. Their first Aristocrat releases were strictly jazz and city r&b, but Sammy Goldstein, the company's talent scout, thought Aristocrat might do well in the blues field and called Sunnyland to arrange a session. It was going to be a duo, with Big Crawford on bass, but late in the game someone, probably Goldstein, suggested the addition of a guitarist, and Sunnyland thought of Muddy. "I caught the streetcar up there to Muddy's house," the pianist recalls, "and Annie Mae told me he was out with the truck. The session was for two o'clock." A friend of Muddy's, Antra Bolton, was there visiting and offered to track Muddy down, and since his delivery routine rarely varied, it didn't take long. Muddy had been disheartened by the Columbia experience and wasn't about to let another opportunity to get on records pass him by. He called his boss, explained in a voice shaking with emotion that his cousin had been murdered in a ghetto alley, turned the truck over to Bolton, who finished the run, hurried home to get his guitar, and made it on time to Universal Studios, on North Wacker Drive in downtown Chicago, for the session.

First Sunnyland recorded two numbers, including one of his best, "Johnson Machine Gun," a violent urban fantasy with a touch of sinister humor. "I'm gonna buy me a Johnson machine gun," he sang, with a high, slightly pinched sound that was more than a little reminiscent of Dr. Clayton, "and a carload of explosion balls / I'm gonna be a walkin' cyclone, from Saginaw to the Niagara Falls." The song began as a boast and ended as a threat: "Now, little girl, the undertaker's been here, girl, and I gave him your height and size / Now if you don't be makin' whoopee with the Devil tomorrow this time, baby, God knows you'll be surprised." After he recorded the more conventional "Fly Right, Little Girl," someone, again probably Goldstein, asked him if Muddy could sing. Characteristically, Muddy was ready, this time with two tightly composed original blues that were much better than the mostly traditional material he'd recorded for Columbia. "Little Anna Mae," the second number he recorded, was a personal account of trouble with his live-in girl friend; "Gypsy Woman" was more intriguing.

You know the gypsy woman told me that you your mother's bad luck child
Well you havin' a good time now, but that'll be trouble after while

Well now you know I went to a gypsy woman to have my fortune told
Say you better go back home, son, and peek through your, your keyhole
You know the gypsy woman told me that you your mother's bad luck child
Well you're havin' a good time now, but that'll be trouble after while

Well now you know I went home, I took the gypsy woman as she said
I peeked through my keyhole, and there was another man layin' in my bed
You know the gypsy woman told me that you your mother's bad luck child
Well you havin' a good time now but that'll be trouble after while

Muddy still thought people wanted to hear modern guitar playing, not his Delta bottleneck blues, and once again he played single-string lead lines. But his work was much improved—he sounded something like Joe Willie Wilkins or perhaps Willie Johnson, two Delta guitarists with backgrounds similar to his who began recording in Memphis a few years later. And he was singing strongly, letting his Delta pronunciations of words like "gypsaay" come out naturally, varying his timbre and playing with pitches to suggest subtle shadings of emotion and meaning. The lyrics were probably inspired by the gypsy fortune-telling salons of the Maxwell Street area and should have been perfect for the black blues audience of the period. But Leonard Chess didn't think much of the record. He let it sit on the shelf for several months before he released it and apparently didn't push it even then.

Then, early in 1948, Aristocrat called Muddy in to do another session. Leonard Chess may have wanted to stockpile material in anticipation of another recording ban by the American Federation of Musicians. In any event, he was still unenthusiastic about Muddy; his partner Evelyn and Sammy Goldstein probably talked him into arranging the session. At the rehearsal that immediately preceded it, Muddy ran through his repertoire. This time, having failed twice in his attempts at contemporary urban blues, he brought his bottleneck and tried some of his old Delta numbers, including several he'd recorded for the Library of Congress. "What's he singing? I can't understand what he's singing," Chess reportedly protested.

"Evelyn was the one that really liked me," says Muddy. "Leonard didn't know nothing about no blues, but she did." And so, despite Chess's skepticism, Muddy recorded "I Can't Be Satisfied" and "I Feel Like Going Home." On a Saturday morning in April 1948, copies of the record went out to Aristocrat's South Side outlets, which included barber and beauty shops, variety stores, and other "mom and dad" businesses, as well as a few record shops. A little more than twelve hours later, the initial pressing was sold out.

The next morning Muddy got up early and went right over to the Maxwell Radio Record Company. The crowded, chaotic little shop was run by one-eyed Bernard Abrams, another of Maxwell Street's Eastern European Jewish immigrants. Abrams had primitive recording equipment in the back and had made acetates for a number of Maxwell Street blues performers. Muddy had played in front of the store in 1947 to help advertise the release of one of two discs Abrams put out in a brief and discouraging attempt to enter the record business, "I Just Keep Loving Her" and "Ora Nelle Blues" by harmonica player Little Walter Jacobs and guitarist Othum Brown. He had been playing with Little Walter off and on for a few years but says he "kind of bypassed around Walter for a while 'cause he had a bad, mean temper, always stayed in fights." He didn't hang around Maxwell Street much, either, but this Sunday morning he wanted a couple of copies of a certain record— *his* record. The crafty Abrams had stockpiled a few and was selling them for $1.10 each, one to a customer (list price was 79 cents). Muddy complained that it was his name on the label, but Abrams adamantly refused to sell him more than one copy or lower the price. Disgusted, Muddy took the one record, went home, and sent Annie Mae over for another one.

Leonard Chess was caught off guard by the success of "I Can't Be Satisfied"/"I Feel Like Going Home," but, like any good businessman, he knew a good thing when he saw it. More copies were rapidly pressed, and soon the disc was selling steadily in Chicago and throughout the South. "I had a hot blues out, man," Muddy says, still feeling cocky about it after all these years. "I'd be driving my truck, and whenever I'd see a neon beer sign, I'd stop, go in, look at the jukebox, and see is my record on there. I might buy me a beer and play the record and then leave. Don't tell nobody nothing. Before long, every blues joint there was, that record was on the jukebox. And if you come in and sat there for a little while, if anybody was in there, they gonna punch it. Pretty soon I'd hear it walking along the street. I'd hear it *driving* along the street. About June or July that record was getting *really* hot. I would be driving home from playing, two or three o'clock in the morning, and I had a convertible, with the top back 'cause it was warm. I could hear people all upstairs playing that record. It would be *rolling* up there, man. I heard it all over. One time I heard it coming from way upstairs somewhere, and it scared me. I thought I had died."

Listening to the record today, it's easy enough to imagine getting a creepy feeling from hearing it echo down some deserted street in the dead of night. The singing is stronger and more commanding than on Muddy's Library of Congress recordings of the same material, and with Big Crawford contributing a firm bass part and Muddy playing more simply and with a heavier rhythmic emphasis, the music has a punching, danceable beat, especially on the up-tempo A side, "I Can't Be Satisfied." But the most striking difference between the 1941 and 1948 recordings is electricity. Muddy had been playing electric guitar since 1944. An acoustic was adequate for apartment parties, but if a guitarist wanted to cut through the noise in a crowded city joint, amplification was a necessity. It lent Muddy's sound a certain weight and density, and it brought out subtleties in his slide playing that had been lost even on the well-recorded Library of Congress sides, including silvery high harmonics that rang out above the notes he was actually playing, sounding like a ghostly second guitar. On "I

Feel Like Going Home," Muddy affected a wide vocal vibrato at the end of certain lines, an effect he may well have picked up from listening to the tremololike sound of his amplified bottleneck playing.

This was the old, deep Delta blues, no doubt about that, but it was also something new. It stood out amid the glut of r&b releases by sax-led jump combos and blues balladeers because of its simplicity, its passion, and its hypnotic one-chord droning. Blacks who lived or had lived down home snapped the record up, and women in particular responded to the music's undercurrent of sexuality. It was no accident that Leonard Chess's partner Evelyn heard Muddy's potential before Leonard himself did; as Howlin' Wolf later sang, "The men don't know, but the little girls understand."

Sometime in 1948 Sunnyland Slim arranged to cut a session for another struggling, and ultimately unsuccessful, Chicago label, Tempo Tone. Once again, his choice of sidemen shaped and hastened the development of the new Chicago blues, for this was the first recorded collaboration between Muddy and Little Walter. The rambunctious young harmonica player was becoming a more frequent associate of Muddy and his now almost constant sidekick, Jimmy Rogers. The one tune issued by Tempo Tone, "I Want My Baby," doesn't sound much like a harbinger of things to come. It's a raucous, jumping novelty number with Little Walter singing lead and Sunnyland and Muddy answering, the kind of light, jazzy hokum Tampa Red and other Bluebird artists were recording in the forties. But the session did demonstrate to Muddy that the wild and frequently contrary Little Walter was ambitious enough to endure the many small (and sometimes not so small) indignities of a professional recording session.

AFTER THE TEMPO TONE SESSION, Muddy and Sunnyland went their separate ways. Sunnyland left Aristocrat after arguing with Leonard Chess over money and went on to record for most of the host of Chicago independent labels that kept springing up, issuing a few records, and then folding. He made plenty of fine records, but the fledgling companies didn't really know how to sell them, and none of them were hits. Muddy stuck with Leonard Chess. "I thought Leonard was the best man in the business," he says. "He did a lot for me, putting out that first record and everything, and we had a good relationship with one another. I didn't even sign no contract with him, no nothing. It was just 'I belongs to the Chess family.' "

The relationship does seem curious. "Leonard had an extraordinarily coarse outer manner," recalls Malcolm Chisholm, an engineer who worked with him frequently at Universal Studios beginning in 1957. "I always wanted to send him a Mother's Day card because he answered the phone that way—'Hello, Mother.' That coarse exterior wasn't altogether phony, but he could be an absolutely charming man, and a master politician. He often was bone-headed and arrogant when running a session, but it wasn't that he was nasty or personally difficult. He was just absolutely sure about what he wanted. In some ways, he was like the blacks he worked with. The blacks say, 'Well, I'll go into my act for this guy,' and they literally change personality, adjusting it to suit. Meanwhile they're sizing you up. You say six words, and they know where you're coming from. Leonard was like that. He learned to be several dozen people. With some of the blues players, the whole session would be Leonard and whoever it was calling each other stacks of motherfuckers. But in the case of Muddy Waters, who was intelligent, perceptive, and all that good stuff, Leonard dealt with him in a very gentlemanly manner, on the basis of absolute mutual respect.

"Another thing about Leonard is that he was genuinely superstitious. He lived in one of those exclusively Jewish villages in Poland until he was about seven, and there was a tremendous amount of superstition involved in that. I think Leonard picked up a great many more superstitions from the blacks with whom he lived and worked, and whom he rather liked, although he didn't admit it much. You would find him acting irrationally in odd ways. He didn't like to record on Fridays, and he would never record on the thirteenth, but the seventh and eleventh were nice. You could dope those out after a while, but in other situations, you would never understand why Leonard would or would not do a given thing. A lot of it was intense, deep-rooted superstition. Well, he eventually sold the company for about fourteen million dollars—maybe he was right."

By the end of 1948 Muddy had a steady working band, with Jimmy Rogers on guitar, Little Walter on harmonica, and Baby Face Leroy Foster doubling on guitar and drums. But Leonard Chess refused to record the group until the summer of 1950, and even then he only used Muddy, Jimmy, and Walter—it was several more months before he allowed them to bring in Foster and then Elgin Evans on drums. The generally accepted explanation is that Chess thought he'd found a winning formula in the combination of Muddy's amplified slide guitar and Big Crawford's bass and didn't want to change it, and while a few records were made in 1949 and early 1950 with Leroy on second guitar and, on one session, Johnny Jones on piano, for the most part Muddy's releases did follow the formula. "You're Gonna Miss Me" was a remake of "I Can't Be Satisfied," with the same guitar and bass parts and different words, and Muddy also recorded "Rollin' and Tumblin' " and other traditional material during this period, even though his band was a popular club attraction on the South Side and had already developed the most original and influential ensemble sound in postwar blues. Malcolm Chisholm offers an alternative explanation for Chess's reluctance to record the band—his superstition. "I've been told that once, and it may have been on Muddy's first successful session, the bass player wore a red shirt. The record sold. The next session, Leonard said, 'Get that bass man. And have him wear a red shirt.' Eventually, I guess his business instincts and the empathy he had for people prevailed. I would argue that Leonard didn't know shit about blues, but he knew an awful lot about feeling. He could *feel* music, although he never learned to read it, and he could feel how people were responding to it. So he *developed* a good feeling for blues, as he went along."

Once the full band began recording, the masterpieces came thick and fast—"Louisiana Blues," "Long Distance Call," "Honey Bee," and "She Moves Me," all from 1951, defined the sound of the new Chicago blues and were soon being imitated in Detroit, in Memphis, down in the Delta, even on the East and

West coasts. They also made Muddy's reputation. "I Can't Be Satisfied"/"I Feel Like Going Home" and the similar singles that followed it had sold almost exclusively in Chicago, Detroit, St. Louis, and the Deep South; it was "Louisiana Blues," his first record to feature Little Walter, that introduced his name to the national rhythm and blues charts. The record also helped establish the Chess label—Leonard and Phil had bought out their partner in the Aristocrat venture just in time to change the logo on the Muddy Waters record that preceded "Louisiana Blues," which was "Rollin' Stone," Muddy's version of "Catfish Blues."

On July 11, Little Walter, who'd been blowing his harmonica through a cheap amplifier since his earliest appearances on Maxwell Street, used an amp in the studio for the first time. The distortion and sustain the amplification added did for Walter's harp what electricity had done for Muddy's slide guitar—it transformed a subtle accompanying style into forceful, big-toned lead work. On the more ordinary of the four songs recorded at the session, "Country Boy" and "My Fault," Walter's harp was recorded at a much higher volume than Muddy's slide guitar. It wrapped itself around the vocals, combining the fluidity of a saxophone with the chordal richness of an organ. In "She Moves Me," which became Muddy's third Top Ten r&b hit in early 1952, the group achieved an almost eerie immediacy. The engineering on the record is brilliant—a touch of echo blends the sounds of the amplified guitars and harp ever so slightly together, and Muddy's vocal is recorded "hot," or close to the overload range, so that it sounds every bit as powerful as the electric instruments. The percussion is a booming bass drumbeat that simply marks each downbeat.

"Leonard Chess played the bass drum," Muddy explains, "because my drummer couldn't get that beat on 'She Moves Me.' The verse was too long. You know, it says, 'She moves a crazy man, he says, Now I'm not so dumb / I took her to a funeral, the dead jump up and run / She spoke to a deaf and dumb boy, he said, Now I can speak,' and that's where he couldn't hold it, 'cause it goes on, 'She shook her finger in a blind man's face, he say, I once was blind, but now I see / She moves me, man. . . .' My drummer wanted to play a turnaround there where I said, and there wasn't no turnaround there. I had to go another six or eight bars more to get it turned around. My drummer wasn't doin' nothin', just dum-chik dum-chik dum, but he couldn't hold it there to save his damn life, and Leonard Chess knew where it was. So Leonard told him, 'Get the fuck out of the way. I'll do that.' "

It was the kind of personal touch that made Leonard Chess a great blues producer. The session concluded with a tune Muddy was using as an in-person showstopper, "Still a Fool," another reworking of "Catfish Blues" that began "Well now there's two, there's two trains runnin' /Well, ain't neither one goin' my way / Well now one run at midnight an' the other one / Runnin' just 'fore day." Little Walter and Jimmy Rogers played electric guitars that meshed into a raw, distorted wall of sound. Muddy turned in one of his greatest vocal performances, but he didn't play on the record, probably because when he did the number on stage, he would put down his guitar, jump up and down, stomp on the floor, and run back and forth like an epileptic suffering a seizure, chanting all the while the concluding litany, "She's all right, she's all right."

The years 1951–53, when Muddy was consistently hitting the national r&b charts with those overwhelming recordings for Chess, were years of war in Korea and prosperity at home. As Mike Rowe points out in the definitive study of Chicago blues, *Chicago Breakdown*, "The non-white unemployment rate dropped . . . to 4.1% in 1953, the lowest ever recorded." But by the end of 1953 the war was over and a particularly grim recession was setting in. Some of the Delta musicians who were recording in Chicago reflected the change by writing blues that were bitterly outspoken. J. B. Lenoir, who was from Monticello, Mississippi, and had played with Elmore James and Rice Miller down home, warned on his Chess release "Everybody Wants to Know": "You rich people listen, you better listen real deep / If we poor get so hungry, we gonna take some food to eat." Floyd Jones and the Kentucky-born John Brim also made records that explicitly protested the hard times. Muddy sailed through 1954 with the biggest r&b hits of his career—"I'm Your Hoochie Coochie Man," "Just Make Love to Me" (which is better known as "I Just Want to Make Love to You"), and "I'm Ready," all of which were written for him by bassist Willie Dixon. The last two records were the only ones Muddy made that cracked the r&b Top Five.

Dixon, a huge, outgoing bear of a man, is an almost exact contemporary of Muddy's. He was born July 1, 1915, and grew up on a farm near Vicksburg, Mississippi, one of fourteen children. During the late twenties he lived briefly in Chicago, and after returning to Mississippi for several years, he settled in the Windy City for good in 1936. His checkered background included singing spirituals and boxing as a heavyweight, but after he got to Chicago he decided to concentrate on music and took up the string bass. During the forties he worked with two popular, slick club blues groups, the Five Breezes and the Big Three Trio, but he liked to keep up with the newer arrivals from his home state, and when starker, more down-home styles began to dominate the blues recording field in Chicago in the late forties and early fifties, he easily adapted. He listened with interest to the development of Muddy's music, for he'd known Muddy's reputation since the thirties. "There was quite a few people around singin' the blues," he says, "but most of 'em was singin' all *sad* blues. Muddy was givin' his blues a little pep, and ever since I noticed him givin' his blues this kinda pep feelin', I began tryin' to think of things in a peppier form."

Early in 1954, Dixon came up with a song he thought might be right for Muddy. "Through many generations," he says, "there has been people that felt like other people could tell them some of the past or the future—even back in Biblical days. Just from thinkin' about all these different things, I got the idea for this song." It was "Hoochie Coochie Man."

"Muddy was working in this big joint at Fourteenth and Ashland," Dixon continues, "and I went over there to take him the song. We went in the washroom and sang it over and over till he got it. It didn't take very long. Then he said, 'Man, when I go out there this time, I'm gonna *sing* it.' He went out and jumped on it, and it sounded so good the people kept on applauding and asking for more, and he kept on singing the same thing over and over again." There was no need for further market research; the audience was made up of the sort of people who were buying Muddy's records, and they weren't at all shy about stating their preferences.

Dixon had already been in the studio with Muddy on January 7, 1954. They recorded his "Just Make Love to Me" at that session, but it wasn't released until after the chart success of "I'm Your

Hoochie Coochie Man." Leonard Chess had been using Dixon on many of his blues sessions because of the bassist's solid playing and reliability, and after Muddy made two of his songs into hits, they recorded together regularly. The band on "Just Make Love to Me," "I'm Your Hoochie Coochie Man," and "I'm Ready" was the finest of all Muddy's groups. Little Walter, who'd left to front his own group in 1952 after he scored an r&b hit of his own with "Juke," was still recording with Muddy, and the rest of the personnel included Jimmy Rogers, Elgin Evans, Dixon, and Otis Spann, a spectacular young pianist from Jackson, Mississippi, who'd learned to play from his father, the Delta bluesman Friday Ford, and from Little Brother Montgomery.

All three of Muddy's Dixon-penned 1954 hits featured stop-time riffs, the whole band phrasing them in unison—dah *dah* dah dat! Similar riffs had long been a part of jazz, and Ray Charles, who was scoring early hits in 1954 in his new, heavily gospel-based r&b style, was fond of stop-time. But the particular riffs that Muddy and his band came up with (according to Dixon these riffs did come from the band and weren't his own inventions) struck a responsive chord in some unlikely places. Out in Los Angeles, two Jewish teenagers, Jerry Leiber and Mike Stoller, were writing r&b tunes and producing discs by black vocal groups for their own Spark label. In 1955 they made a record called "Riot in Cell Block Number Nine" with a group called the Robins, using a Muddy Waters stop-time riff as their instrumental backdrop. The record was one of the first r&b hits to feature extensive use of sound effects and precisely timed comedy hits. The next year, the Robins disbanded, and Leiber and Stoller formed a new group using some of the original Robins—the Coasters, who became one of the most popular black groups of the rock and roll era under Leiber and Stoller's direction. A little later Muddy and Willie Dixon were surprised to hear one of Muddy's stop-time patterns pop up in the jazz soundtrack to the film "Man with the Golden Arm." "We felt like this was a great achievement, for one of these blues phrases to be used in a movie," says Dixon, diplomatically. These riffs, particularly the dah-*dah*-dah-dat! from "I'm Your Hoochie Coochie Man," were soon absorbed into the lingua franca of blues, r&b, jazz, and rock and roll.

Stop-time wasn't Muddy's only rhythmic innovation during the mid-fifties. "I had to find me a drummer that would *drive*," he says. "My drummer [Elgin Evans] was straight right down—bop bop bop bop. I had to part from him 'cause he just couldn't hit the backbeat. The blues *do* have a backbeat to it, you know, *today*." Muddy found a solid backbeat drummer in 1954 in Francis Clay, who stayed with him until the early sixties. Again, putting a back-beat (heavy emphasis on the second and fourth of every four beats) behind the blues didn't originate with Muddy, but once he made the move, other musicians followed, and the sound rapidly filtered into the emerging rock and roll idiom. "You know," Willie Dixon reflects, "when you go to changin' beats in music, you change the whole style. The difference in blues or rock and roll or jazz is the beat. The beat actually changes the whole entire style. Muddy was able to change these various styles of music because he was always lookin' for something unique, and I learned very early that when you're able to create something that's good and different also, you don't have very much trouble sellin' it."

Dixon's songs, especially "I'm Your Hoochie Coochie Man," are the songs people most readily associate with Muddy, and this is ironic, for their flamboyance, macho posturing, and extra-gener-ous helping of hoodoo sensationalism are much less subtle than Muddy's own material. During the same period, for example, Muddy wrote a song that he recorded twice with somewhat differ-ent lyrics, once as "Clouds in My Heart" and once as "Flood." It was never a hit, but he thought enough of it to put it back in his repertoire and perform it for college audiences during the sixties, and in its own modest way, it's one of the finest of all his blues. "Flood," recorded with a watery tremolo on the guitar, goes like this:

So cloudy, so cloudy, I believe it's gonna rain
So cloudy, so cloudy, I believe it's goin' to rain
I don't believe my woman love me, she's in love with another man

Go look at the weather, I believe it's goin' to be a flood
Go and look out at the weather, I believe it's goin' to be a flood
I believe my baby gon' quit me, because I can feel it all in my blood

Oh, stop and listen, don't you hear how the thunder roar
Oh, stop and listen, don't you hear how the thunder roar
I'm so blue and lonesome, don't you hear how the wind is blowin'

Anyone who's lived in the country, and particularly in an area like the Delta where almost everyone depends on the weather for his livelihood, is sensitive to atmospheric changes. The first time I heard Muddy's "Flood," I remembered an afternoon, years before, when I felt an overcast sky dropping lower and lower, increasing a peculiarly disturbing pressure I could feel physically, in my blood. I was sure the heavens were going to pour down rain and lightning bolts at any moment. But the storm never came—it was inside me, a perception of a gathering emotional storm that I'd unconsciously projected into the cloudy skies. "Flood" brought back that afternoon so vividly I could taste it. The song delineates, in three felicitous, formally perfect verses, an intimate and immutable linkage between the worlds outside and inside our bodies that city dwellers aren't always attuned to and country people simply *know*.

Living in the city, Muddy adapted to survive. He sang Willie Dixon's songs, which gave him a repertoire loaded with crowd-pleasers and transformed his personal magnetism (which he'd projected in a more understated manner in songs like "Gypsy Woman" and "Louisiana Blues") into a marketable image. For the public, Muddy became the bedroom root doctor, the seer-stud with down-home *power* and urban cool. But he never lost sight of the Delta foundations he mined so deeply in his singing and playing and in lyrics like "Flood," and his audience loved him for that, too. Through all the changes—the rhythmic "pep," the flashier lyrics, and a more and more flamboyant performing style—he kept playing his unmistakable slide guitar and singing his old Delta favorites, and this fidelity to tradition was especially appreciated in the Delta itself, where many of the younger blues musicians were breaking away from the styles and songs that had been the common property of their predecessors for several generations. The breakaway was prodded along by Robert Johnson's stepson and chosen musical heir, Robert Jr. Lockwood.

PART
III

CHAPTER 5
King Biscuit Time

"Helena was a little Chicago back in the thirties and forties," says a lifelong resident. "We had nine, maybe close to ten thousand people living here then, and around seventy percent was black." The blacks came from rural Arkansas and from the Mississippi Delta just across the river because they knew they could make money. There were boats full of cotton to be unloaded, a cotton-processing complex that covered several blocks just south of the center of town, railroad yards, and other industries, including, for a time during the forties and early fifties, a West Helena Chrysler plant. And of course there were other ways to make money—bootlegging, gambling, playing the blues.

The town was wide open. Cherry, the main street, which parallels the levee a block to the west, is reputed to have had forty or fifty white saloons in operation during the years preceding World War II, and Elm, which parallels Cherry a block farther west, probably had a comparable number of black joints. Because of its unusual, dappled residential pattern, Helena had black joints all over town. There were joints north of downtown, amid the rows of one-story shotgun houses and vacant lots planted in peas and corn that clustered up against the north side of Walker Levee, a steep ridge of sod designed to keep floodwaters out of the white neighborhoods to the south. Farther north, where the houses start thinning out as the land rises abruptly, forming Crowley Ridge, there were joints. At the opposite, southern end of town, where cotton warehouses, small factories, and rambling railroad yards cluster in a kind of industrial suburb ringed by ramshackle black housing, there were more joints. Farther south, almost out in the country, was Helena Crossing, a black residential enclave whose day laborers might work harvesting cotton in the spring and commute in to town jobs the rest of the year. In West Helena, more black housing and more joints clustered around a railroad switching yard. Wherever blacks could find work and wherever they lived, they didn't have to go far to spend their paychecks on liquor, women, and music.

"Helena was a pretty nice-sized town then," says bluesman Johnny Shines. "Had its own bus service, I remember. And lots of places to play there, too. Juke joints, I guess you'd call them. The guys running them had the protection of the police—not state protection but the local police—so they kept the places open through those means. Beer was served in cups. Whiskey you had to drink out of the bottle. See, they couldn't use mugs in there because the people would commit mayhem, tear people's head up with those mugs. Rough places they were. When you were playing in a place like that, you just sit there on the floor in a cane-bottomed chair, just rear back and cut loose." Guitarists like Shines, Robert Johnson, his stepson, Robert Jr. Lockwood, and Howlin' Wolf played in the rougher places, while many of the gambling dens along Walnut and the side streets closer to the river employed pianists like Sunnyland Slim, Memphis Slim, and the Helena-born Roosevelt Sykes.

The music wasn't confined to the joints. "On a Saturday afternoon or a Saturday night, all you had to do was go down to the landing where the boats docked, or down along Walnut Street, and these guys would be out on the corner singing," says Sonny Payne, a white radio announcer and former swing band bassist who's lived in Helena most of his life. "Or you could go down to the railroad depot south of the main part of town, and there'd be some guys sitting there playing harmonica and guitar. Play half an hour, people come by and drop something in the hat. Down at Cherry and Elm, right by where you drive through the gap in the levee down to the ferry landing, the kids would get together and sit on the sidewalk across from the Illinois Central ticket office and the main telegraph office. Most of us couldn't afford radios back in the thirties when I was growing up, so we'd sit there and wait for the telegraph operator in St. Louis to telegraph the innings in the baseball game. 'Two balls, two strikes. Uh-oh. They got a man on base.' This is how we used to listen to baseball, by Morse code. And there'd be musicians around there. These people played so beautifully. They would come into town in the evening after picking cotton all day, sit right on the piers down by the river with their guitars and their harmonicas and even with Jew's harps, and they would sing the blues and make it sound like something out of Hollywood, like somebody really *produced* it. It was unrehearsed. It was the way these people lived. Back in the thirties and forties we had the best music in the world, right here in this town."

In November 1941, Helena began sharing some of this music with the rest of the northern Delta. Sam Anderson, a white businessman with homespun features, a receding hairline, and ears that seemed to stick out almost at right angles from the sides of his head, had begun putting together a studio, staff, and program schedule for the town's first radio station around the beginning of the year. Local residents who owned sets could pick up the more powerful Memphis stations, but a station right in the center of town was something else again. The news spread like wildfire.

One afternoon two black musicians who'd been performing together on Helena street corners for several years showed up at Anderson's office and asked to see him. One of them, who was known variously as Rice Miller, Willie Miller, and Little Boy Blue, was a tall, lanky harmonica player in his mid-forties. Even for a man who was six foot one or two, Miller had enormous hands. The weathered lines in his face and his prominent eyelids—droopy above the eyes, pouched and puffy below—made him look older than he was. His friend and guitar accompanist, twenty-five-year-old Robert Lockwood, was known among the musicians in town as Robert Jr. After his father, Robert Lockwood, Sr., and his mother separated, Robert Johnson began courting his mother and entered into an intimate, ongoing relationship with her. Robert Jr.—the Jr. was added to his name in recognition of his stylistic and personal debt to Robert Johnson—was quiet, a little withdrawn in fact, with close-cropped hair that was already thinning on top and bright, piercing eyes. He'd recorded for Bluebird in Chicago the previous July, and one of his songs, "Take a Little Walk with Me," a sexy come-on that was musically and lyrically in the Robert Johnson tradition, was already well on its way to becoming a Delta blues standard.

Miller and Lockwood both knew blues musicians who'd broadcast over the radio. As early as 1935, the washboard player, blues singer, drummer, and tap dancer James "Peck" Curtis had been on the air in Blytheville, Arkansas. The show didn't last long, but Curtis later bragged about how many people he'd been able to attract to his juke joint performances by announcing them in advance over the radio. The garrulous Rice Miller, who always seemed to do most of the talking when he was with Lockwood, had a proposition for Sam Anderson: the two of them would perform on his radio station every day if he'd let them announce where they'd be playing at night.

There are several versions of what happened next. According to Sonny Payne, an original KFFA staff announcer, "They came in and talked to my boss one day, asked him could they get on the radio and play blues. Sam told 'em, 'The first thing you have to do is get you a sponsor.' He sent 'em over to the Interstate Grocery Company to see Max Moore, the owner, and Max gave 'em a little break." Max Moore's account, as published in the English magazine *Blues Unlimited,* has Miller and Lockwood auditioning live in Sam Anderson's office and Anderson calling Moore, who had been considering sponsoring a show in order to advertise his King Biscuit Flour. At any rate, Anderson and Moore were both impressed—like Sonny Payne, they'd been listening to the blues on the streets of Helena all their lives—and the two musicians signed contracts with Interstate, becoming the King Biscuit Entertainers.

In 1979 I stopped in Cleveland, Ohio, to talk to Robert Lockwood, who'd been living there since 1960 or '61. He met me at the front door of his comfortable, two-story frame house in a deteriorating but still pleasantly tree-shaded black residential area, bald head glistening in the overhead light of his vestibule, biceps flexing as he rubbed an afternoon nap out of his eyes, the scowl familiar from photographs darkening his face. His only published interviews were fragmentary at best, and he had a reputation for being outspoken and difficult. "People say that I'm arrogant, mean, selfish," he noted matter-of-factly a little later. "I learned not to let it bother me. People accept me like I am or leave me alone."

Once Lockwood learned I was interested in *him* rather than in the Robert Johnson legend he's perennially quizzed about, he became friendlier. He wasn't any less stern or plainspoken, because that's his way, but as he warmed to the subject of his early years in the Delta, he began remembering stories, laughing, getting a kick out of telling them for the first time in years. I asked him about the beginnings of King Biscuit Time. "I left Chicago in 1941," he said, "after I made those records. When I got back to Helena, I remember I was walkin' on Elm Street when Sonny Boy spotted me. He grabbed me, had me up off the ground, and said, 'You ain't gonna leave here.' And I was stuck with him for about two years."

"Sonny Boy" is of course Rice Miller, not the then-popular blues recording star John Lee "Sonny Boy" Williamson; how Rice Miller became Sonny Boy Williamson "the second" is something of a mystery. Max Moore claimed a few years before he died that it was *his* idea for Miller to broadcast as "Sonny Boy Williamson," and none of the many bluesmen who knew Miller from the late twenties onward remember him using the name before the early forties. On the other hand, Miller insisted until his dying day that he was "the only Sonny Boy, *the* Sonny Boy," and that John Lee Williamson, who was at least fifteen years his junior, had appropriated the "Sonny Boy" tag from him before moving to Chicago in 1937. The musical evidence indicates that Miller had perfected his uniquely sensitive and speechlike harmonica style long before he heard John Lee Williamson's more instrumentally conceived harp solos on records. One searches Miller's recordings in vain for hints of John Lee Williamson's influence, but in 1947 John Lee apparently attempted to cash in on Miller's popularity in the South by recording a version of the King Biscuit Time theme song as "King Biscuit Stomp," with Mississippi guitarist Big Joe Williams accompanying him. In the harp solo on that tune, there are gritty tremolos that suggest Williamson was copying Miller's style, and one can hear even more vivid Miller echoes in Williamson's "Alcohol Blues," made the same year.

In any event, Rice Miller's personality and remarkable harmonica playing made King Biscuit Time an immediate success. The show was broadcast live from 12 noon to 12:15 (changed to 12:15–12:30 a few years later) out of KFFA's studio in the Floyd Truck Lines building, two or three blocks from the ferry landing. As soon as it went on the air, sales of King Biscuit Flour skyrocketed, and Interstate soon began marketing Sonny Boy Corn Meal, with a picture of a smiling Rice Miller, cradling his harp in one of those oversized hands and sitting astride a gigantic ear of corn, on every bag. The new Sonny Boy and Robert Lockwood became the Delta's first media-made blues stars.

Lockwood, who was already impatient with the Delta's traditional blues forms and was spending his nights off tuning into network radio broadcasts by Count Basie and other jazz bands, was about to play a crucial if largely unsung role in modernizing Delta blues. He was the first electric guitarist heard over the radio in the Delta, and the first many younger guitarists in the area heard anywhere. He was the first Delta guitarist to popularize a jazz-influenced, single-string lead guitar style. His pupils included the future King Biscuit Time guitarist Joe Willie Wilkins, a somewhat reluctant Muddy Waters (who learned Lockwood's song "Black Spider Blues" from hearing him play it over KFFA but resisted Robert's offer to teach him the jazzier elements of his style), and the most popular and influential blues guitarist of the last three decades, Riley "B. B." King.

LOCKWOOD WAS BORN ON A FARM between Aubrey and Marvell, Arkansas, around twenty-five miles from Helena, on March 27, 1915. Like pianist Sunnyland Slim, but unlike his guitar-playing contemporaries Muddy Waters, Johnny Shines, and Honeyboy Edwards, Robert grew up on a farm his family owned. And he probably would have become a pianist rather than a guitarist if it hadn't been for Robert Johnson. "My grandfather had this farm," he explained, settling back onto a couch in a living room that was crowded with furniture left him by several recently deceased relatives, amplifiers, a guitar, a portable phonograph, and a collection of jazz and urban blues records. "A hundred and sixty acres. And he had an organ, the kind you pump. That's the first thing I learned to play a tune on, when I was around twelve.

My mother and father split up before that. My mother had a high school education, and she knew shorthand, but you know how it was down there—she couldn't get jobs that paid more than three dollars a week. She lived in Helena, and when I got to be school age, she came and got me so I could go to school nine months out of the year—out in the country, it was seven months. We lived in St. Louis for a little while when I was seven, but then we moved back to Helena. And around 1928 or '29, when I was thirteen or fourteen, was when Robert Johnson came along."

It seems more likely that this was in 1931 or '32, when Lockwood was in fact sixteen or seventeen. Johnson, only four years his senior, would have been nineteen or twenty and recently returned to the northern Delta from his mysterious stay in Hazelhurst. "At the time," Lockwood recalls, "my ambition was to play a piano or an organ. I had heard a lot of guitar players, but I wasn't interested in 'em. I didn't want to play an instrument if I had to have help, and all the guitar players I would see were in string bands or at least they had another guitar player to complement. But then Robert came along, and he was backin' himself up without anybody helping him, and sounding *good*. He would go somewhere to play for people and tear up the house. So I got right on top of that. By him having a crush on my mother, I got a chance to be around him a little bit. I think I'm about the only one he ever taught."

Numerous musicians learned to play something like Johnson by watching him or studying his recordings, but Lockwood is the only musician Johnson is known to have actually given lessons to. "He would sit down and show me, real simple, the simpler things that he'd do. One of these things was 'Mr. Down Child,' the way he done that." The song, a Johnson classic that its composer never recorded, has been preserved on recordings by Rice Miller, Lockwood, and other artists. Its opening verse was one of the most emblematic in Johnson's repertoire: "Mr. Down Child, Mr. Down Child, please take a fool's advice/Don't never let no one woman, man, misuse you twice."

"Robert was like a father to me," Lockwood continued, "or a big brother, and he accepted me like a baby brother or a son. He was real open with me, and he had me playin' inside of six months. In fact, I had learned three of his tunes inside of two weeks. I was already musically inclined. I'd been messing around with the old organ. And also, I had an ailment, diarrhea, and I couldn't walk or stand too much for goin' to the bathroom. So I didn't have no other kind of job. My mother had tried and tried to get me cured. When I got on the guitar, she'd let me play all day. Robert wouldn't show me stuff but once or twice, but when he'd come back, I'd be playing it.

"Better than a year passed, and then he took me to Mississippi to play with him. We went down along the Sunflower River, and he said, 'Junior, you stay on this side. I'm bound for the other side. Let me show you something about competition.' But then when we decided to hang it up, we both had made a little better than fifteen dollars. That night we played at a place called Davenport, Mississippi, and I think he was really surprised, 'cause till then he never really knew how well I could play. I hadn't let him know 'cause I figured that would really bother him, that he taught me and then I did as well as he did. On a lot of things, you know, Robert kind of messed the time around, and I played perfect time. And by that time, I was playin' almost everything he played." This sounds like boasting, but Lockwood's 1941 recordings, especially "Take a Little Walk with Me" and the bottleneck piece "Little Boy Blue," feature dazzlingly intricate guitar accompaniments, articulated cleanly and with exemplary tonal richness. His work was probably never as intense and desperate sounding as Johnson's; he was a cooler player. But his blues had their own brand of intensity. They were a slowly burning flame rather than an explosion that flared, consumed, and then winked out.

During the next few years Lockwood made several more excursions into Mississippi with his stepfather. "In Clarksdale," he remembers, "Robert pushed me out from under a knife once. We were playing on the streets, and later on I remembered that everywhere, every street corner we had been on that day, this lady was there. I didn't notice her, wasn't paying her no attention, and all of a sudden, she came at me. Robert shoved me. If he hadn't, she would have cut me." These adventures ended abruptly with Johnson's death. Lockwood's playing had been patterned wholly in Johnson's image, and their repertoires were virtually identical; musically, as well as personally, the younger man was devastated.

"I didn't go near his funeral," Lockwood says. "I guess maybe I would never have been able to play again if I had. As it was, it took me a year and a half before I could play in public. Everything I played would remind me of Robert, and whenever I tried to play, I would just come down in tears. That's really what inspired me to start writing my own material."

The songs Lockwood says he wrote over the next few years—they include "Take a Little Walk with Me," "Black Spider Blues" (or "Mean Red Spider," as Muddy Waters called it when he recorded it in 1948), "Little Boy Blue," and "That's All Right," all of which became blues standards—used a number of Johnson's melodic ideas and basic guitar patterns, including some musical material that originated, on records at least, with Leroy Carr and Scrapper Blackwell. It's been widely assumed that several of these songs, and particularly "Take a Little Walk," were in fact unrecorded Johnson compositions. They're certainly in the Johnson tradition, and some of them may well have been at least partially borrowed, in familiar blues fashion. But whether any of them originated with Johnson or not, Lockwood made them all his own. He tamed Johnson's polyrhythmic ferocity, substituting a refined, almost classical counterpoint and a slower, more deliberate walking tempo. These innovations later served as a model for countless Delta and Chicago blues guitarists who would have had trouble (as more slavish Johnson imitators like Johnny Shines did) integrating the careening Johnson style into band accompaniments.

Lockwood's lyrics carried on Johnson's simultaneous fascination with and distrust of women, but they evidenced little of Johnson's tortured, driven quality. For the most part, the songs Lockwood sang were disillusioned but assertive dispatches from the sexual battlefield. At times they were aggressively misogynistic. "Black Spider," for example, compared a manipulative woman to a spider ("Her web's all over town"), while simultaneously playing on in-group color prejudice ("black" vs. "red"). In "Little Boy Blue," Lockwood indulged in a scabrous phallic fantasy that Johnson probably wouldn't have stated so baldly: "I'm gonna take my whip and whup her, I'm gonna whup her down to the ground/I'm gonna take my dirk and stab her, you know I'm gonna turn it round and round. . . ." This verse comes in the middle of a song based on a familiar children's nursery rhyme! In "That's All Right," on the other hand, Lockwood affected icy disdain: "Every now and then I wonder who's lovin' you tonight."

During the last year or two of his life, Robert Johnson performed and traveled from time to time with Chester Burnett (Howlin' Wolf), a hulking, sandpaper-voiced former student of Charley Patton's who'd been farming in Arkansas since the early thirties, and Rice Miller. Around 1934 or '35, Miller began showing up at Lockwood's front door, begging his mother to let her son go out and work as his accompanist. "I started going to places in Arkansas with him," Robert recalls, "but he worried my mother for about two years before she let me go to Mississippi with him. And sure enough, we had some pretty strange experiences there. One time we left the Delta and went up into the hill country, and in Sardis they put us in jail for vagrancy for twenty-one days. That was on a Friday. On Saturday, we went up on the second floor and raised the jailhouse windows and started playing.

"In a matter of minutes, the jailhouse was surrounded with people. There was a little fence down there, about as big as the one on the side of my yard, and the people started throwing nickels and dimes and quarters and dollars over that fence. The trusty went out there and picked the money up, and we knew he didn't bring it all to us. We knew *he* got fat, but when he turned it in to us, we had made four hundred dollars. That day. The next night, the high sheriff and the deputy sheriff came and asked us did we want to go out and make some money. Sid and Ed was their names. And for the next twenty-one days, they took us out to serenade for the whites, every night but Sunday. They'd take up the money for us, pass the hat, make the people not put nothin' less than a dollar in it. And then they'd take us back and put us in jail. Now, mind you, they was bustin' places for corn whiskey right and left, and they gave us a whole gallon of that. We had girls comin' to the jailhouse and spendin' the night. We was eatin' from a hotel down the street. So it really wasn't like bein' in no jailhouse. But it was terrible 'cause it was against our will."

Lockwood told me this story with a mixture of amusement and bitterness. "See," he added, "this particular part of Mississippi was really starved for music. And the police officers, they liked the way we sounded and just took advantage of bein' police officers.

They knew the only way they was going to be able to enjoy us was to lock us up. Sonny Boy was doing quite a few country and western things—'You Are My Sunshine' and stuff like that—but we would do the blues for them, too. Them white people down there always did like the blues. They just didn't like the people who *created* the blues." Lockwood laughed drily. "Well, by the time our twenty-one days was up, we had close to a thousand dollars apiece. So old man Ed asked me and Sonny Boy at the same time, 'Look, if I turn y'all loose, what y'all gonna do?' And I mean I'll tell you the truth, even if it hurt me. I grew up like that. I said, 'Mr. Ed, I'm gettin' the hell outta here.' Sonny Boy said, 'Whoahhh, I'm gonna stay around awhile.' They laughed and let us out. Knew damn well he was lying. And as soon as we got out, we hit the highway."

The story is typical of Rice Miller, who often found himself in a jam and usually was able to talk his way out. He is remembered with mixed feelings by many people who knew him. "He wasn't hard to get along with," says Houston Stackhouse, who played guitar behind him on the radio and throughout the Delta beginning in 1946, "but he'd just work you, get you, talk you sweet and everything. Then when he'd get that money in his hand, he'd get away with the money. . . . Him and Elmo James was workin' together, and he beat Elmo James out of fifty dollars or somethin'. Elmo cracked him 'cross the head with his mike stand. Knocked a hole in his head. Yeah, Sonny Boy, he'd just get that money from you if he could." Paul Oliver, in an article written shortly after Miller's death, quoted an unnamed Delta blues singer as saying "He was real evil," and added some observations of his own: "It needed very little—a misplaced word—for him to take offense, whether from a stranger or from another blues singer. He was involved in more than one fracas when in Europe, and though perhaps it is still too soon to relate the incident, he 'jumped' another blues singer with a knife at a London hotel and had to be forcibly separated from him before the consequences proved serious. He had been drinking heavily at the time, but he was always a steady drinker, carrying a hip flask of whiskey and pulling from it continually. It had severe effects on his temper and loosened the few controls on his language."

Miller was suspicious of interviewers and rarely told many details of his early life. He was born in the very heart of the Delta, out in the country between Glendora and Tutwiler, around 1897–99 and raised by his mother, Millie Ford, and stepfather, Jim Miller. His family began calling him "Rice" when he was a baby. Unlike most Delta blues singers, who seem almost without exception to have come from broken homes, Miller apparently enjoyed a stable family life. In fact, he lived with or near his mother and stepfather until he was around thirty, but there must have been tensions under the surface, for in the late twenties he had a decisive, violent confrontation with his stepfather and abruptly left home.

He was already playing the harmonica, though apparently he performed only church music and had devoted most of his first thirty years to working on the various plantations where his family lived as sharecroppers. After the split, the harmonica became his livelihood. Throughout the Depression he lived by his wits, riding the rails, singing and playing the harp on street corners for handouts, teaming up with guitarists like Robert Johnson, Elmore James, and Robert Nighthawk from time to time but most often keeping to himself. Sometimes he would piece together a drum set and play it while wailing away on harmonica and kazoo. He was basically a loner, trusting no one, and this probably accounts for the development of his uniquely orchestral harmonica style. He alternated quavering, vocally inflected melodies and rich chords, sometimes thickened with his humming, and he alternated them so skillfully the music took on an almost hypnotic ebb and flow. Sometimes he would "spread" a chord, articulating the notes in it one at a time but hitting each one while the one before it was still ringing. This effect gave his sound the presence and sustaining quality of an organ.

"His large, callused lips enfolded the cheap harps he played," wrote Paul Oliver, "and he seemed to mould the notes through the long fingers of his hands, which were laid palm in palm as if he were to take a long drink of water from them. He would utter the words of his blues from the side of his mouth, slipping the harp between his lips as he finished a vocal phrase so that the melody was sustained on the instrument. When he sang, his voice was husky, sometimes almost guttural, at other times near a whisper. And through everything he sang and played, his impeccable sense of timing pervaded." In his band recordings of the fifties and sixties, Miller played with tremendous drive and spirit, though he dropped a bar of music here and there, throwing his accompanists into confusion. When he played unaccompanied, he was a power-house. On "Bye Bye Bird," a solo recording from 1963, he turned in an astonishing simulation of a guitar shuffle, replete with bass runs, chopped-off chording, and wah-wah-inflected melodic punc-tuations.

He was also an extraordinary showman. He would play without his hands, snapping his fingers just in front of the microphone to provide percussive cross-rhythms, or he would play with the har-monica in his mouth sideways, like a cigar. Sometimes he played a harmonica that was entirely hidden inside his mouth, smiling a sly, enigmatic smile. During the thirties and forties he would play anything anyone requested—popular Tin Pan Alley numbers, hillbilly, spirituals, blues hits. But when he didn't have to please crowds in order to survive, and especially after he finally began making records, he sang only his own blues. The lyrics tended to be directly, unselfconsciously autobiographical, at a time when blues singers were de-emphasizing overtly personal or regional lyrics in favor of topics of more general interest, particularly the vagaries of love. Although he was one of the very first musicians to amplify the harmonica and one of the first bluesmen to realize the value of radio as a medium for gaining a wider audience, he was much older than the other blues musicians who began recording in the fifties. He was over fifty years old when his first 78-rpm discs were released by the Trumpet label of Jackson, Mississippi, in 1951; Charley Patton would have been no more than twelve or thirteen years his senior.

MILLER CLAIMED TO HAVE MADE unissued test recordings during the late twenties, but his recording career was still almost ten years in the future when he began performing regularly with Lockwood on King Biscuit Time. The routine varied little from show to show. A few minutes before noon, Miller and Lockwood would arrive at the Floyd Truck Lines building, a two-story com-posite of wood and brick with the trucking company's loading docks on the first floor and the KFFA studios upstairs. They would trudge up the rickety wooden steps, which squeaked noisily from the day KFFA began broadcasting until the building was condemned and the station moved twenty years later, and take their places in the cramped but modern studio along with the show's announcer (usually Herb Langston after Sonny Payne went into the service in 1942). The first words, spoken with great gusto, were the announcer's: "Pass the biscuits, 'cause it's King Biscuit Time!" Miller and Lockwood would immediately launch into the show's theme, a jump-tempo blues. The version Lockwood recorded in 1975 went like this:

Good evenin' everybody, tell me how do you do
Good evenin' everybody, tell me how do you do
We're the King Biscuit Boys, and we've come out to play for you

Every mornin' for my breakfast, put King Biscuit on my table
Every mornin' for my breakfast, put King Biscuit on my table
I'm invitin' all my friends, and all my next door neighbors

We're sellin' King Biscuit Flour, money back guarantee
We're sellin' King Biscuit Flour, money back guarantee
And if you find you don't like it, send it on back to me

Every mornin' for my breakfast, I eat all the way from nine to ten
Every mornin' for my breakfast, I eat all the way from nine to ten
Every time you look across the table, I'm reachin' over in the pan again

The show consisted of songs by Sonny Boy and Robert, many requested in cards and letters sent in by listeners, and florid commercials, read by the announcer, that were the work of Interstate's Max Moore. "Light as air! White as snow! Yes, friends, that's King Biscuit Flour, the perfect flour for all your baking," one of Moore's scripts began. "Friends, do you like honest to goodness Southern cornbread, corn sticks, corn muffins, corn pone, or just skillet cornbread?" asked another. "Well, say no more, just step out and get yourself a bag of that fine, white, fancy Sonny Boy Meal, and start baking. Yes, you can bake the best cornbread you ever tasted with Sonny Boy Meal. When you buy Sonny Boy Meal from your grocer, you get the finest, whitest, and cleanest meal packed in bags. And remember, Sonny Boy Meal is guaranteed to give you perfect satisfaction." Despite the hyper-bole, most of the musicians who played on the show seem to have believed in the product. Guitarist Houston Stackhouse, who in-tensely disliked Max Moore, told Jim O'Neal of *Living Blues*, "King Biscuit Flour was some good flour; Sonny Boy Meal was some good meal, too." When the show's time was almost up, the engineer would signal from the control booth, and the musicians would quickly reprise the theme, with a final verse: "Good-bye, everybody, if I never see you no more/Buy King Biscuit Flour, I don't care where you go."

At first the show went surprisingly smoothly. Rice Miller wasn't exactly celebrated for his reliability or for staying in one place for very long, but King Biscuit Time was bringing him immense pres-tige, and no matter how much he'd had to drink the night before, he rarely failed to make it to the studio by twelve noon. When the program went on the air, KFFA was broadcasting at only two hun-dred and fifty watts, which gave it a range of around thirty-five or forty miles in each direction, sixty on a good day. The broadcast range was increased to eighty miles in 1944, but Helena was so ideally situated that, from the very beginning, the show reached into an enormous number of black homes. And during much of the forties it was broadcast simultaneously over WROX in Clarks-dale. Between them, the two stations effectively blanketed the upper Delta. The musicians' pay was minimal, but since they an-nounced every day where they would be playing that night, they drew large crowds and were able to command substantial perform-ance fees. Lockwood reports that during the early forties, the pair asked for, and got, seventy-five dollars apiece for a night's work. "Most of the people who had good jobs was makin' forty-five dol-lars a week," he adds.

Miller spent money as fast as he made it, usually on gambling, whiskey, and women, but the more career-minded Lockwood saved and was soon the proud owner of a 1939 Pontiac, which he bought from a white woman in Helena. "The car was a six," he re-members, "but it had been all psyched up. It was super fast, used to have it on the polices in Mississippi." The two men needed a fast car, for their nightly jobs were often in Mississippi, and the ferry back across the river to Helena stopped running sometime between one and two A.M. There was no bridge until the mid-fifties. If a job ran late, they might spend the night near Lula, Mississippi, with pianist and juke joint proprietor Henry Hill. But most nights, Sonny Boy and Robert would pile into the Pontiac and go racing down the highways, often taking short cuts along dirt roads, trying to make the last ferry back to Arkansas.

"One night," says Lockwood, "we played Tutwiler, and on the way to the ferry, I passed the highway man, you know, the police. He must've been parked off by the side of the road 'cause I didn't see nobody. I looked back and seen some lights and said, 'Sonny Boy, somebody's really coming back there. It's got to be the highway man.' He looked and said, 'It's got to be.' Well, that Pontiac could run, and I got a jump on the law. There was two ferries to Helena, one that left from the Mississippi side right across from Helena, one that left further down the river from Friar's Point, Mississippi. When I got to the fork in the road at Lula, instead of keepin' on to the Helena ferry, I cut my lights out and come back down the riverside to Friar's Point. I ran that car up onto the boat, and Charlie, the guy that ran the ferry, was messin' around there. I said, 'Man, get this goddamn thing out in that river. The goddamn highway man is chasing me.' Well, when the police got there, we was halfway across the river. They started talkin' on this little electric thing they had, on the horn, tryin' to get the boat to turn around and go back. I said to Charles, 'You take this goddamn boat back to the Mississippi side, and I won't be on the motherfuckin' thing.' Charles laughed, man. He just cracked his side."

The boat eased into Helena's harbor, a natural inlet around an eighth of a mile long that was protected from the river's swift current by a fingerlike promontory overgrown with willows. Robert and Sonny Boy drove off the deck of the boat onto the gravel landing and stopped for a moment to take a deep breath. The willows, birches, and sycamores that grew right down to the water were waving gently in the late night breeze off the river. The two men laughed, Robert gunned the Pontiac, and they drove up the gravel embankment, through the gap in the concrete-topped sod levee, and down the deserted streets of Helena toward their homes. "A couple of days later," Robert recalls, "I was back over in Mississippi, and the highway man walked up to the car. He said, 'Wasn't you over here the other night?' I said, 'No, sir.' After that, Charles teased us about it all the time."

Lockwood enjoyed being a regional media celebrity, but he was already plotting to modernize the sound of the two-man King Biscuit Entertainers. Early one afternoon in 1942 he drove west from Helena almost as far as Marvell and then north up Route One, intent on convincing percussionist and vocalist James "Peck" Curtis to join the group. It was a part of Arkansas he knew well, the part he grew up in. As he left the vicinity of Helena, the dark, low shape of Crowley's Ridge, which runs from northern Arkansas down the riverside as far as Helena, began to recede to the east. The land abruptly grew flatter, like the Mississippi Delta on the other side of the ridge and the river but with more frequent patches of uncut woods. Huge plantations stretched for mile after mile along the straight two-lane blacktop—one Arkansas Delta plantation, founded by Robert E. Lee Wilson in 1886, spread over thirty-six thousand acres and was the home of around ten thousand black tenant farmers and day laborers. Other plantation land in the vicinity was owned by the Dockery family and visited frequently by Joe Rice Dockery, who made periodic trips back and forth across the Mississippi to supervise his vast holdings. But all one could see of these places from the highway were occasional roadside stores, most of them operated by the plantation owners, though a few were owned by enterprising Chinese families like the Fongs, and here and there a gravel road leading off into the fields. Robert knew most of these back roads by heart, but he was heading for Marianna, a picture-postcard town with a well-kept square and, well away from that, a number of black cafés and honky-tonks.

It didn't take Robert long to locate "Peck" Curtis, who was tired of making a precarious living playing in the juke joints and gladly accepted the offer of a regular radio spot in Helena despite the fact that money was not discussed. Curtis, who was born March 7, 1912, in Benoit, Mississippi, but raised mostly in the Arkansas Delta, had played drums or washboard with Robert Johnson, Memphis Slim, and the Memphis Jug Band and was also an accomplished singer, dancer, and all-around entertainer. "He was really a carnival man, vaudeville shows and stuff. He traveled with them," says Lockwood. "I was out there as a dancer for a little while before I got on that guitar, and we had teamed up together. So I went and got Peck, and he played washboard on the show for about six months. Then I said, 'Man, can you play drums?' He said he could, and I went out and paid for a snare, a sock cymbal, a couple of ride cymbals, a hi-hat, and a bass drum. Paid fifty or sixty dollars for them. And Peck gave me one five-dollars! At that time, we was payin' Peck ten dollars a day, seven days a week, which was a lot of money then, and he would not have money no further than one day to the next. Sonny Boy hadn't wanted to pay him at all, and we didn't at first, but I sat down with old Sonny Boy one day and said that the two of us ought to each pay him five dollars, and that's what we did."

Curtis played drums like a dancer, scattering accents right and left, executing sudden and unpredictable crescendos, abruptly dropping out only to come charging back in. "James 'Peck' Curtis couldn't keep a straight four beat if he had to," Sonny Payne maintains, "but the beat he kept for these particular tunes, no-body could top him." The density of his accompaniments would vary radically within a single song—one verse would be backed by volleys of rimshots, the next by a repeatedly smashed cymbal, the next by an erratic bass drum and cowbell pattern, and so on. "Peck would near 'bout make a band out of the drums," Houston Stackhouse has remarked. At its most orchestral, his playing re-calls the timbral layering within an African drum ensemble, and it's interesting that another early Delta blues drummer whose work survives on a few recordings, Joe Martin, also played in a multi-textured style. Both men were used to drumming with and against the complex, often polyrhythmic accent patterns of tradi-tional Delta blues, and though they were utter primitives as far as technical rudiments were concerned, their freely responsive ac-centing and instinctively orchestral use of the drum kit made them sound more like Max Roach or Elvin Jones, modern jazz drummers who have studied African and Afro-Caribbean tradi-tional drumming in depth, than like the metronomic shuffle drummers heard on most blues records of the fifties and sixties.

At first Curtis was something of a problem when it came to broadcasting. "He used to bust more hides," says Stackhouse. "Done always be drinkin' and feelin' good, and he'd get drunk and

stomp that drum, boom! Knock a hole." But there were compen-
sations. Having broadcast as early as 1935, Curtis knew how to
adjust his dynamics to the demands of the medium, and when he
was sober, he did so. He was also a capable blues singer, and occasionally he would amuse and amaze King Biscuit Time's listeners
by dancing over the air. Stackhouse says, "He had him a piece of
plywood board. It was five feet, I think, each way. He'd get on that
board, plates on his shoes and things. You could pick it up just as
clear as a bell."

Not long after Curtis joined, the group was further augmented
by the addition of pianist Robert "Dudlow" Taylor, an immense,
introverted man the show's regulars soon began calling "Mr. Five
by Five." Sonny Payne remembers him as "a man that had no personality, nothing whatsoever but a good mind for the blues, a good
heart, and a good pair of hands. He didn't know an A-minor chord
from a B flat. He knew nothing about phrasing compared to a
master of phrasing like Sonny Boy. I would not classify him as a
piano *picker,* which is what someone like Memphis Slim is. He
was strictly a piano player." Influenced mostly by the Helena
blues pianist Roosevelt Sykes, though he probably was from Louisiana originally, Dudlow is remembered as a competent, dependable sideman. Despite his nickname, which was synonymous with
the word "boogie," his forte was slow blues. He seems to have
been hired away from a medicine show by Max Moore; the regular
King Biscuit Entertainers might have preferred working with a
more versatile stylist. In 1943 they brought in Joe Willie "Pinetop" Perkins, who was to become a mainstay of the Muddy Waters
band beginning in 1969, as the show's second pianist and resident
boogie specialist. Another Delta pianist, Willie Love, was a frequent guest performer, along with a minstrel-style comedian and
a trumpet player whose names nobody seems to remember. But
Dudlow stayed on as a King Biscuit Time regular well into the fifties.

Most of Rice Miller's sidekicks probably had to run at one time
or another—even the huge, customarily placid Dudlow. One night
in the late forties, guitarist Joe Willie Wilkins was sleeping with a
woman in the servants' quarters behind a white family's house
near Glendora, when he heard a commotion coming from the
front yard. Sonny Boy, Peck, and Dudlow needed him for a job,

and Sonny Boy had driven a battered Buick with half a muffler up into the yard. The man of the house yelled out the window demanding that the interloper identify himself, and Miller, drunk as a lord, yelled back, "This is Sonny Boy Williamson from Helena, Arkansas. Sonny Boy on King Biscuit Time."

"You can be Johnny Boy from hell for all I care," the white man replied. "If you don't get the hell outta my yard, keepin' up all that racket, I'm gon' kill you. Hand me my shotgun, wife." Stackhouse, who related this tale to interviewer Jim O'Neal, laughed uproariously. "God dog! Dudlow and old Peck was in the car. Peck fell outta one side and Dudlow out' the other one. They took off and went clear up the road. Peck said he was in good shape then. He could run, sure enough, but he said Dudlow kept up with him. Old Dudlow done run till he give out of breath, Peck said. Dudlow got there, laid up on the bed, 'Hahh! He gon' get somebody killed!'"

BY THE TIME PECK AND DUDLOW became King Biscuit Time regulars, the show was so popular it had been flattered by several imitations. In 1942 Robert Nighthawk returned to Helena and settled at 308½ Franklin Street, where he was to live until 1948. Within a year of his arrival he was broadcasting over KFFA for Bright Star Flour, the product of one of the Interstate Grocery Company's rivals. Bright Star was happy to have him, for unlike Sonny Boy, who had yet to make a record, Nighthawk had recorded a number of sides for Bluebird and Decca, both on his own and as backup guitarist for John Lee Williamson and other popular artists. His "Prowling Nighthawk" (1937) was fondly remembered, and it was around this time that Robert, who was born Robert Lee McCollum and had recorded as Robert Lee McCoy and Peetie's Boy, decided to start calling himself Robert Nighthawk. He preferred not to use his real name, apparently for a very good reason.

Nighthawk was born in Helena on November 30, 1909, and grew up on nearby plantations. By the time he was fourteen, he had left home and was supporting himself by playing the harmonica. It wasn't until the early thirties that he took up the guitar, initially under the tutelage of Houston Stackhouse. At the time, young Stackhouse was still mesmerized by the blues of his south Mississippi neighbor Tommy Johnson, and the songs he taught Nighthawk were mostly Johnson staples—"Big Road Blues," "Big Fat Mama," "Maggie Campbell." "I taught him how to play all that," says Stackhouse, "and then he could work out from then on like he wanted to. We was day-workin' on Mr. Toy Woods' farm out there at Murphy Bayou. Plowin' mules, gettin' a dollar a day . . . Two weeks' time, boy, we was playin' them two guitars good. And we'd make them days and then go play at night somewhere."

In 1932 Nighthawk's brother, Percy McCollum, joined the duo on harmonica, and with Stackhouse playing fiddle and mandolin as well as guitar, they were probably a fine and fairly typical southern Mississippi string band. But later that year, a series of troubling events broke up the team. On the way south to New Orleans, the trio got drunk in Brookhaven, Mississippi, and found themselves in jail. "Well," says Stackhouse, "what it was, they said three colored boys had ravished some white girls down in there. And they thought maybe it might have been us." The three were threatened and intimidated, and even though they were saved when a patrolman who knew them from Hazelhurst vouched for them and got them released, the experience apparently terrified them, especially Percy, the youngest. "Just hit the highway and walk where everybody can see you. Better not catch nothin'," the Brookhaven police told them, and they walked the thirty-three miles back to Stackhouse's (and Tommy Johnson's) home town, Crystal Springs. Percy quit playing the harmonica following this incident; Stackhouse speculates that it "probably just scared music out of his mind."

Robert left southern Mississippi soon after that, stopping to play in Friar's Point, meeting and working briefly with the young John Lee Hooker in either Clarksdale or Memphis, hooking up occasionally with carnivals and medicine shows. In the mid-thirties, he left the South. He would only say that he'd been in "deep trouble." Stackhouse claimed "it was something about a pistol, but they didn't say where he killed nobody." In any event, Robert adopted his mother's maiden name, McCoy, and settled in St. Louis for a time. There he met several Mississippi-born bluesmen, including Henry Townshend and Big Joe Williams, who had recording contacts in Chicago, and on May 5, 1937, he took part in the marathon session in Victor's Aurora, Illinois, studio with Williams and John Lee "Sonny Boy" Williamson. Nighthawk sang and played on six of his own blues, including "Prowling Nighthawk" and "Tough Luck," songs that reflected two sides of his complex and customarily veiled personality. Like Rice Miller, he had grown withdrawn and suspicious during his years on the road, and like Miller, he would never stay in one place for very long. "Prowling Nighthawk" celebrated his rambling nature. "I have been ramblin' and prowlin'," he boasted, "ever since I was twelve years old / And I wouldn't stop ramblin' for all my weight in gold." "Tough Luck" was no less appropriate to the life he had lived, but it was more a complaint than a boast: "Now I got in tough luck, all my people dead and gone / And I haven't got any money, no place to call my home."

John Lee Williamson's numbers, especially "Good Morning, School Girl" and "Blue Bird Blues," were the session's biggest hits, but Nighthawk impressed blues producer Lester Melrose as an adept guitar and harmonica accompanist and a better than average singer, and between 1937 and 1940 Robert commuted regularly between St. Louis and Chicago, recording on his own and behind a number of other artists. When he returned south, he brought a band with him consisting of a second guitarist, a string bassist, and a drummer. The group worked mostly around Clarksdale, where Nighthawk's electric guitar, purchased shortly before he left Chicago, stirred considerable interest, and where Son Sims, the veteran blues fiddler, played with them. (At some point, perhaps as early as 1941 and perhaps several years later, Sims attached a pickup to his fiddle, plugged into an amplifier, and appeared with the Nighthawks as one of the earliest electric violinists.) Robert and his band also spent time working at Jim Seals's Dipsy Doodle Club in Osceola, Arkansas, where his audience included Jim's youngest son, Frank, then less than a year old. Frank, who was nicknamed "Son," later played drums behind Nighthawk and Albert King and eventually developed into the finest young blues guitarist to emerge during the 1970s.

Nighthawk returned from Chicago a master of the slide or bottleneck guitar style. Houston Stackhouse had introduced him to the technique, but Nighthawk perfected his slide work in Chicago by watching and listening to Tampa Red. Once he began broadcasting from Helena over KFFA, his versions of the Tampa Red hits "Anna Lou Blues" (changed by Nighthawk to "Anna Lee") and "Black Angel Blues" became local favorites, requested again and again by the Bright Star Show's listeners. According to Stackhouse, Robert could and occasionally did play them in an uncannily exact imitation of Tampa's style, "and then he'd get back to his style: 'Well, I'm gon' get back in my own style now. I'm just showin' you I can do it.' " Nighthawk recorded "Anna Lee" and "Sweet Black Angel" in 1949, his way, and anyone who listens to these performances back to back with Tampa Red's originals will immediately appreciate the qualities that indelibly stamped Nighthawk as a *Delta* stylist. In both versions of "Black Angel Blues," the fifth note of the scale marks the apex of the melody. But while Tampa Red sang this melody evenly and lightly, Nighthawk added pitch shadings, especially the flattening around the fifth so characteristic of Delta blues. When Tampa Red approached the third note of the scale, he either flattened it slightly or sang an ordinary major third, but all Nighthawk's thirds were heavily flattened and "blue." The contrast in their slide guitar work was just as marked, with Tampa playing loosely and with an almost airy tone and touch while Nighthawk's notes seemed to drip slowly out of the amplifier like thick, oozing oil.

While Nighthawk was establishing himself on Helena radio and taking advantage of his local notoriety to work lucrative engagements in the upper Delta with a band that at various times included pianist Pinetop Perkins and drummer Kansas City Red, Rice Miller was feeling the tug of that old wanderlust. Now that Peck Curtis was a regular on the King Biscuit show, there was another vocalist and front man; Sonny Boy could skip broadcasts occasionally without disrupting the routine or incurring the wrath of Max Moore.

Actually, Moore and the KFFA staff seem to have expected erratic or at least contrary behavior from Sonny Boy. "Sometimes," says Sonny Payne, "when he felt like it, Sonny Boy would write down the songs he was going to do and give them to us. Then we would say, 'Now here's Sonny Boy and all the gang to do such and such a tune.' Well, if he wasn't in the right mood, he'd do something else, and then I'd have to come back after they played it and say, 'We-e-ell, that's Sonny Boy for ya. He didn't want to play the tune he said he was gonna play after all, for the simple reason that he wasn't in the mood.' Let me put it this way: he had a mind of his own. He was moody. He was a boozer. He loved his booze, couldn't get up in the morning without it. But, and you may think I'm crazy when I tell you this, he was *not* an alcoholic. In the old days, right at first, Sonny Boy and Robert would get drunk and thrown in jail, but once he found out that he could play and sing over the radio, he *found* himself. He would drink, but after the earliest days of the show, I never saw him drunk."

Having his picture carried far and wide on trucks full of Sonny Boy Meal must have done as much to bolster Miller's self-confidence as the show itself. He was recognized throughout the Delta now, and not just by the juke joint regulars. On Saturday mornings the King Biscuit Entertainers would put on the special shirts Max Moore had had made for them—yellow short-sleeved shirts with each musician's name knitted on the back, along with the words King Biscuit Flour or Sonny Boy Meal—and pile into an Interstate Grocery truck. They would make a number of stops, playing in front of country grocery stores, at gas stations, just about anywhere a crowd could be expected to gather. Their schedule was always announced in advance on King Biscuit Time, and audiences tended to be large and enthusiastic. Before long, Max Moore decided to present the King Biscuit Entertainers in regular Saturday morning stage shows at Helena's Plaza Theater. Admission was free, and the theater was always packed.

Between these wearing Saturdays, the broadcasts five days a week, and nights spent performing, drinking, and gambling, it was an exhausting life, and though the musicians made plenty of money from their nightly performances, the grueling work for Interstate paid only a pittance. According to Stackhouse, who began playing regularly on King Biscuit Time in 1946, Max Moore was a tightwad who wouldn't even buy the musicians a bottle of whiskey for their Saturday promotional tours. Being a Delta radio personality wasn't exactly a bed of roses, then, and in 1944 Sonny Boy hit the highway. He played as far east as Florida, broadcast for a time from Monroe, Louisiana, and then tried his luck with a radio show out of Little Rock, where he also found work at night in various joints. King Biscuit Time went on as before, with Peck Curtis leading the band and singing the theme song. Once in a while, Sonny Boy would show up, take over the show for a short time, and vanish again.

In 1945, irked by Sonny Boy's disappearances and anxious to play a different brand of music, Robert Lockwood quit King Biscuit Time to broadcast over KFFA for yet another brand of flour, Mother's Best. "I had myself, piano, bass, drums, trumpet, and trombone," Lockwood recalls. "We was playing jazz—'One O'Clock Jump,' 'The Sheik of Araby,' 'Stardust,' all that kind of stuff." King Biscuit Time fans who tuned in to the Mother's Best show must have been shocked, although Lockwood's pianist, James Starkey, was a fine blues player, and there was blues as well as jazz and standards in the group's repertoire.

By this time Robert was taking confident single-string solos on his electric guitar. Guitarists like jazzman Eddie Lang and the versatile Lonnie Johnson had been playing improvised solos that were more or less hornlike in conception since the twenties, and guitarist-trombonist Eddie Durham recorded some single-string solos on an amplified instrument with the Kansas City Five and Six (small groups that featured the Count Basie rhythm section and tenor saxophonist Lester Young) in 1938. In 1939 a number of electric guitarists recorded, including the seminal modern jazz stylist Charlie Christian (with Benny Goodman's popular big band) and Christian's friend and former musical associate Aaron "T-Bone" Walker, who was with the band of Les Hite. Lockwood says he never heard Christian, who made only a few records and died young, until some fans gave him a Christian reissue lp in the mid-seventies. But he heard T-Bone Walker, whose electric lead style grew out of the early Texas guitar blues as played by Blind Lemon Jefferson. Walker actually led Jefferson around the streets of Dallas for a time during the twenties, and he was playing an electric guitar as early as 1935. His single-string lead style was fully mature when he first recorded under his own name in 1942.

How early Lockwood heard Walker is unclear. Robert says, "I heard T-Bone all my life, but I never really liked the way he played. I just liked the songs he wrote." Several blues guitarists have confirmed Robert's contention that in the mid-forties, when he was working out his own jazz-influenced lead guitar style, he played with his fingers and not with a pick. "I never really listened to guitar players after Robert Johnson," Lockwood claims. "I listened to horns. I'd tune in Count Basie or somebody like that and sit and try to copy the licks the horns were playing. I've just found out in the last few years that Charlie Christian was originally a horn player." I mentioned that Eddie Durham doubled as a trombonist. "Well," he said, "see, it had to be a horn player to create that. That's where all the good electric guitar players get their ideas, from other types of instruments." The earliest recordings of Lockwood's electric lead playing, made after he moved to Chicago at the beginning of the fifties, do sound more horn-influenced, in their uneven and sometimes erratic phrasing, than Walker-influenced. T-Bone's work had a decisive impact on the younger generation of Delta blues guitarists who matured during the late forties and the fifties, but Lockwood seems to have developed mostly on his own.

CHAPTER 6
I Believe I'll Dust My Broom

With Lockwood, Nighthawk, and, when he was in town, Rice Miller all broadcasting over KFFA, Helena began to attract aspiring blues musicians from throughout the Deep South. Among the players who came in the mid-forties to listen and learn were the future mainstays of Muddy Waters' first electric band, Jimmy Rogers and Little Walter. Rogers was born in Ruleville, in Sunflower County, Mississippi, on June 3, 1924. During the thirties his family lived in the Delta near Vance, and it was there that he began playing his first instrument, the harmonica. During the mid-thirties he sometimes played in impromptu groups with three or four other harmonica players, including a future Chicago blues associate, Snooky Pryor. And around the same time he took up the guitar, learning initially from Arthur Johnson, a musician who played around Greenwood. Johnson never recorded, but his nephew, Luther Johnson, also known as Guitar Junior, played with the Muddy Waters band in the sixties and seventies.

Around 1939 or 1940 Jimmy heard Rice Miller play near Minter City, Mississippi, and was impressed. When Miller and Lockwood began broadcasting over KFFA, the eighteen-year-old harmonica player, now a budding guitarist as well, knew Helena was where he belonged. "The radio station drew quite a few musicians to Helena," he says. "For blues, that was the spot, the headquarters." A number of young musicians who were still in their teens, many of them children of broken homes and already living on the road, were in and out of town during the early and mid-forties. They would congregate at the radio station, and sometimes they were allowed in to watch the broadcasts. At night, they would follow Sonny Boy and his band to their gigs, waiting for a chance to sit in. Jimmy would stay around Helena for a short while and then return to his family, but when he was at home, he would never miss Sonny Boy's show. "I would rush home every day around twelve to hear him," Rogers says. "I'd be diggin' every inch of his sounds."

Around 1944 Jimmy was back in Helena, hanging out, picking up pointers from Robert Lockwood, and occasionally playing guitar behind Sonny Boy and Nighthawk when more accomplished musicians weren't available. The experience with Nighthawk would prove invaluable in later years when Rogers played second guitar behind Muddy's slide stylings; Muddy himself picked up a few pointers from Nighthawk between 1942, when Robert returned to the Delta, and 1943. Muddy would return the favor in 1949 by arranging for the Chess brothers to record Nighthawk doing "Anna Lee" and "Sweet Black Angel." The two men's styles were different—Muddy stayed much closer to the basics he'd learned from Son House and the recordings of Robert Johnson, while Nighthawk's more fluid and polished approach fitted readily into changing band styles. But as Rogers says, "By the time I got to playin' with Muddy, I could back up a slide guitar good, even though I didn't play that way myself. That's why it wasn't too complicated to stay with Muddy and background him in that way."

It was in Helena in 1944 that Jimmy first encountered Little Walter Jacobs, who was born May 1, 1930, near Marksville, Louisiana. By the time he arrived in Helena, the fourteen-year-old Walter had been on his own for two years and had gained experience playing the harmonica on the streets and in several clubs in New Orleans and Monroe, Louisiana. (The latter, a town just across the Mississippi line, was a hot spot for blues at the time and is celebrated in Robert Johnson's "Dust My Broom.") The harp style that would revolutionize the blues in ten years' time wasn't yet formed.

Walter had been imitating John Lee Williamson, but after he arrived in Helena he fell under the spell of Rice Miller. Years later, traces of Miller's phrasing would continue to show up in Walter's virtuosic amplified solos. At first, Sonny Boy and the other musicians in his charmed circle—Lockwood, Nighthawk, Peck, Dudlow, and the rest—ignored Walter; he was little more than a street urchin. "He'd go around these musicians," says Rogers, "and they didn't want to recognize him, but he was learning something, see." Walter would wait patiently for Sonny Boy to leave the bandstand for the crap tables, and then, if nobody objected too violently, he would sit in. Sonny Boy began hearing snatches of Walter's rich-toned, technically assured playing and began instructing him in some of the fine points of harp technique. Their friendship was cemented one night in a West Helena juke joint when a woman lunged at Walter with a knife, and Sonny Boy, who was known to draw a blade himself from time to time, stepped in.

During his first year or so in Helena, Walter usually slept on a pool table in whatever joint he happened to be in, and he seems to have depended on the generosity of various gamblers, hustlers, and musicians for cigarettes and meals. Gradually his situation improved. He found work with Stackhouse and with pianist Henry Hill, and before long he had an avid local following. He was quite a bit younger than any of the musicians he worked with, and he had a younger style, for while he was still absorbing the influence of Rice Miller and studying the latest recordings by John Lee Williamson, he was also listening to jump blues.

The most influential artist then working in the jump blues idiom was Louis Jordan, a singer and alto saxophonist who was born in Brinkley, Arkansas, in 1908 and retained a gritty sound and vocalized inflection in his sax playing despite years of experience as a section musician and soloist with big bands like Chick Webb's. Jordan's Tympani Five, actually a seven- or eight-piece group, featured two or three riffing horns, boogie-woogie-style piano, and a light, jazzy rhythm section, all subordinated to the leader's knowing novelty vocals and alto breaks. By 1945 Jordan had appeared in several Hollywood films and was riding high on one of his biggest hits, "Caldonia," a rolling boogie with humorous lyrics ("What make your big head so hard?") that soon found its way into the repertoires of numerous Delta singers. Little Walter, who had an exceptionally quick and accurate ear for music, began imitating Jordan's saxophone solos on his harmonica.

In 1945 Walter landed his own radio show on KFFA, broadcasting for Mother's Best. Lockwood had had the show earlier that year, but then he found better-paying work outside music, a train crew job that took him as far west as Nevada and Wyoming. Walter, with Dudlow as his accompanist, was happy to take over the show, and with his youthful enthusiasm and unusual style, which combined deep blues feeling with the lighter phrasing he'd absorbed from Louis Jordan's records, he was an immediate hit. In fact, he was soon drawing more fan mail and requests than Sonny Boy and the King Biscuit regulars—probably another reason Sonny Boy was seen around Helena less and less often.

Honeyboy Edwards was an occasional guest on Walter's show, and sometime around 1946 or 1947 Walter left Helena to join him in St. Louis. Edwards announced that he was Chicago bound, and Walter decided that sounded good to him, too. "We caught a ride," says Honeyboy, "out from East St. Louis, and come into Decatur, Illinois, about broke. Stopped in a train station and played there in the depot. The man let us play in there. So we made some money and made it on into Chicago. Now Little Walter, he would never stay still. He'd walk the streets all the time. We got us a room down there near Maxwell Street, and that Sunday morning I was laying up there sleeping. He comes in there, says, 'Man, come on. Get up. Let's make us some money. These streets is full of people.' I said, 'I ain't got no shirt to put on.' He said, 'I'll get you one,' went down there and got me a second-hand shirt off the street for fifteen cents. We went downstairs and hooked up on the street, and I guess we made about fifty or sixty dollars that Sunday. We made a cigar box full of money three times, went around the corner to a place called Goldberg's three times to cash in those nickels and quarters for some bills. Then one lady come out there. She was a preacher, sanctified. She wrote Walter some cards asking him to come out to her house, and he said O.K. He didn't come back until that Thursday. She had bought him a new suit, new shoes, dressed him up all sharp, cable stitches on."

Walter began frequenting the Maxwell Street area with a group of Mississippi musicians that included Othum Brown, Johnny Williams, Johnny Young, and Moody Jones. They could often be found in or around Bernard Abrams's Maxwell Radio Record Company, where Walter sometimes ran into Jimmy Rogers; Jimmy had left Helena for West Memphis and St. Louis and finally settled in Chicago in 1945. Abrams thought he heard commercial potential in these neighborhood musicians, and in 1947 he recorded several of them on the acetate disc cutter in the back room of his store. A duet by Walter and Jimmy Rogers remained unissued, but Abrams did put out two records, one of which featured Walter and guitarist Othum Brown, with a vocal from each.

Walter's number was the jumping "I Just Keep Loving Her," probably a representative example of the Sonny Boy–Louis Jordan synthesis he'd been working on since he got to Helena. Brown sang "Ora Nelle Blues," apparently giving Abrams's Ora Nelle label its name. The song was actually Robert Lockwood's "That's All Right," and Brown's guitar accompaniment echoed Lockwood's more restrained version of the Robert Johnson style. The record didn't sell despite live promotions in front of the store that included one of Muddy Waters' handful of Maxwell Street performances. Neither did the other Ora Nelle release, which featured Johnny Young and Johnny Williams. Walter, whose argumentative nature always seemed to get him in trouble, secured and then lost a job playing at the Purple Cat on West Madison, and he spent the latter part of 1947, and perhaps early 1948, back in Helena.

LOCKWOOD HAD RETURNED to the Delta as well, following an unexpected interlude as guitarist and vocalist with an otherwise all-white band. "I was out west with the Union Pacific work train," he explains, "and one night I went into a club in Casper, Wyoming. This band was playing there, and I came back the next night to listen to them again. Finally the piano player came over and said, 'Man, you must be a musician.' I said, 'Oh, I just try to play the guitar, you know.' Well, the man who owned the place had a beautiful guitar and amplifier, and they rolled that shit out on the stage for me to play. I went up on the bandstand, and I sang and played 'Caldonia' by Louis Jordan, something by Eddie 'Cleanhead' Vinson, and 'Things Ain't What They Used to Be.' And the house came down. I got ready to leave the stage, and the man said, 'You comin' down? You better stay on up there. I'm gonna give you fifteen dollars for the day.' That was a very decent salary. So I played that man's guitar for almost a year. That was a nice bunch of dudes. They went out and bought me about five suits of clothes, brought 'em back, and said, 'You gonna wear these.' But then we started playin' down in Texas, the shows started getting held up, thirty minutes in one place, an hour in another—because I was black. I assumed I was bad news for the band, and I slipped off from them. They never would have let me go."

After a brief stay in St. Louis, Robert spent several months around Memphis and West Memphis. One afternoon in 1947 he was playing solo in the little park just off Beale Street. Five or six of the Memphis Jug Band musicians were wailing away in another corner of the park, but Robert was playing a more up-to-date mix of blues and jump tunes, and he pulled most of the Jug Band's crowd away. After he'd finished and was counting the change he'd collected, a young man walked up and sat down on the park bench beside him. "You know," the man said, "you raise hell with that goddamn guitar all by yourself." Lockwood thanked him for the compliment and there was an awkward pause. "Don't you want a band?" the man finally asked. Lockwood said no. "Motherfucker, you got one. We got a lot of jobs, and you gonna help us do 'em." Lockwood, always ready for a new adventure, said, "Tell me how much I'm makin' and all that. And by the way, what's your name? What do you play?" "I'm a piano player. My name is Bill Johnson, but they call me Destruction."

Destruction turned out to be a formidable blues and boogie pianist, and something more. Like Lockwood, he had grown up playing country blues and then developed a taste for jazz. He had a band together, two saxophones, piano, bass, and drums, and they were playing music in the jump style popularized by Louis

Jordan. They had been promised work at Jim Lindsay's club in North Little Rock and offered a radio spot there on KXLR, but they needed a front man, preferably one with a reputation; Robert's record of "Take a Little Walk with Me" was still a regional jukebox favorite.

Lockwood played with Destruction and the band over KXLR for more than a year, into 1948. "That 'Struction, he could play," Robert remembers admiringly. "He could play guitar, too. You know, I was still playing with my fingers, and he was the first one to put a straight pick in my hand. I couldn't hold that pick for nothing at first, but he said, 'Goddamn it, you gonna use it.' " Lockwood's transformation from a Robert Johnson–style country bluesman into the Delta's first modern lead guitarist was now complete.

While Robert was perfecting his lead picking, Sonny Boy was on the air again, but not for the Interstate Grocery Company. In 1947 he'd settled in Belzoni, Mississippi, and renewed his prewar acquaintance with guitarist Elmore James, a Robert Johnson disciple who didn't share Lockwood's infatuation with jazz. Elmore was born January 27, 1918, on a farm near Richland, Mississippi. His mother, who was all of fifteen, probably hadn't expected to start raising a family so soon, but she gamely set up housekeeping with Joe Willie James, the man who was thought to be Elmore's father, and they supported themselves precariously as sharecroppers, moving from plantation to plantation in Holmes County. Elmore taught himself to play by stringing broom wire on the wall of one of their cabins, and by the time he was nineteen, he was a reasonably competent young blues guitarist.

Elmore's family lived near Belzoni for a while, and it was there that he met Rice Miller and Robert Johnson. The slippery Johnson probably didn't give him any actual lessons, and in any case Elmore wasn't a fast learner, but he did manage to pick up some of the rudiments of Robert's style, including the stinging slide guitar riff for "Dust My Broom." By 1939 Elmore was already playing and singing with a full band that included saxophone, trumpet, a second guitarist, and drummer "Frock" O'Dell. The group played for dances at various Delta theaters and cafés and was one of a number of early attempts to fit traditional Delta blues into a band context—Robert Johnson had worked with backup musicians occasionally, and Honeyboy Edwards was playing with a saxophonist and drummer around this time.

Elmore went into the Navy in 1943, and shortly after he returned from the South Pacific (where he took part in the invasion of Guam), he ran into his old friend Rice Miller. They played together off and on for the next two years, and then, in 1947, Miller moved into the Belzoni boardinghouse where Elmore was staying. Before long the celebrated harmonica ace had landed a local radio show advertising Talaho, a locally manufactured patent medicine with a high alcohol content. O. J. Turner, Talaho's inventor and entrepreneur, owned a drugstore in Belzoni, and it was from there that Miller began broadcasting once more, over a hookup to Yazoo City's WAZF and Greenville's WGVM. Elmore would occasionally come on the show to play and sing—he had made infrequent guest appearances when Miller was on KFFA—but anything related to broadcasting or recording seems to have made him nervous, and he much preferred working in the local juke joints. By this time he was a formidable *electric* bluesman, crying out traditional lyrics in a high, forceful, anguished-sounding voice over his screaming, superamplified slide guitar leads.

Sonny Boy and Elmore began working frequently with another guitarist who was now living in the area, Arthur "Big Boy" Crudup. Crudup had made a number of successful records for Bluebird, including "Rock Me Mama" (1944), the prototype for the postwar blues standard "Rock Me Baby," and "That's All Right" (1946), an up-tempo blues with a hillbilly tinge that had little to do with the Robert Lockwood tune of the same name and was recorded in 1954 by a young and previously untried white singer, Elvis Presley. Crudup was an atmospheric but erratic guitarist who didn't feel comfortable in any key other than E, but he was a strong singer and a popular recording artist and could probably have worked steadily in Chicago if he'd wanted to. He chose to remain in the Delta, and with Elmore and Sonny Boy packed into his car, he would drive as far west as Little Rock to dance jobs.

The biggest surprise of Sonny Boy's Belzoni period—it probably surprised him as well as his friends—was that he fell in love. The fifty-year-old bluesman was so smitten with Mattie Gordon, the recently divorced daughter of a Silver City, Mississippi, preacher, that he took a day job for a while, driving a tractor in the hot Delta sun. Late in 1948 he left for West Memphis, found a job broadcasting over KWEM for Hadacol tonic, rented a house at Ninth and Polk, and sent for Mattie. On June 4, 1949, they were married, and though their relationship would prove erratic, his affection for her was lasting. One of the last songs he recorded, at his final Chicago session in August 1964, was "Mattie Is My Wife."

WEST MEMPHIS, a wide-open Arkansas town across the Mississippi from Memphis, was beginning to rival Helena as a regional blues center by the time Sonny Boy moved there. Howlin' Wolf had finally given up farming for a full-time musical career (at the age of thirty-nine) and was broadcasting over West Memphis's KWEM at three P.M. daily. Lockwood was in and out of West Memphis in 1949, and so were his disciple Joe Willie Wilkins (an influential guitarist in his own right), Elmore James, pianist Willie Love, harmonica player Forest City Joe, the one-man band Joe Hill Louis, and the drummer Oliver Sain, later a successful record producer, bandleader, and soul saxophonist based in St. Louis.

Riley ("B. B.") King, an ambitious young singer and guitarist from Indianola, Mississippi, who'd worked in various gospel quartets and sung for tips on Delta street corners and occasionally ran with a circle of Memphis musicians that included the stand-up vocalist Bobby Bland and pianist Johnny Ace, was working at the Square Deal Café in West Memphis and making occasional guest appearances on Sonny Boy's Hadacol-sponsored show early in 1949. He was attempting to play in the modern single-string lead style but was having problems adjusting to band accompaniment, so he began taking informal lessons from Lockwood. "His time," Robert notes, "was apeshit. I had a hard time trying to teach him." Later in 1949, King left town to live and work in Memphis, where he soon landed his own radio show on WDIA advertising Pepticon tonic. He became well known for spinning the latest jump blues—records by southwestern-born, California-based boogie pianists and blues shouters like Amos Milburn and Little Willie Littlefield, the mellow Texas blues of T-Bone Walker and Lowell Fulson, the latest Louis Jordan hits. The Pepticon show helped him learn to fit his guitar into jump and jazz-oriented band backing. He'd plug in at the studio and play along with the records as they went out over the air.

Toward the middle of 1949, Sonny Boy lost the sponsorship of Hadacol, and before long he and Mattie were fighting. After a particularly nasty spat, she left for Memphis, and while Sonny Boy was there attempting to track her down, their house in West Memphis was struck by lightning and burned to the ground, an event later commemorated in his "West Memphis Blues." The pair tried to patch things up, and eventually they were reunited, but for the time being, Sonny Boy was perturbed and restless, and he took to wandering off for months at a time. Meanwhile, Lockwood tired of the West Memphis scene. He was really getting tired of living in the Deep South, but instead of returning north, to St. Louis or Chicago, he drifted back to Helena.

There, in October 1949, he ran into Jimmy Rogers and Little Walter again. They'd come to town with Baby Face Leroy and Muddy Waters on a kind of extended Southern tour promoting Muddy's early Aristocrat records. The quartet had spent the last half of 1948 and most of 1949 working at the Do Drop Inn, the Club Zanzibar, and other Chicago night spots and terrorizing competing blues bands on their off nights. They would drop into local taverns, ask to spell the resident band, blow them away, and gleefully announce the place and time of their next regular gig. Musicians began calling them the Headhunters.

Walter in particular had developed astonishingly. "We'd do a lot of rehearsin' durin' that time," says Jimmy Rogers. "The three of us. And Walter wanted to learn. His ears were open, but he just didn't have nobody to sit down and really teach him. He was mostly playing between Rice Miller and that saxophone sound of Louis Jordan; after he came with us, we developed him mostly into a harder sound."

"He was a good boy," Muddy adds, "but he had that bad, mean temper, that kind of thing, like 'You don't mess with me too much.' Then when we got it together, I found out I was the only somebody that could do anything with him when he really got out of hand. He began acting like I was his daddy. And when we was sitting around the house playing together, or on the bandstand, that's when he worked out all that stuff that he did on our records later on, all them tricks with harps and so on. He was a man that was always thinking of something. His mind just kept going, learning more and more and more. But we was all into it. We all wanted to work, and we learned how to play up *tight* with one another. We would rehearse and rehearse. It was hard work, man. *Hard* work. But we had three naturals. Me, Little Walter, and Jimmy. Natural from our hearts."

When the band took off for the South in 1949, packing their few changes of clothes, small amplifiers, and drum set into Muddy's new convertible and Walter's 1941 Buick Special, Helena seemed the best choice as a kind of base camp. Muddy had listened to King Biscuit Time regularly before he left Stovall's plantation in 1943, and he knew broadcasting over the radio from such a central location would enable the band to draw crowds throughout the area. As soon as he got to town, he went around to several local merchants, and Katz's Clothing Store on Cherry Street agreed to sponsor a program on KFFA. There was one hitch—the only available time slot was six A.M., a good time for reaching farm workers who had to get up with the sun but a daunting hour for musicians who worked and partied late. Muddy and his band would take the ferry to Mississippi, play until close to one A.M., and race back, like Lockwood and Sonny Boy before them, to catch the last ferry from Dundee or Friar's Point. They'd have to get up before daybreak in order to make it down to the Floyd Truck Lines building for their show. On one occasion Jimmy and Walter overslept and slipped into the studio twenty minutes late while a commercial was being read, but the band was determined to succeed and such incidents seem to have been rare. Muddy and his men also worked at the Owl Café in Helena, where Houston Stackhouse and Peck Curtis often sat in. Lockwood would come around, scowling dourly at the down-home directness of the music until he'd had a few drinks and relaxed. Often these sessions would end with Robert, Muddy, Walter, Jimmy, and Stackhouse roaring around in one of their automobiles to various late-night jukes, laughing drunkenly and singing as loudly as they could.

Muddy and his group returned to Chicago in January 1950, and once they'd left Helena, the place seemed dead. Sonny Boy was rattling around Florida, Louisiana, and Texas. Robert Nighthawk had a minor r&b hit with "Black Angel Blues," recorded for Aristocrat in Chicago in 1949, and though he was in and out of Helena, most of his work was elsewhere. Lockwood decided it was time to make a move, and early in 1950 he left once again for Chicago, this time to stay for a decade. On August 15, just a few months after Robert's arrival, Jimmy Rogers made his first solo recording for Chess—Robert's "That's All Right." Commercially it followed the pattern of Muddy's more successful records up to that time, selling well and steadily in Chicago, St. Louis, a few other Middle American cities with large black populations, and in the Deep South—this was before Muddy's first band recordings and his first nationwide hit. Rogers has often claimed "That's All Right" as his own. "I built the song," he told two interviewers from *Living Blues*. "It was in between Robert Lockwood, Willie Love, ideas comin' in verses, like I put some verses with it and built it that way." Rogers's "That's All Right" probably did differ somewhat from the version Lockwood was singing around Helena; this seems to be another example of the way blues singers shape existing material to their own individual style and consider this process to constitute authorship. On the other hand, Muddy Waters says flatly, " 'That's All Right,' that's Robert Jr.'s song."

On the record, Rogers accompanied his vocal with a Lockwood-like mix of single-string fills and shuffle-rhythm chording. Little Walter contributed an intricate counterpoint, complete with speechlike inflections in the Rice Miller manner. The singing contrasted tellingly with Muddy's style. It was lighter, with a clean tone, deliberately clear phrasing and pronunciation, and a more understated use of blues inflections. "That's All Right," along with its flip side, "Ludella," can be heard as both a summation of the modern Delta style that developed in and around Helena in the forties and a milestone in the formative period of contemporary Chicago blues. In fact, to a considerable extent, the Helena style and the music that's now universally recognized as Chicago blues were one and the same.

In May 1952, Little Walter recorded a rocking instrumental at the end of a Muddy Waters session, with Muddy and Jimmy on guitars and Elgin Evans on drums. The band had been using the number as a kind of theme song, and they recorded it as "Your Cat Will Play." Leonard Chess decided to issue it under Walter's name and to title it "Juke." Again, "Juke" is both a Helena-style record and a Chicago classic. On it, Walter reverted to the jump-oriented style that made his reputation in and around Helena; most of the phrases he played were saxophone phrases. His harp was amplified, and the electricity and his masterful manipulation of both the instrument and his microphone brought out a richness of tone and subtlety of inflection that hadn't been evident in his acoustic playing on earlier records. And beginning with the second verse of the record, Elgin Evans broke into a light triplet figure on his ride cymbal that set a pattern for much subsequent Chicago blues drumming and seems to have prefigured one of the most characteristic rhythms of early rock and roll. Even more effectively than "That's All Right," "Juke" synopsized the immediate past while pointing unerringly toward the future. It also broke up Chicago's number-one blues band.

"We was down around Monroe and Shreveport, Louisiana," Muddy recalls. "Had a little tour down there with a disc jockey, called him the Groovy Boy. 'Juke' had just come out, and we went in this club one night and the people were *playing* that record. Every time the jukebox would ring, 'Juke,' 'Juke,' 'Juke.' Little Walter couldn't stand that jive. The next day he grab a train, pssssssshhhhh, back to Chicago. When me and Jimmy got back, Walter asked me, 'Wh-wh-where my money?'—like for the rest of the tour. I said, 'I thought you brought it witcha.' " Walter rejoined Muddy's band for a few weeks, but as "Juke" climbed the national r&b charts, he grew more and more restless, and finally he left. In a switch that's typical of Chicago's inbred blues scene, Walter took over a band called the Aces that was being fronted by a young harmonica player from West Memphis, Junior Wells. Muddy hired Junior. When Walter was in town, he still recorded with Muddy, but by late 1952 "Juke" was the number-one r&b record in the country, and it stayed in the Top Ten for sixteen weeks. Walter had the biggest hit any of the Delta or Chicago bluesmen had managed to chalk up, and soon he was touring the country with the Aces.

The band consisted of Louis and David Myers, two guitar-playing brothers from Byhalia in the northern Mississippi hill country, and Fred Below, a former jazz drummer who had turned to blues because blues bands were working more steadily than jazz groups in the Chicago of the early fifties. At first Below found playing the blues difficult, but once Walter began leading the Aces, everything fell into place. Between them, Walter and Below laid down a light, jazzy swing, while the Myers brothers held the groove together with solid shuffle patterns. At a time when Muddy Waters was just beginning to peak as a nationally known entertainer, Walter and the Aces were bringing electric blues into towns and cities that had never heard anything like it. The popular black bands of the period were mostly jump combos, with piano, string bass, drums, saxophones and brass, and perhaps a single, understated electric guitar, and Walter's little four-piece band was playing louder and harder than any of them. In a 1967 interview, Walter and Louis Myers remembered getting into a battle of the bands with Ivory Joe Hunter's mostly acoustic group in Dallas. "The cat [who] was bookin', Owl Lewis, was bettin' this other cat that owned the place that our band was gonna beat this nine-piece band," Myers laughed. "Below come in, nothin' but the drum. Dave comin' down. Finally I had an amplifier." Walter mimicked the club owner: "Where the horns at, the bass?" Myers continued: "He said, 'Where is the band?' And them cats bet us six hundred dollars, didn't they? And Below held the money. These cats, man, was heavy. . . ." Walter: "We stole the show." Myers: "And man, when we play, they don't want to hear that twelve-piece band no more." Because they were loud, jazzy, and jumping, Walter and the Aces got over even in Harlem's Apollo Theater, where Muddy's more down-home band, with James Cotton on harp, was practically booed off the stage a few years later.

By the mid-fifties Sonny Boy and Elmore James had joined Walter, Jimmy Rogers, Lockwood, and most of the other Helena regulars in the North. They'd made their first recordings in Jackson, Mississippi, in 1951, almost in spite of themselves. The first session, held on January 5, 1951, was Sonny Boy's. Lillian McMurry, who owned a furniture store and record shop in Jackson and had just launched her Trumpet label, knew him from his many radio broadcasts and had been scouring the Delta looking for him when she finally located him, in the back room of a Greenville juke joint, in December 1950. Sonny Boy brought Willie Love, Joe Willie Wilkins, Elmore, and "Frock" O'Dell, the drum-

mer in Elmore's first band, to Jackson with him, and although the
first session yielded nothing McMurry considered worth issuing,
she persevered.

During the next few months, Rice Miller finally recorded for
posterity some of his brilliant harmonica playing and engagingly
original lyrics. His first single, "Eyesight to the Blind," was a solid
regional hit, selling well in areas where he had performed or
broadcast. "You're talkin' about your woman," he began. "I wish
to God, man, that you could see mine / Every time the little girl
start to lovin', she bring eyesight to the blind." Sonny Boy blew
flat out in the instrumental chorus, interrupting himself to shout,
"What a woman! What a woman!" "We gotta get out of here!" he
yelled before lunging into the final harp solo. "Let's go! Let's go
now!"

The other Trumpet recordings Sonny Boy made during 1951
ranged from jumping up-tempo numbers with Joe Willie Wilkins
on fleet-fingered lead guitar to the astonishing "Mighty Long
Time," an unaccompanied vocal and harmonica showpiece with
overdubbed bass singing by Cliff Bivens. Sonny Boy's singing is so
deeply intimate on "Mighty Long Time," and it segues into and
out of his chordal harp playing so seamlessly, that the two
"voices" seem to become a single instrument. His control of vocal
nuance was fully mature—he was around fifty-five years old—and
on this performance, as well as on several others from the same
period, he modified the sound of his voice syllable by syllable,
passing from a gritty moan to a pure falsetto, thickening and then
thinning out his textures, ranging from breathy to heavier phrasing, playing with subtleties of inflection and intonation, all in the
course of a single line. His autobiographical lyrics bristled with
sharp, private images at a time when the lyrics on most commercial blues records either repeated traditional formulas or dealt
with male-female relationships in a less specifically personal manner. Scattered among the Trumpet sides are the first recorded
versions of tunes Sonny Boy would later remake for Chess, tunes
that have become blues standards—"West Memphis Blues,"
which describes the burning of his West Memphis home in 1949;
"Pontiac Blues," a sexy automotive jump tune that was probably
inspired in part by Lockwood's '39 Pontiac; the vivid "Nine Below

Zero"; the tall-tale telling of "She Brought Life Back to the Dead"; and the Robert Johnson–inspired "Mr. Down Child."

ELMORE JAMES OFTEN VISITED Scott's Radio Service in Jackson when Sonny Boy was recording. His version of "Dust My Broom," which retained some of Robert Johnson's lyrics and that characteristic slide guitar riff but transformed what had been a brisk country blues into a rocking, heavily amplified shuffle, was celebrated throughout the Delta by this time, and Lillian McMurry asked him to record it. He wouldn't, but in October he was tricked into rehearsing it in the studio with Sonny Boy and Frock while McMurry surreptitiously ran a tape. She had already recorded a dark, atmospheric version of "Catfish Blues" by an otherwise obscure singer named Bo Bo Thomas, so she put out a record with Elmore's "Broom" on one side and "Catfish" on the other. To everyone's surprise, "Dust My Broom" entered the national r&b charts. By April 1952 it was in the r&b Top Ten. Chess and other independent labels began trying to sign James to a contract, and apparently Joe Bihari of Los Angeles's Modern label recorded him clandestinely several times that spring, backed by Ike Turner's Kings of Rhythm. Sometime within the next few months, Bihari lured Elmore north to Chicago, where he joined the local chapter of the American Federation of Musicians on June 2.

As soon as he arrived in Chicago, Elmore moved into a rooming house where his uncle and Howlin' Wolf were staying. He soon made contact with the Jackson-born pianist Johnny Jones, who had already played with Tampa Red, Muddy, and other established artists. The two of them put together a band and began working at Sylvio's, where they alternated sets with the headlining group, usually Muddy's or Wolf's. Before long they were one of the most popular blues combos in Chicago. The combination of Elmore's slashing slide playing, Jones's two-fisted, rocking piano, the curious, nanny-goat saxophone sound of Mississippi-born J. T. Brown, and Odie Payne, Jr.'s crisply propulsive drumming was irresistible, especially when Elmore was singing with his usual overpowering intensity. Beginning in late 1952, the group recorded for Modern's subsidiary label, Meteor, and "I Believe," a "Dust My Broom" variant but with a heavier, wilder sound and a much stronger vocal, equaled the success of the earlier record. Subsequent releases didn't do as well, but James and his Broomdusters recorded prolifically, and the basic quartet stayed together, with occasional additions such as Eddie Taylor or Homesick James on second guitar, until 1960. The music didn't change much during this time, but it didn't really have to. The Broomdusters rocked harder than any other Chicago blues band; their music still sounded contemporary when copied by white rock groups twenty-five years after "Dust My Broom" was an r&b hit.

Throughout the fifties Elmore suffered from a heart condition, exacerbated by his drinking, and he returned south a number of times, sometimes recording while he was there in a Mississippi juke joint or another makeshift location under the aegis of Modern's Delta talent scout, Ike Turner. Then he would return to Chicago, refreshed by his "vacation" down home, and reassemble his band. From 1960 until he suffered a fatal heart attack on May 24, 1963, Elmore recorded mostly in New York and New Orleans using a variety of sidemen. His music remained basically unchanged, and several of his masterpieces, including "The Sky Is Crying," "Shake Your Moneymaker," "It Hurts Me Too," and the supremely powerful "Something Inside of Me," date from this period. These and Elmore's earlier sides with Johnny Jones, along with the best fifties discs by Muddy, Wolf, Sonny Boy, Little Walter, Jimmy Rogers, Robert Nighthawk, and perhaps a few others, constitute the recorded pinnacle of Chicago blues.

Sonny Boy bought a home in Milwaukee and began recording for the new Chess subsidiary label, Checker, in 1955. His first single, "Don't Start Me to Talking" ("Because," he warned, with perhaps a hint of irony, "I might tell everything I know"), with Muddy and Jimmy Rogers on guitars, Otis Spann on piano, and the Aces' Fred Below on drums, became a Top Ten r&b hit toward the end of the year, and Sonny Boy, now approaching sixty, suddenly found himself on the verge of stardom. By this time Robert Lockwood had established himself as a valued lead guitarist at Chess and other Chicago studios. He played on most of Sonny Boy's subsequent Chess singles and frequently backed Little Walter as well. For five years, the three most influential musicians that emerged from the fertile Helena blues scene of the forties worked together frequently in Chicago. Each was, in his own inimitable way, proud, suspicious, and argumentative. Walter continued to talk his way into fistfights and cutting scrapes regularly, Sonny Boy was too fractious to stay with any of the r&b package tours he was booked on for very long, and Robert's contempt for most other blues musicians—the few who had some working knowledge of jazz were excepted—kept him trapped in a sideman's role. Times were increasingly tough for all three, as well as for Jimmy Rogers, who was never able to get a band of his own going on a permanent basis after he left Muddy in 1958, and soon dropped out of music. In 1960 Sonny Boy convinced Lockwood to move with him to Cleveland, Ohio, where they worked together for thirteen months. Then, as usual, Sonny Boy left, but Robert had bought a house and moved his wife and children in, and he stayed on, working mostly outside music until his reemergence on the blues festival and club circuit in the 1970s.

Rock and roll, which Chess helped introduce and popularize by recording Chuck Berry and Bo Diddley, hit the older Delta bluesmen hard. A number of them—Nighthawk, Sonny Boy, Elmore— went back south and performed there when times were toughest up north. Others stuck it out. Even Muddy found the going rough, but he maintained his loyal ghetto audience in Chicago, and gradually he began to realize that there was another audience for his music, a white audience. A "blues revival" was brewing—actually the discovery by whites of a music that had been under their noses, shaping the popular music they listened to, for decades. In order to understand the roots of that revival, which was an inevitable outgrowth of rock and roll, we'll have to backtrack one more time, back to the early fifties and Memphis, Tennessee.

CHAPTER 7
Kings of Rhythm

One March afternoon in 1951, a Delta highway patrolman spotted a flagrantly overloaded sedan wallowing up Highway 61 toward Memphis. Seven black teenagers were crammed inside, and a string bass, three saxophones, a guitar and amplifier, and a set of drums were partly crammed in with them and partly lashed to the vehicle's roof. The patrolman pulled out onto the highway and turned on his siren, and as the sedan shuddered to an ungainly halt on the shoulder, several pieces of equipment, including the guitar amp, tumbled off the roof and onto the ground.

Eighteen-year-old Ike Turner, the ringleader of the group, was a Clarksdale native and something of a personality around town. He worked as a disc jockey for Clarksdale's WROX, spinning records by nationally popular black performers, and he played piano with Delta bluesmen like Robert Nighthawk. His band, the Kings of Rhythm, was a popular local attraction. The group played jumping dance music, including versions of the latest r&b hits, and were popular with some white teenagers as well as with younger blacks. The handsome, pencil-moustached Turner was already a charmer. He explained to the patrolman that he and his band were on their way to Memphis to make their first record. This was their big chance! Only a cop with a heart of stone would have denied them their shot at the big time, and before long they were back on the road, having tied their gear to the top of the car more securely.

Ike knew just which way to go once they'd come up out of the Delta into the hillier country just south of Memphis. He headed due west toward downtown Memphis, skirted the center of town, and finally pulled up at 706 Union Avenue, where a small radiator shop had been meticulously converted into the Memphis Recording Service—the city's first permanent, professional recording studio. The man who'd designed the studio and built it with his own two hands also held down an engineer's job at WREC Radio and supervised the public address systems for the Peabody, the most opulent of the downtown hotels. His name was Sam C. Phillips, and he was a striking, energetic man of twenty-eight, with a shock of bright red hair, a pair of piercing blue eyes, and a gift for oratory worthy of a country preacher. He was glad to see Turner and his ragged-looking band; he'd built his studio so that he could record some of the Memphis area's wealth of black music.

"I thought it was vital music," Phillips says today. "I don't know whether I had too many people agree with me immediately on that." This is an understatement. Phillips's co-workers at WREC, who couldn't understand why a white man with a good job would get involved in a risky venture recording black musicians, would tell him, "You smell O.K. today. Must not've been recording those niggers." Phillips, who grew up in the country near Florence, Alabama, didn't let it bother him. "I thought it was vital," he reiterates, as he is wont to do, "and although my first love was radio, my second was the freedom we tried to give the people, black and white, to express their very complex personalities, personalities these people didn't know existed in the fifties. I just hope I was a part of giving the influence to the people to be free in their expression." Phillips's interest in black people and their music wasn't particularly unusual for a white man of his age and background. What is unusual is that he did something about it and, in doing so, revolutionized American popular music.

Sam Phillips was born January 5, 1923, and grew up on a small Alabama farm near a bend in the Tennessee River. As a child, he worked in the cotton fields, like most of the black and white artists he later recorded. "I never did see white people singing a lot when they were chopping cotton," he says, "but the odd part about it is, I never heard a black man that couldn't sing *good*. Even off-key, *their* singing had a spontaneity about it that would grab my ear." Later he would linger outside black churches to listen to the singing and preaching and spend hours with Silas Paine, an elderly black man with an apparently bottomless repertoire of blues and folk songs. A leadership role in his high school band led him directly into local radio, and by 1945 he was working in Memphis. A year later he began engineering live remote broadcasts for a CBS network hookup. "It was the big-band era," he says, "and it was a *good* era. I loved the big bands, but I found myself feeling that they were letting me down because there was not enough innovation there."

Phillips found innovation in the black music he heard around Memphis. The black theaters on Beale Street put on regular shows for whites, or roped off a section of the balcony for them, and it was at one of these shows that Sam first heard B. B. King. He liked what he heard and was impressed when King landed a spot on WDIA Radio advertising Pepticon tonic. WDIA had begun its black programming on October 25, 1948, with a thirty-minute show hosted by a high school music teacher, Nat D. Williams. The response from the city's black community, and from the thousands of blacks in western Tennessee and the upper Delta who could pick up the signal, was overwhelming, and in 1949 WDIA became the first radio station in the United States to adopt an all-black format. A number of the shows featured recorded music, but others were live.

Once Phillips had heard B. B. King, he began to realize that there were scores of talented black musicians in the vicinity of Memphis, and that there was no place for them to make records. He rented the premises at 706 Union late in 1949 and put all his engineering expertise into designing and building a tiny studio just behind the receptionist's desk, and in January 1950 he opened for business. He provided acetate discs of speeches, weddings, funerals, and other notable events for a modest fee, supported his growing family with the pay from his jobs at WREC and the Peabody, and talked to several local black musicians, among them B. B. King, about making records. He knew the independent record companies that had sprung up since the war, companies like Chess in Chicago and Modern in Los Angeles, would be receptive to the music he was recording.

That summer, Saul and Jules Bihari of Modern came to town and booked Phillips's studio to record B. B. King and another locally popular entertainer, the Memphis-born boogie pianist Roscoe Gordon. Sam had made tentative arrangements with both musicians to produce their recordings, but he didn't get anything on paper, and he agreed to engineer for the Biharis on the basis of a handshake. The King sessions featured backup by some of the city's most gifted young jazz musicians, including trumpeter Willie Mitchell (later a successful record producer for, among other artists, Al Green), saxophonist Hank Crawford, and pianist Phineas Newborn. But young Newborn's phenomenally fluent playing didn't please the Biharis, who wanted a simpler, more down-home blues sound. They began looking around for a basic, dependable blues pianist, and within a year they'd found their man—Ike Turner.

Ike was born November 5, 1932, in Clarksdale. He was a town kid, not a country boy, and his first exposure to the blues came over the radio via King Biscuit Time. Sonny Boy Williamson was wailing away, but Ike's attention was captured by the clean, polished boogie-woogie played by the show's featured pianist, Pinetop Perkins. A few years later Ike found himself at a dance near Moorehead, where the Southern crosses the Dog. Sonny Boy was playing, and the pianist was Pinetop, who took a liking to the precocious Turner and offered to give him lessons.

The piano-dominated jump blues of the mid-forties was blasting out of jukeboxes throughout the black sections of Clarksdale, and Ike supplemented his lessons with Pinetop by imitating the latest hits. Before long he felt confident enough to put together a big band with some of his school chums. The Tophatters included up to eighteen musicians, but soon most of them left to play jazz, and a smaller group, with three saxes, guitar, bass, drums, and Ike's piano, reorganized as the Kings of Rhythm. At the same time, around 1947 or 1948, the sixteen-year-old Ike began doing his own disc jockey program over WROX. This gave him access to the latest jump blues records by Louis Jordan, Amos Milburn, Charles Brown, Joe Liggins, and other popular r&b artists. Like B. B. King (whom he befriended when King was passing through Clarksdale with only four strings on his guitar, headed for Memphis), Ike listened carefully to the records he played. At the same time, he worked a few local gigs with musicians like Robert Nighthawk and Sonny Boy Williamson and visited Helena, where he heard and probably picked up a few pointers from Robert Lockwood.

Ike's closest friend in the Kings of Rhythm was Jackie Brenston, the baritone saxophonist and occasional vocalist, who lived across the street from him in Clarksdale. Some of the other musicians were from out in the country. The guitarist Willie Kizart grew up around Tutwiler and Glendora. His father, Lee Kizart, was a well-regarded local blues and boogie pianist, and from his earliest years Willie had been exposed to the Delta's finest blues guitarists, who would work at his father's café in Glendora or come by the house to pick and drink. In particular, Willie had learned a great deal from Earl Hooker, a fluent, sophisticated young slide and single-string lead guitarist whose principal teacher was Robert Nighthawk. Raymond Hill, the Kings' ebullient tenor saxophone soloist, had learned to negotiate chord progressions by getting the patient Houston Stackhouse to strum the chords and then finding the corresponding notes on his horn. All these musicians could play the natural blues in a manner even the most scrupulous of the older Delta bluesmen found acceptable, but when they were among themselves, they would sometimes laugh about the way the older musicians mangled chords and broke time. Their idols were Louis Jordan and the other nationally known jump combo leaders of the period. In this, they were typical of a new generation of young Delta musicians—the first generation to break away from the oral tradition that had sustained Delta blues and left it relatively unchanged for decades, the first to draw their inspiration primarily from radio and records.

They were cocky and sure of themselves, with their shiny instruments and their encyclopedic knowledge of the latest jump blues sounds from Texas and California and New York. They were also, thanks to Ike Turner's organizational abilities and somewhat militaristic tendencies, very well rehearsed. "Ike had the best-prepared band that ever came in and asked me to work with them," says Sam Phillips. "They had a hell of a good band sound. And Ike! What a piano player he was! People don't know that Ike Turner was the first stand-up piano player. Man, he could tear a piano apart and put it back together again on the same song. But I could not hear Ike as a solo vocalist. Now I dealt with these people honestly. I said, 'Well, Ike, you've got a good band. It's got a feel, but we've got to have a vocalist.' He said, 'Oh, yeah, man, me and Jackie.' Even then he had a lot of confidence in his ability, and he's one of the great musicians of our time. Anyway, he put Jackie up there to sing, and I heard this 'Rocket 88.' And man! They had a little guy that played sax with them, Raymond Hill. He wasn't over sixteen, but you think he couldn't blow the reed out of the barrel of that damn horn? He could flat do it."

Everyone was excited and ready to record "Rocket 88," but there was a problem. Willie Kizart's guitar amp had been damaged when it fell off the top of the car and was emitting static and fuzz. "When it fell," Sam explains, "that burst the speaker cone. We had no way of getting it fixed. I guess we probably could have hustled around some way, but it would have taken a couple of days, so we started playing around with the damn thing. I stuffed a little paper in there where the speaker cone was ruptured, and it sounded good. It sounded like a saxophone. And we decided to go ahead and record. Because the thing is, I didn't want to get these people in some stupid-assed studio and lead them astray from what they had been used to doing. To put it another way, I didn't try to take them uptown and dress them up. If they had broken-down equipment or their instruments were ragged, I didn't want them to feel ashamed. I wanted them to go ahead and play the way they were used to playing. Because the *expression* was the thing. I never listened to the sound of one instrument. I listened for the effect, the total effect."

So, with Kizart playing a boogie bass figure and sounding for all the world like an electric bass with fuzz-tone (neither the electric bass nor the fuzz-tone had been invented yet), the Kings of Rhythm and Sam Phillips recorded "Rocket 88." It was a rocking little automobile blues, squarely in the tradition of Robert Johnson's "Terraplane Blues." "Step in my rocket and don't be late," Brenston offered. "Baby, we're pullin' out about half past eight / Goin' round the corner and get a fifth, everybody in my car's gonna take a little nip / Movin' on out. . . ." Raymond Hill blew a tough, screaming tenor solo, Ike pumped the piano hard against the back beat, and the string bass and Kizart's loudly distorted guitar doubled the irresistible bass line, a trick Ike may have learned from listening to the rhythm and blues records that were coming out of New Orleans, if he didn't think it up himself. The record fairly sizzled, and Sam sent it to the Chess brothers in Chicago. The Biharis hadn't paid him for the use of his studio and had, he felt, snatched B. B. King and Roscoe Gordon from under his nose.

Leonard Chess had made several field trips looking for Southern blues talent, passed through Memphis, and asked Sam to send masters for possible release. When he received "Rocket 88," he was ecstatic. Chess rushed the record out, and by the beginning of May it was on the national rhythm and blues charts. It eventually hit Number One, remained on the charts for seventeen weeks, and emerged as one of the biggest r&b hits of the year, and the only Number One recorded in the South. Chess was scoring with Muddy Waters' "Louisiana Blues" and "Long Distance Call" in 1951, but neither of these records came close to equaling the sales of "Rocket 88."

A number of people, including Sam Phillips, have called "Rocket 88" the first rock and roll record. In 1951 there wasn't any such thing as rock and roll, of course, but "rocking and rolling" was a phrase everyone who listened to r&b records understood. It was a euphemism for having sex. Another of 1951's Number One r&b hits was "Sixty Minute Man," recorded by a New York vocal group, the Dominos. "Looka here, girls, I'm tellin' you now, they call me lovin' Dan / I rock 'em and roll 'em all night long, I'm a sixty minute man," sang the lead vocalist, bass man Bill Brown. But musically the record wasn't rock and roll. It had a light, bouncy, jazz-related groove, and the only electric instrument was a trebly, discreetly amplified guitar. "Rocket 88," with its furious drive, heavily amplified guitar, and screaming saxophone solo, rocked out.

Delta bluesmen had been rocking for years—the term was understood there musically as well as sexually at least as early as the thirties. There was nothing particularly startling about the way "Rocket 88" moved, and in fact several boogieing West Coast r&b artists, especially Amos Milburn, had made records that rocked just as hard even if they weren't as electric. But a massive shift was taking place in the listening habits of young white Americans, and the shift was felt very early in and around Memphis. Whites in the area had been hiring black entertainers for their school dances, country club parties, plantation cookouts, and other festivities for decades, and by the beginning of the fifties, most of the jukeboxes in recreation parlors, soda fountains, swimming pool club rooms, and other spots frequented by white teenagers were stocked almost exclusively with records by black artists. Country and western music was for countrified, lower-class kids. The teenagers who considered themselves sophisticates danced and drank and necked to a soundtrack of "nigger music." Sam Phillips remembers that at the time "distributors, jukebox operators, and retailers knew that white teenagers were picking up on the *feel* of the black music. These people liked the plays and the sales they were getting, but they were concerned: 'We're afraid our children might fall in love with black people.' " Even then, Phillips was looking for an entertainer who could bridge the gap—a white singer with a natural "feel" for black rhythms and inflections. In 1954 he would find Elvis Presley.

Even as early as 1951, the change was in the air, and not just in the south. In the spring of 1951, when "Rocket 88" was scaling the r&b charts, a white disc jockey who also led a jazz- and cowboy-influenced country band decided to add the number to his repertoire. His name was Bill Haley, and he was broadcasting over WPWA in Chester, Pennsylvania. His band, the Saddlemen, were recording for a Philadelphia label, Holiday, and they soon cut their own disc of "Rocket 88" for the country market. This was Haley's first "cover" recording of a rhythm and blues hit. In 1954 his cover of Joe Turner's "Shake, Rattle and Roll" would climb to the top of the nation's pop charts, creating a climate in which Elvis Presley and Chuck Berry could explode into overnight successes.

But Haley's unsuccessful recording of "Rocket 88" wasn't the most significant event of 1951 as far as the emergence of rock and roll was concerned. In June, Alan Freed launched a radio show called "The Moon Dog House Rock 'n' Roll Party" over Cleveland, Ohio's WJW. On it, he played r&b records for both white and black listeners. He wasn't the first disc jockey to do so, but he would soon become the most successful. And he *was* the first disc jockey to start calling r&b "rock and roll." In mid-1951, with the help of Freed and other like-minded disc jockeys, the Dominos'

"Sixty Minute Man" became the first r&b hit to cross over to the national pop charts in a big way—*Billboard* listed it for twenty-three weeks on the same chart as the white crooners and dance bands who then dominated American popular music.

Rock and roll was inevitable, but Sam Phillips understood that it needed a charismatic white performer to really get it across, and it's difficult to imagine the music catching on the way it did in 1955 without Phillips and Elvis Presley. By that time, Sam's blues recordings had largely become a thing of the past, but from 1950 to 1954, Phillips and Ike Turner recorded the most outstanding blues performers to be found in Memphis and the Delta.

"THE MISSISSIPPI DELTA," David L. Cohn has written, "begins in the lobby of the Peabody Hotel in Memphis." Tommy Johnson, Willie Brown, and other Delta originals made their early recordings in the Peabody, while planters from the Delta socialized in its spacious salons and dining rooms and the hotel's celebrated ducks swam lazily in the fountain that graced its immense lobby. But Memphis hadn't always been so opulent. It was founded in 1819, when Helena, Arkansas, was already a busy river port and New Orleans boasted its own opera company and resident orchestra. At first, the inhabitants were limited in their musical tastes. They sang lustily and enjoyed dancing to the banjo and fiddle. Some of the banjoists and fiddlers were undoubtedly slave musicians, and Memphis's early music seems to have been heavily black-influenced no matter who was playing it. In 1838, when the Norwegian concert violinist Ole Bull became the first classical musician to perform in Memphis, the locals received him coolly. "If he had only struck up 'Lucy Neal' or 'Buffalo Gals,' and played a nigger fiddle," a budding local critic complained, "the Norwegian would have captured our . . . amateurs."

By the 1850s, cotton and timber had made Memphis a thriving commercial center. The most popular entertainments were minstrel shows, which often arrived by Mississippi River steamer and featured white imitations of black dialect and plantation music. But now Memphians seemed to crave music of all sorts. In 1851 Jenny Lind, the Swedish Nightingale, drew a thousand people to her first Memphis concert—an eighth of the town's total population. Tickets were scalped at up to thirty dollars each. Ballroom dancing was popular among well-to-do Memphis whites, many of whom profited from extensive land holdings in rural Mississippi and Arkansas. The music was provided by local orchestras, some of them black. In 1858 the luxurious, newly renovated Gayoso Hotel staged a gala reopening and introduced its black ballroom orchestra. Since this was the most popular spot in town for monied whites, one assumes the musicians played waltzes, quadrilles, and other dance music in something approximating the European manner. But perhaps they played some hotter music as well.

Apparently white Memphians were willing to spend their money dancing to black orchestras but not on badly needed civic improvements. The town's sketchy sewage system was a disgrace and seems to have been at least partly responsible for the disastrous yellow fever epidemic of 1878–79, which sent most of the population fleeing into the countryside. The dislocation following this pestilence was so wrenching that Memphis went bankrupt, and the state of Tennessee revoked its town charter. But the Southern economic recovery that came with Reconstruction eventually brought better times. The planters who'd managed to hold on to their Delta cotton land had to have some place to spend their money, and by the mid-1880s Memphis was once again in full swing. Musical diversions included brass bands, vaudeville and burlesque entertainments, Mozart and Mendelssohn societies, Wagner and Beethoven clubs, visiting opera companies, and a small local orchestra. An opera house was built in 1889 at the corner of Main and Beale Streets, an area then fashionable and white. During the 1890s the Lincoln and other early black theaters opened on or near Beale, which, in its downtown blocks, was turning into a regional center of fashionable black night life.

When W. C. Handy and his black dance band from Clarksdale settled in Memphis, around 1909, they chose Pee Wee's Saloon on Beale as their headquarters. Pee Wee's was a twenty-four-hour musicians' hangout where whites or blacks in a partying mood could call, strike a bargain, and hire a band on the spot. The tavern's regular patrons were entertained by a succession of versatile pianists who tended to favor the blues, but Handy and most of the other players who spent idle hours there were not bluesmen as the term would have been understood in the Delta. They were trained reading musicians who could play anything from the "Poet and Peasant Overture" to "Turkey in the Straw." Up and down Beale Street, the nightlife was as glittering and urbane as the theater owners and entertainers could make it. The Palace, the street's most popular vaudeville house in the early twentieth century, boasted an accomplished pit band that could sight-read the arrangements brought in by visiting singers and comedy acts or improvise hot jazz, as required. When blues was heard at the Palace and neighboring theaters, it was the jazz-accompanied blues of vaudeville entertainers like Ma Rainey and Bessie Smith, both of whom were Beale Street favorites. Handy did hear plenty of down-home blues in Memphis, and strains of it found their way into many of his compositions. But he heard this rougher, funkier music in back-street gambling dens, pool halls, and cafés. On Beale Street itself, country blues was decidedly unwelcome.

During the twenties and thirties Memphis turned out a number of polished, successful jazz musicians, including the clarinetist Buster Bailey and the swing band leader Jimmie Lunceford. Local bluesmen with country roots organized various jug bands—informal groups that played a mixture of blues, ragtime, minstrel tunes, and pop music and usually featured several stringed instruments and a jug blower instead of a bassist. But Memphis developed no single, identifiable blues idiom of its own. The city's blues fans—mostly hardworking, undereducated blacks with rural backgrounds—listened to blues musicians like Sleepy John Estes and the members of Gus Cannon's various jug bands, who came from western Tennessee and played lilting string band music while singing in a liquid, crying style. Or they danced and partied to the strong, declamatory singing and thumping rhythms of two-guitar teams from the north Mississippi hill country, the most famous of which consisted of Frank Stokes and Dan Sane, the Beale Street Sheiks. Barrelhouse pianists, many of them Delta-bred, passed through town as well. But despite occasional visits by the likes of Charley Patton and Robert Johnson, deep Delta blues doesn't seem to have gained much of a foothold in Memphis until the late thirties and the forties, when improved highways and the lure of wartime jobs brought Delta blacks into the city in great numbers.

WDIA occasionally gave time to Delta performers like Rice Miller after it switched to its all-black format in 1949. One of the station's most popular regulars was Joe Hill Louis, "the Be Bop Boy," who was born near Memphis but learned to play raw, driving blues in West Memphis and the upper Delta during the thirties and forties. With the coming of amplification, Louis became a one-man band, playing rocking boogies on electric guitar, blowing wild solos on the harmonica he wore in a neck rack, and operating a small drum set with his feet. Sam Phillips and his friend Dewey Phillips (no relation), a white Memphis disc jockey who played black records on his show, decided to try their hand at launching a local label in 1950, and the man they chose to record was Louis. His "Boogie in the Park" featured roaring, distorted electric guitar and an irresistible boogie beat, but it wasn't much of a success, not even locally, and was both the first and the last release on the Phillips label.

The rest of the WDIA regulars offered a more urbane brand of music, including B. B. King, who was born between Itta Bena and Indianola, Mississippi, on September 16, 1925, and was raised in a typical Delta environment. King's grandfather was a bottleneck guitarist, and both his parents sang. But before he had a chance to learn much about the blues, his precocious singing talent led him into a succession of young gospel quartets and featured spots with church choirs. By the time he began teaching himself guitar in the early forties, he was already a gospel-style singer, and an avid radio and jukebox listener who was more impressed by the stylings of T-Bone Walker and other modern lead guitarists than he was by local Delta musicians. Robert Lockwood helped him straighten out his time and his chording in West Memphis in the late forties, and of course Robert encouraged his predilection for a jazzy single-string lead style. In time, B. B. absorbed some jazz influences from the recordings of Charlie Christian and the French gypsy guitarist Django Reinhardt. He never really rejected his Delta roots, which are evident in his singing and playing today, especially in his fine ear for pitch shadings and subtle vocal and instrumental inflections. But he was a young man, still in his early twenties, when he first arrived in Memphis in 1946, and he knew he didn't want to spend the rest of his life plowing mules, chopping cotton, and singing for whiskey in Delta juke joints. He made

it a point to learn and perform the latest r&b hits, and when he hit
Memphis, one of the first things he did was to enter the weekly
amateur contest at Beale Street's Palace Theater.

Rufus Thomas, a singer, dancer, comedian, and future WDIA
air personality, was master of ceremonies at the Palace Theater
amateur nights when B. B. first began competing. The audience
was ruthless—inferior or uncertain performers would be pelted
with flying objects and booed off the stage—but there was more
involved than getting experience and competing; there were
prizes of up to five dollars for the night's winner. Even second or
third prize would buy a man several square meals. So B. B. entered practically every week, working as a stand-up singer and
doing mostly ballads and novelty numbers. "At that time," Rufus
Thomas recalls, "the bigger and better black clubs in Memphis
had a big band and a floor show. We had people like Duke Ellington and Count Basie coming through with their bands and playing
in some of the theaters. The blues, with harmonica and guitar and
so on, that was in the juke joints. Now I was born in the country,
but I never lived there. I was raised in town. A person like me
might want to go out and dig some blues occasionally. People from
the so-called best of families did that from time to time. It was just
a part of living. But that would be what they call slumming. When
you decided you wanted to go slumming, that's when you went
out to dig some blues."

Occasionally B. B. would take his guitar down to Handy Park
and play for tips. That was where the country bluesmen tended to
congregate when they came to town and where members of the
old Memphis Jug Band could still be found on balmy evenings and
weekend afternoons. But mostly B. B. hung out with the sophisticated younger crowd that listened to the big bands and frequented
the larger clubs. There and at the Palace Theater amateur nights
he began to meet other young musicians who were similarly anxious to break into the big time. Among them were Bobby "Blue"
Bland, a gospel-rooted singer from Rosemark, Tennessee, near
Memphis, who was five years B. B.'s junior; John Alexander, who
was born and grew up in Memphis, sang sentimental ballads in a
wistful, crooning style, and achieved fame as Johnny Ace before
ending his life in a game of Russian roulette at the end of 1954;
Herman "Little Junior" Parker, a teenage harmonica player

who'd learned from Rice Miller in West Memphis and worked with Howlin' Wolf but had his sights set on a career as a citified stand-up blues and ballad singer; and the West Memphis–born pianist Roscoe Gordon, whose blues shuffles had a rolling, almost Caribbean lilt.

People began calling these and associated musicians like drummer Earl Forest and saxophonist Billy Duncan "the Beale Streeters" because of their taste for the high life of black Memphis's main thoroughfare. B. B. often played gigs with backing by Forest, Duncan, and Johnny Ace on piano, but it's typical of his associations and ambition that when he became the first of the Beale Streeters to record, for the Nashville-based Bullet label in 1949, his accompaniment was arranged by Tuff Green, a bassist and leader of one of the city's finest big bands.

In 1951 B. B. recorded "Three O'Clock Blues," which was Number One on the national r&b charts before the end of the year and launched the most successful show business career in blues history. Nothing about the record sounded particularly like the Delta or Memphis. B. B.'s lead guitar betrayed strong T-bone Walker influences, though his tone was bigger and rounder and his phrasing was somewhat heavier. His singing made extensive use of melisma (bending and a stretching a single syllable into a convoluted melodic phrase), a gospel technique. Such singing was being popularized by the New Orleans–based r&b star Roy Brown, who'd scored an r&b hit in 1947 with "Good Rocking Tonight," and at this early stage B. B. sounded very much like Brown. But during the next few years, as he consolidated his nationwide appeal with a string of Memphis-recorded r&b hits, King's delivery grew more polished and original—the vocals soulful and pleading, the guitar cutting through with a clean, punchy attack. T-Bone Walker's lead playing began to sound rambling and discursive by comparison, and B. B. became a black matinee idol. The younger singers who still competed for prizes at Palace Theater amateur nights, among them future blues stars Bobby "Blue" Bland and Fenton Robinson, now attempted to win over the crowd with renditions of B. B.'s latest hits. King himself was out on the road, working a succession of one-night stands. He's been on the road ever since.

THE NEXT NATIONAL BLUES STAR to emerge from the Memphis milieu couldn't have been more unlike B. B. King and the hip young Beale Streeters. He was Chester Burnett, the Howlin' Wolf, who had been Charley Patton's student on Dockery's in 1929, Robert Johnson's and Rice Miller's road partner in the mid-thirties, a teacher to younger musicians like Johnny Shines and Floyd Jones, and, mostly, a farmer until he came to West Memphis in 1948. Wolf was born in June 1910, five years before Muddy Waters, Robert Lockwood, Johnny Shines, and Honeyboy Edwards, so it isn't surprising that he remained a traditionalist. When he settled in West Memphis and decided to try a full-time career in music at the age of thirty-eight, he was still playing Charley Patton and Tommy Johnson numbers and hypnotic one-chord drone pieces like "Smokestack Lightnin'." But he'd bought an electric guitar and listened with interest to his old friend Rice Miller's broadcasting band. He decided that what he needed was a group of his own and a radio show to help spread his reputation.

The band came first. Wolf told interviewer Peter Welding that the original group included Willie Johnson and M. T. "Matt" Murphy on guitars, the teenaged Junior Parker on harmonica, Destruction on piano, and drummer Willie Steel. The personnel shifted somewhat, but between 1948 and 1950 Wolf molded his musicians into the most awesome electric blues band the Delta had seen. Muddy, Jimmy Rogers, and Little Walter were shaping *their* definitive ensemble sound during these years, and, as another amplified group playing updated versions of traditional Delta blues, Wolf's band, one would think, should have been comparable. In fact, it was both more primitive and more modern than Muddy's group, for while Wolf was moaning and screaming like Charley Patton and Son House and blowing unreconstructed country blues harmonica, his band featured heavily amplified single-string lead guitar by Willie Johnson and Destruction's rippling, jazz-influenced piano. The result was an unlikely but exceptionally powerful blend, and it perfectly mirrored the dialogue between tradition and innovation that was beginning to transform the Delta's music. Wolf and his group could sound exceptionally down-home, especially when they were performing "Pony Blues" and other Patton numbers, and they could swing, jump-blues fashion. But most of the time, Wolf strutted and howled, Willie Steel bashed relentlessly, and Willie Johnson, his amp turned up until his tone cracked, distorted, and fed back, hit violent power chords right on the beat. Wolf's band rocked.

Even before they began broadcasting over KWEM, Wolf and his cohorts were a popular attraction around Arkansas and Mississippi. The group was incomparable, but the real attraction was Wolf, a showman of the Patton school who had made up as many tricks as he'd learned and would do almost anything to drive an audience into a frenzy. Eddie Shaw, a saxophonist from Greenville who left the Delta with the Muddy Waters band in 1957 and joined Wolf the following year, states flatly, "Muddy never had the energy Wolf had, not even at his peak. Muddy would rock the house pretty good, but Wolf was the most exciting blues player I've ever seen." These are the words of a Wolf loyalist; during the fifties Muddy was a powerful performer indeed. He would dart around the stage, chanting a key phrase over and over, his face bathed in sweat, eyes rolling back in his head, while his band riffed one chord and the audience swayed as if in a trance. But no matter how hard he worked, Muddy simply would not go to the lengths Wolf *habitually* went to. Muddy was superstud, the Hoochie Coochie Man; Wolf was a feral beast.

In later years, and especially after he began working mostly for white audiences, Wolf would take it easy. A little of the old ferocity was enough to ignite the most jaded college crowd. But I'll never forget a 1965 performance when Wolf played Memphis on a blues package show. This was several years before the blues revival made much headway among local whites, and there were only three or four of us, huddled right up front in the theater's most expensive seats. Wolf was halfway down the bill, which also included Big Joe Turner, T-Bone Walker, and headliners Jimmy Reed and Little Milton. This sounds like an impossible dream show now, but younger blacks were deserting blues in favor of soul, even in the Deep South, and most of the stars on the bill were probably glad to be doing short theater sets instead of grueling club dates.

The MC announced Wolf, and the curtains opened to reveal his band pumping out a decidedly down-home shuffle. The rest of the bands on the show were playing jump and soul-influenced blues, but this was the hard stuff. Where was Wolf? Suddenly he sprang out onto the stage from the wings. He was a huge hulk of a man, but he advanced across the stage in sudden bursts of speed, his head pivoting from side to side, eyes huge and white, eyeballs rotating wildly. He seemed to be having an epileptic seizure, but no, he suddenly lunged for the microphone, blew a chorus of raw, heavily rhythmic harmonica, and began moaning. He had the hugest voice I have ever heard—it seemed to fill the hall and get right inside your ears, and when he hummed and moaned in falsetto, every hair on your neck crackled with electricity. The thirty-minute set went by like an express train, with Wolf switching from harp to guitar (which he played while rolling around on his back and, at one point, doing somersaults) and then leaping up to prowl the lip of the stage. He was The Mighty Wolf, no doubt about it. Finally, an impatient signal from the wings let him know that his portion of the show was over. Defiantly, Wolf counted off a bone-crushing rocker, began singing rhythmically, feigned an exit, and suddenly made a flying leap for the curtain at the side of the stage. Holding the microphone under his beefy right arm and singing into it all the while, he began climbing up the curtain, going higher and higher until he was perched far above the stage, the thick curtain threatening to rip, the audience screaming with delight. Then he loosened his grip and, in a single easy motion, slid right back down the curtain, hit the stage, cut off the tune, and stalked away, to the most ecstatic cheers of the evening. He was then fifty-five years old.

"A disc jockey from West Memphis told me about Chester Burnett's show on KWEM," says Sam Phillips, "and I tuned him in. When I heard Howlin' Wolf, I said, 'This is for me. This is where the soul of man never dies.' Then Wolf came over to the studio, and he was about six foot six, with the biggest feet I've ever seen on a human being. Big Foot Chester is one name they used to call him. He would sit there with those feet planted wide apart, playing nothing but the French harp, and, I tell you, the greatest show you could see to this day would be Chester Burnett doing one of those sessions in my studio. God, what it would be worth on film to see the fervor in that man's face when he sang. His eyes would light up, you'd see the veins come out on his neck, and, buddy, there was *nothing* on his mind but that song. He sang with his damn soul."

Wolf first recorded for Phillips toward the end of 1950, and in January 1951 Chess released a single, "Moaning at Midnight," with "How Many More Years" on the flip. The music was astonishing, and Phillips never did a better job of capturing a mood. "Midnight" began with Wolf alone, moaning his unearthly moan. Willie Johnson's overamplified guitar and Willie Steel's drums came crashing in together and then Wolf switched to harp, getting a massive, brutish sound and pushing the rhythm hard. "How Many More Years" featured Willie Johnson more prominently, and his thunderous power chords were surely the most *electric* guitar sound that had been heard on records. Wolf's rasping voice sounded strong enough to shear steel; this music was heavy metal, years before the term was coined. The record shot into the r&b Top Ten.

Chess and the Bihari brothers' Modern label were still competing for Sam Phillips's services, with Ike Turner beginning to work independently as a Modern talent scout and A&R man. During 1951 and most of 1952 Wolf recorded several lengthy sessions. Some songs were cut at Sam Phillips's studio and sent to Chess, some were recorded there and ended up with Modern, and some were recorded by Ike Turner under makeshift conditions, probably at KWEM in West Memphis. Modern's RPM subsidiary competed with Chess's "Moaning at Midnight" by releasing a similar version, transparently retitled "Morning at Midnight." The two companies were also wooing Roscoe Gordon, whose jump blues "Booted" was issued by both companies and went to Number One on the national r&b charts in the spring of 1952.

Wolf enjoyed the sudden celebrity. He would do a session for Phillips, pocket the cash, and be ready to do another session for Ike Turner, if the price was right. Chess and Modern threatened legal action. But the end result of all this wrangling is that today we have an extensive recorded portrait of the music of Wolf's Delta band. No single performance quite matches the raw power of "Moaning at Midnight"/"How Many More Years," but there are plenty of highlights. "Riding in the Moonlight," the flip side of RPM's "Morning at Midnight," is an awesome indication of the band's force and drive. "Crying at Daybreak" was Wolf's first and, in many ways, his best recording of the brooding theme he later cut for Chess as "Smokestack Lightnin'," and, on "House Rockers," Wolf gabbed and shouted while the band rocked harder than ever: "Play that guitar, Willie Johnson, till it smoke. . . . Blow your top, blow your *top*, blow your TOP! . . . Good evenin', kids, the Wolf is in your town. . . . I know you want to see me. . . . ARRRRGHHHHH! [a bloodcurdling roar] . . . That's so sweet. . . ."

Wolf's Memphis recordings, and the equally raw sides he made for Chess after he moved to Chicago at the end of 1952, seldom made it onto *Billboard*'s national r&b charts. After "Moaning at Midnight"/"How Many More Years" in 1951, Wolf had to wait until 1956 to score another national hit, with "Smokestack Lightnin'." But these records found their way into a surprising number of white record collections, especially the collections of young rock and roll guitarists. The first white rocker to reflect the impact of Wolf's music was a Memphis guitarist named Paul Burlison. During 1952, Paul, the brothers Johnny and Dorsey Burnette, and Elvis Presley were all working for the Crown Electric Company in Memphis. Elvis harbored musical ambitions but performed mostly in his bedroom at home; the Burnettes and Burlison were playing country music semiprofessionally in a Hank Williams–derived style. But Burlison, a tireless experimenter, began visiting KWEM in West Memphis, which broadcast country as well as blues shows, and on several occasions he performed on the air with Wolf's band. The edge this experience brought to his playing became evident early in 1956, when Presley was enjoying his first nationwide smash after switching from Sam Phillips's Sun label to RCA Victor and Burlison began recording with the Burnette brothers as the Rock and Roll Trio. The most distinctive feature of the Trio's records, which included the classic "The Train Kept A-Rollin'," was Burlison's fuzzed-out, distorted lead guitar playing. There had been nothing like it in white popular music, and although Burlison claims to have discovered the sound when he accidentally knocked a tube loose in his amplifier, it strikingly resembles the sound Willie Johnson got on Wolf's early records.

In England, a group of young rockers called Johnny Kidd and the Pirates began picking up discs by the Rock and Roll Trio, who never enjoyed a substantial U.S. hit, and were mesmerized. During the late fifties and early sixties, when English rock and roll was generally a pale imitation of American originals, the Pirates were rocking for all they were worth. Their guitarist, Mick Green, developed a style that was modeled almost entirely on Burlison's and combined lead and rhythm functions. He soon became the idol of a younger generation of English guitarists, among them Eric Clapton, Jeff Beck, Jimmy Page, and Pete Townshend. Some of these musicians later picked up on Green's idols; the Yardbirds, with Clapton and later Beck, made "The Train Kept A-Rollin' " their concert showstopper.

Meanwhile, young white guitarists all over America were carefully studying Wolf's records, and especially Willie Johnson's work. One was Robbie Robertson, who joined Ronnie Hawkins and the Hawks in the early sixties and can be heard playing what amounts to a Willie Johnson homage when he solos on Hawkins's 1963 rave-up "Who Do You Love." Roy Buchanan, who played lead for Dale Hawkins and other white rock singers beginning in the late fifties, was heavily influenced both by Wolf's records and by Elmore James, the other really *electric* Delta guitarist of the fifties. Robertson and Buchanan went on to become two of the most influential and respected American rock guitarists of the sixties and seventies, Robertson with The Band and Buchanan as a legendary bar-band recluse and, later, a solo recording artist.

When Wolf settled in Chicago near the end of 1952, his reputation had preceded him, and he soon found work in the same South and West Side clubs that featured Muddy Waters. He continued to howl the deep blues, and his backing groups continued to combine traditional blues playing with contemporary jump, jazz, and r&b styles. In 1955 Muddy brought Chuck Berry to the attention of the Chess brothers, thereby almost cutting his own throat, for with Berry and Elvis Presley at its forefront, rock and roll *arrived* in 1955, bringing with it harder times for bluesmen. Wolf maintained his popularity, though, and throughout the late fifties, when Muddy's records seemed to be settling into formula (with a few notable exceptions), Wolf made some of the finest sides of his career. "Smokestack Lightnin' " and the Tommy Johnson–derived "I Asked for Water" came in 1956, the old Mississippi Sheiks hit "Sitting on Top of the World" became an r&b hit for

Wolf in 1957, and then in 1960–61 he really hit his stride with a succession of tough, pounding classics, many of them written by Willie Dixon—"Wang Dang Doodle," "Back Door Man," "Spoonful," "The Red Rooster," "I Ain't Superstitious," "Goin' Down Slow." Most of these numbers found their way into the repertoires of the early English "r&b" groups—the Yardbirds, the Rolling Stones, the Animals. When the Stones first toured America, they were asked to appear on a nationally syndicated television pop show called "Shindig." Only, they said, if they could bring Howlin' Wolf in to do a guest spot. Howlin' Who? Few American teenagers had heard of the man, but there he was one night in prime time, moving his great bulk around the "Shindig" stage with unbelievable agility and screaming the blues for the millions.

WOLF'S DEPARTURE FOR THE NORTH was a blow to Sam Phillips, who says he "would have loved to have recorded that man until the day he died." But there was plenty of blues talent in and around Memphis. Between 1950 and 1954, Phillips made dozens of great blues records, some for Chess, some for his own Sun label, and some, which waited more than twenty-five years to see the light of day, for his own personal satisfaction. He recorded the Beale Streeters—Bobby "Blue" Bland and Junior Parker sharing the vocals, with Johnny Ace on piano—early in 1952, before Bland went into the Army and Ace signed with the new Duke label. He recorded Junior Parker with his Blue Flames in 1953, and these sessions yielded both "Feelin' Good," a rocking boogie that became a national r&b hit, and the original "Mystery Train," a tune Parker and Phillips hammered out from traditional sources and, to many, the most metaphysically potent song in all of rock and roll. Early in 1954 Phillips recorded the young harp man James Cotton, with lead guitar by Auburn "Pat" Hare. Both musicians went on to play with Muddy Waters during the late fifties and early sixties, but neither ever quite equaled their Sun record "Cotton Crop Blues." "Pat Hare had a small Fender amp and a pretty good guitar," says Phillips. "His pickup was pretty powerful, and I think he had a mismatch of impedance. It was a little more than his amp could stand, but it felt good." Hare's gritty, roaring sustain and

aggressive lead lines and chording were even rawer and more
electric than Willie Johnson's work with Wolf, and the song's
lyrics explained with admirable directness why blacks were leaving the Delta.

Ain't gonna raise no more cotton, I'll tell you the reason why I said so
Ain't gonna raise no more cotton, I'll tell you the reason why I said so
Well, you don't get nothin' for your cotton, and your seed's so doggone
    low

Well, like raisin' a good cotton crop's just like a lucky man shootin' dice
Well, like raisin' a good cotton crop's just like a lucky man shootin' dice
Work all the summer to make your cotton, the fall come, still ain't no
    price

I have plowed so hard, baby, corns have got all in my hands
I have plowed so hard, baby, corns have got all in my hands
I want to tell you people, it ain' nothin' for a poor farmin' man

Hare also recorded, on his own, an even more staggering record,
"I'm Gonna Murder My Baby." Here the guitar was so distorted it
cut like barbed wire, and the homicidal lyrics caught the mood of
the playing perfectly. Not even Sam Phillips dared to release this
record, and it only came to light twenty years later on a Dutch
album bootlegged from the Sun archives. Years after he recorded
for Sam Phillips, after he'd played with Junior Parker's Houston-
based band and contributed lead guitar to Muddy Waters'
ground-breaking *At Newport* album, Hare was convicted of mur-
dering his girl friend and sent to Stillwater Prison near Minneapo-
lis.

During 1953 and 1954, Phillips recorded Little Milton Campbell, a guitarist from Inverness, Mississippi (near Greenville and
Leland), who went on to a successful career as a soul-tinged blues
vocalist for Chess. He made extensive recordings of Ike Turner's
Kings of Rhythm. He recorded Elmore James's cousin, Boyd Gilmore, who sang in a similarly impassioned style, fronting a combo
that included one of the Delta's most gifted younger guitarists,
later the most virtuosic blues guitarist in Chicago, Earl Hooker.
He recorded Walter Horton, the harmonica player, who is often
called Big Walter and who is one of the three great harmonica soloists of modern blues, the other two having been Little Walter

and Rice Miller. He recorded Joe Hill Louis, the rocking one-man band, and "Doctor" Isaiah Ross, another one-man band from Tunica County in the upper Delta, whose records of 1951–54 rock furiously and document the deleterious effects of "The Boogie Disease." "I may get better," the Doctor sang jubilantly, "but I'll never get well." The Palace Theater's MC, Rufus Thomas, recorded several animal specialties—"Bear Cat," an answer to Big Mama Thornton's r&b hit "Hound Dog," and "Tiger Man (King of the Jungle)." Sam Phillips put Thomas together with a downhome band that included Joe Hill Louis, much to Rufus's disgust. And he recorded many other Delta musicians, among them Honeyboy Edwards; Robert Lockwood's star pupil, Joe Willie Wilkins; the popular drummer-vocalist Willie Nix; and barrelhouse pianists Pinetop Perkins, Henry Hill, and Albert "Joiner" Williams.

Meanwhile Ike Turner was busy working for Modern. He recorded several of Elmore James's most impressive sides in a Canton, Mississippi, nightclub and in Clarksdale, with backing by the Kings of Rhythm. He recorded Boyd Gilmore singing a wild, careening rendition of a traditional Delta blues that would become a postwar standard, "Look on Yonder's Wall" (released as "Just an Army Boy"). Turner or one of the Bihari brothers performed a neat trick of studio surgery by grafting a bloodcurdling guitar introduction recorded by Gilmore's cousin Elmore James onto the beginning of another Gilmore classic, "All in My Dreams." The otherwise obscure Charley Booker recorded under Turner's direction a sinister, smoldering remake of the Delta standard "Special Rider Blues" as "No Riding Blues." "Greenville's smokin' and old Leland's burnin' down," Booker chanted evilly, as if, in his mind's eye, he could see the entire Delta in flames. Turner also converted a North Little Rock furniture store into a makeshift studio so that he could record Elmon Mickle, a friend of Rice Miller's who was broadcasting locally as Driftin' Slim. The band included Sonny Blair, a lunging harmonica player and intense vocalist who took over the King Biscuit Time show for a short while later in the fifties and died following an attack of delirium tremens in 1966, at the age of thirty-four. In Helena, Ike even recorded the King Biscuit regulars, with Peck and Dudlow taking the vocal leads and the wily Sonny Boy, still under contract to Trumpet, contributing unmistakable harmonica obligatos.

Turner never had a regular studio to work in, but his productions for the Biharis' various labels maintained a high standard, and almost every record featured his sturdy barrelhouse piano. Throughout the early fifties, though, he was learning guitar, principally from Willie Kizart, and as early as 1953 he was making experimental recordings at Sam Phillips's studio as lead guitarist and vocalist with his expanding Kings of Rhythm. By 1954 he felt that he was ready for bigger and better things, and that summer he took his entire band, which still featured saxophonist Raymond Hill, north to St. Louis. They quickly established themselves as the most popular black dance band in the area. Ike's saxophone section riffed with deft, swinging precision, his rhythm section cooked, and he had attracted several powerful, shouting vocalists, including Billy Gayles, Clayton Love, tenor saxophonist Eugene Fox, and, following several unsuccessful years milking ever-diminishing returns from his one hit with "Rocket 88," Jackie Brenston, who rejoined the fold in time to make an extensive series of recordings for the Federal label in August and September of 1956.

These Federal sessions, which produced the national r&b hit "I'm Tore Up" and have been reissued on an English album of the same name, were rock and roll milestones. Turner combined pop and blues song structures, extroverted vocals in the Little Richard manner, and some of the most shattering, kinetic guitar solos ever put on wax. Instead of playing a telling phrase, laying back and waiting for an answer, and then responding, like B. B. King or any other modern blues guitarist, Turner would keep up a machine-gun-like barrage of tortuously twisted high notes, bent and broken chords, and reiterated treble-string riffing at the very top of the neck. The 1956 Kings of Rhythm records were influential among blues guitarists everywhere, but for sheer demented recklessness, Turner's solos on discs like "I'm Tore Up," "Sad as a Man Can Be," and "Gonna Wait for My Chance" weren't equaled until Clapton, Beck, and other English rockers perfected the string-bending orgasm and the amphetamine stutter in the mid-sixties. By that time Ike had discovered Tina Turner, and the two of them were making tough, wholly contemporary soul records, some of which still included flashes of the dynamic Ike Turner guitar.

By the time Ike Turner left Memphis, Sam Phillips had grown discouraged with making blues and r&b discs and was turning increasingly to white country artists—especially if they had some blues feeling. This shift wasn't creeping conservatism, as many have assumed. Phillips simply couldn't hold onto his best black artists; the Deep South couldn't hold onto its most ambitious blacks. Memphis was a growing metropolis and there were jobs to be had, but the wages and opportunities couldn't compare with reports that continued to filter back from Chicago and other Northern cities. One by one, Phillips's favorites left him. The Sun label had always suffered distribution problems, and by 1954 Sam had realized that he would never be able to market r&b discs as successfully as Atlantic in New York, Savoy in New Jersey, King-Federal in Cincinnati, or Specialty, Aladdin, and Modern/RPM in Los Angeles.

Still, "weeping steel guitars and cornstalk fiddle" (Phillips's scornful description of conventional country music) held little interest for him. As early as 1951, he'd recorded a white hobo guitarist and harmonica trickster named Frank Floyd—Harmonica Frank, who performed black blues in an old-time black idiom and even sang, in his prophetic "Rockin' Chair Daddy," "I never went to college, and I never went to school/But when it comes to rockin', I'm a rockin' fool." Then a painfully shy but flamboyantly dressed young man named Elvis Presley walked into Sun to make an acetate record for his mother's birthday. That was sometime early in 1954, and on July 5, during a casual, bantering moment in the little studio, Presley, guitarist Scotty Moore, and bassist Bill Black began jamming on a Delta blues hit from 1946, Arthur "Big Boy" Crudup's "That's All Right." Phillips excitedly told them to cut it, just that way, and the record they came up with sounded like nothing that had been heard before. It wasn't a country-swing version of r&b, like Bill Haley's records, it wasn't country music (no fiddle, no steel guitar, too much rhythmic emphasis), and it wasn't r&b (too acoustic and lilting and, besides, the musicians were white). In its own odd way, it was country blues. It resembled Muddy's earliest sides in its combination of a strong blues vocal with stark electric guitar and prodding string bass backing. It was also the beginning of something very, very big, something anybody could have predicted, nobody could have stopped, and perhaps only one person, Sam Phillips, could have started.

CHICAGO AND MEMPHIS attracted most of the ambitious blues musicians who wanted to get out of the Delta during the fifties, but not all of them. Several settled in Detroit, including John Lee Hooker, who was working as a janitor in a Detroit steel mill in 1948 when he made his first records; Dr. Ross, who found work at a General Motors plant in nearby Flint; Baby Boy Warren and Calvin Frazier, two Delta singer-guitarists who'd been associated with Howlin' Wolf, Rice Miller, and Robert Johnson during the thirties and forties; and Alabama-born Bobo Jenkins, who played guitar and harmonica in the Delta during the thirties and was a Detroit filling station attendant when he began recording for small local labels in 1954. For a while, in 1953–54, Rice Miller lived in Detroit, where he worked and recorded with Warren and Frazier, but the familiar wanderlust caught up with him soon enough. Of the musicians who stayed, only John Lee Hooker achieved significant commercial success, and it came with his very first recording.

Hooker was born in Coahoma County, near Clarksdale, on August 22, 1917. His stepfather, Will Moore, was a popular blues guitarist in the immediate area and occasionally worked with Charley Patton when Patton was up from Dockery's. Hooker remembers Moore playing Patton tunes like "Pony Blues" around the house, but Moore had grown up in Shreveport, Louisiana, and the brand of blues he'd learned there was very different from what was current in the Delta. It was basically hypnotic, one-chord drone blues, with darkly insistent vamping, violent treble-string punctuations, and songs that fitted both traditional and improvised lyrics into a loose, chant-like structure. "My style come from my stepfather," Hooker says. "The style I'm playing now, that's what he was playing." Robert Pete Williams and other Louisiana country bluesmen have recorded in a somewhat comparable style, but Hooker's guitar playing really doesn't sound like anyone else's. His heavy, dramatic vocals are more recognizably in the Delta mold; he sometimes sounds a little like Muddy Waters, who considers him one of the deepest of blues singers, and, like Muddy, he was a regular churchgoer from childhood through his early teens. Hooker even sang solos with various church choirs, and he'd performed at church functions with several informal gospel groups before he left home at the age of fourteen.

During the thirties Hooker lived in Memphis, where he worked as an usher in a Beale Street movie theater and performed at occasional house parties. He was still learning to play the guitar and wasn't yet thinking of music as a full-time occupation. From Memphis he went to Cincinnati to stay with relatives, and there he worked for a cesspool-draining firm as well as in another theater. He arrived in Detroit in 1943, and with the city's factories cranking out tanks and other vehicles at peak wartime capacity, he had no trouble finding work. Playing the blues was still an avocation; he'd boogie at house parties on weekends and occasionally sit in at one of the clubs along Hastings Street, black Detroit's main drag. This went on for five years, and then one night in 1948 a black record store owner heard Hooker playing in someone's living room and took him to meet Bernie Bessman, a local record distributor. Like the Chess brothers in Chicago and the Biharis in Los Angeles, Bessman was interested in breaking into the wide-open rhythm and blues market, and he had enough sense to realize that Hooker's sound was unique and compelling. John Lee made a demo tape, Bessman placed it with the Biharis' Modern label, and the company decided on an up-tempo stomp called "Boogie Chillen" as the first release. "The thing caught afire," Hooker recalled in a *Living Blues* interview. "It was ringin' all around the country. When it come out, every jukebox you went to, every place you went to, every drugstore you went, everywhere you went, department stores, they were playin' it in there. I felt good, you know. And I was workin' in Detroit in a factory there for a while. Then I quit my job. I said, 'No, I ain't workin' no more!' "

"Boogie Chillen" wasn't the first guitar boogie on record; there had been dozens of records by black and even white country guitarists playing boogie-woogie patterns in emulation of the popular piano style. But Hooker wasn't copying piano boogie. He was playing something else—a rocking one-chord ostinato with accents that fell fractionally ahead of the beat. The closest thing to it on records is "Cottonfield Blues," recorded by Garfield Akers and Joe

Callicott, two guitarists from the hill country of northern Mississippi, in 1929. Essentially it was a backcountry, pre-blues sort of music—a droning, open-ended stomp without a fixed verse form that lent itself to building up a cumulative, trancelike effect. On later records, Hooker would use his boogie form to build moods that suggested dark, sudden violence, but "Boogie Chillen," despite its undertone of danger, was a Detroit ghetto travelogue. John Lee described walking down Hastings Street and dropping into Henry's Swing Club, took time out to shout "Boogie, chillen!" before executing a simple but effective guitar break, and then delivered his coup de grace, a dialogue that has been echoed in countless blues and rock performances down through the years.

"One night I was layin' down," he began. "I heard Mama and Papa talkin'. I heard Papa tell Mama to 'let that boy boogie-woogie! 'Cause it's in him and it's got to come out!' " Five years later, Junior Parker would construct a similar monologue over a similar one-chord boogie riff for his "Feelin' Good," and fifteen years after that, the rock group Canned Heat popularized the same guitar boogie, amplified to thunderous volume, all over again. It's been a standard rock and roll rhythm pattern ever since.

Bernie Bessman was a smooth operator. He paid Hooker well—the first recording session brought him a thousand dollars advance—and leased his masters to numerous small labels under a variety of pseudonyms, including Texas Slim, Delta John, Birmingham Sam and his Magic Guitar, the Boogie Man, and the whimsical John Lee Booker. But Modern seemed to get the best sides, or do the best selling job, and they put Hooker on the national r&b charts again between 1949 and 1951 with "Hobo Blues," "Crawling Kingsnake Blues," and the spookily echoed "I'm in the Mood," which featured Hooker's foot stomping on a piece of plywood thoughtfully provided by Bessman. During the years when Muddy was developing his blues band sound in Chicago and Wolf was fusing old-time Delta blues with jump and jazz in West Memphis, Hooker continued to record with only his own electric guitar as accompaniment. Gradually the sound filled out—a harmonica here, piano or second guitar there, occasional drums—until, in the mid-fifties, Hooker switched to the new Chicago label Vee Jay. There he began recording with larger bands that included Delta musicians Eddie Taylor and Jimmy Reed and a sophisticated lead guitarist, Lefty Bates. He also made more rhythm and blues hits, most notably the rocking "Boom Boom" (1962), a sexy stop-time number that was done to death by English and American rock groups for the next ten years. Like Muddy Waters and only a handful of other Delta bluesmen, Hooker adapted to changing times, becoming a "folk bluesman" when folk was in fashion, assembling rock-oriented backing groups during the sixties, and eventually settling in San Francisco, where he recruited road bands from his suburban neighborhood. The young white audiences he plays for now demand "the boogie," but Hooker often dangles his slower, deeper blues as bait.

Hooker often names Albert King as one of his favorite blues guitarists and singers, and Albert is one of a group of Delta musicians who made St. Louis their headquarters during the early fifties. The sound of sax-heavy jump bands with high-voltage guitar leads was the dominant sound of St. Louis blues in the fifties, and while Ike Turner and his Kings of Rhythm were probably the primary local influence at the time, both Albert King and Little Milton Campbell made exciting, innovative records there from the mid-fifties through the early sixties, for the Bobbin label. Albert arrived in St. Louis by a circuitous route. He was born Albert Nelson near Indianola, Mississippi, on April 25, 1923. His claim that he is B. B. King's brother or half-brother is hotly disputed by B. B. His early life involved hard farm work on various plantations (as one of thirteen Nelson children) and singing in country churches. Around 1931, the family moved to the vicinity of Osceola, Arkansas, a popping blues spot not far from Memphis and the Missouri state line, and Albert chopped and picked more cotton, played guitar and sang the blues in the joints, and continued to sing gospel music as well. During the late forties he tried living in St. Louis, but he was a country boy, and soon he was back in Osceola, gigging with a local jump band called the In the Groove Boys at clubs like the T-99 and the Dipsy Doodle. He tried the North again in 1952–53, and in Gary, Indiana, he met and performed with Jimmy Reed, who'd moved there from the Delta in 1948. In 1953 Albert arranged to make his first recordings, for the Parrot label of Chicago. Johnny Jones, the brilliant pianist from Elmore James's Broomdusters, was on the session, which revealed

that Albert was still under the sway of Elmore and Robert Nighthawk. The records didn't sell, and Albert returned to Osceola one
more time, staying a couple of years before he drifted back to St.
Louis in 1956.

During the next ten years Albert refined his own style. He evidently listened hard to B. B. King's light, skipping lines and increasingly woody tone, but he'd already absorbed too much of the
heavier lead playing of Elmore, Nighthawk, and Willie Johnson to
become a B. B. imitator. Instead, he created a unique synthesis,
playing single-string leads but with a broadly metallic tone and
brawny, heaving phrases that seemed to dig into the beat from
underneath. In 1962 he achieved fleeting national recognition
with "Don't Throw Your Love on Me So Strong," a medium-slow
blues with a strongly implied triplet feel that introduced the "Albert King signature"—*dah*-dah-dah, a three-note lick falling from
a flattened third down to the tonic. The record made it to Number
Fourteen on the national r&b charts, but it wasn't until Albert
hooked up with Memphis's Stax label in 1966 that his career really
took off. Backed by the premier soul rhythm section of the period
(Booker T. and the M.G.'s) and the strutting Memphis horns, he
cut the venerable Delta blues "Crosscut Saw" (performed by Sam
Chatmon, Tommy McClennan, and other Mississippi bluesmen at
least as early as the thirties), updating its rhythmic pulse with a
quasi-Latin beat; "Laundromat Blues" ("You better hear my
warning, I'm gettin' madder every day / I don't want you to get so
clean, baby, you just might wash your life away"); and "Born
under a Bad Sign," a fortuitous commercial stroke that combined
a menacing rock riff, a bulldozer rhythm, high-energy guitar
leads, and fashionable lyrics with astrological overtones. All these
songs were national r&b hits, and in 1968 they were collected on a
Stax album, *Born under a Bad Sign,* perhaps the most influential
blues album of the sixties. When Eric Clapton left the Yardbirds to
form Cream, he turned increasingly to Albert King–style playing;
Cream's "Strange Brew" and "Born under a Bad Sign" were
practically Albert King parodies. Albert began performing at rock
halls like the Fillmore East while maintaining his large down-
home black following, and he has managed to please both audiences ever since without quite attaining B. B. King's show business stature.

Albert is a solid, no-frills blues shouter who doesn't go in for B. B. King's gospelish melismata, but he is important as one of the premier guitar stylists of modern blues. His playing evidences a sharp ear for the subtle pitch shadings and voicelike inflections that make blues deep. Often he will "worry" the fifth or another note, bending and twisting it this way and that while punching at the rhythm with a finesse none of his legion of imitators has been quite able to match.

Little Milton Campbell, who was born September 7, 1934, and raised around Greenville and Leland, Mississippi, was never as original. His blessing and his curse was that he could sound like almost any other blues artist, and his early recordings, made for Sun, the Memphis-based Modern subsidiary Meteor, and later Bobbin, included faithful reproductions of the styles of B. B. King, Roy Brown, even Fats Domino. In 1963 he left St. Louis for Chicago, where his records for the Chess subsidiary Checker took on a pronounced soul-gospel coloration. His "Feel So Bad" and "Grits Ain't Groceries" were soul-blues hits in 1967 and 1969, and he has continued to perform for an almost entirely black following without crossing over to the white audience enjoyed by B. B. and Albert King.

It seems strange that New Orleans, the metropolis at the mouth of the Mississippi River, didn't attract more Delta bluesmen. Rice Miller and Elmore James performed there frequently during the forties, playing in the streets before they graduated to club engagements, and other Mississippi bluesmen paid occasional visits. But New Orleans had its own indigenous brand of blues, a jazz-oriented style that had more to do with Texas and Kansas City music than with the Delta and often made use of the Afro-Caribbean rhythm patterns that have survived in the city's folklore since the celebrated slave gatherings that took place in Congo Square. Only one Delta bluesman left his mark on New Orleans music. His name was Eddie Jones, and he was born in Greenwood on December 10, 1926, and raised in southern Mississippi near Hollandale. Like Hooker and the Kings, Jones sang in church before he sang the blues, but in his case the experience seems to have left a deeper impression. By the time he arrived in New Orleans in the late forties and put together a trio with the future rock and roll star Huey "Piano" Smith, Jones was singing the way sanctified preachers preached—groaning, screaming, torturing almost every syllable, investing even the most shopworn blues lines with what would later be called "soul power." He was also an astonishing lead guitarist with his own almost frighteningly intense version of the T-Bone Walker style and an individual way of wresting screaming high-note sustains from his overworked amplifier. Since he was tall, skinny, good-looking, and a flashy dresser, he soon acquired a nickname—Guitar Slim.

Some of the earliest Delta blues singers were inspired by sacred singing—Patton, Rubin Lacy, Son House, and on down to Muddy Waters and John Lee Hooker. Beginning in the late forties, the New Orleans–based singer Roy Brown popularized a crying, occasionally overwrought vocal style with a lot of gospel in it, and by the early fifties blues singers like B. B. King and Bobby "Blue" Bland were stretching and pummeling syllables and letting hoarse, tearing textures creep into their voices, betraying an even stronger church influence. Guitar Slim took this evolution, which has been one of the most significant developments in the history of black popular music, a crucial step further. In Nashville in 1952 he recorded an eight-bar ballad, "Feelin' Sad," for the Bullet label. It began with wordless moaning, and the wrenching vocal performance that followed wasn't gospel-blues, it was unadulterated backcountry gospel with secular lyrics. The song's eight-bar verse form and melody line, the piano accompaniment, the discreet horn section, which contributed chords the way an organ might have—almost everything about the record was gospel rather than blues or pop. Yet the lyrics were autobiographical blues lyrics: "I was in Korea in '51 / I had no love, and I was so alone / I was sending you all my money, baby / And all the time, you was doin' me wrong." This was using the Lord's music to do the Devil's work, and many musicians and listeners found it shocking. One who didn't was a blind pianist from Florida named Ray Charles. Beginning in 1949, the musically sophisticated Charles, who was capable of scoring complex jazz arrangements in braille, had recorded for several California and New York labels. A few of his sides were gritty urban blues, but most were smooth blues-ballads in a Nat "King" Cole–Charles Brown vein. Then Charles ran into Guitar Slim.

In October 1953, Slim recorded in New Orleans for the new Los

Angeles–based Specialty label. He brought Ray Charles to the session, along with a group of crack r&b musicians who recorded regularly with Fats Domino and other local artists. According to Jerry Wexler, who was co-producing Charles for Atlantic at the time, Ray "sketched out a head arrangement for Slim's 'The Things I Used to Do,' playing piano at the date and directing things at the keyboard. This record was to sell a million copies for the Specialty label. Nobody knew it then, but this was a big breakthrough for Ray—he had, in effect, written his first commercial hit arrangement." Even before "The Things I Used to Do" became one of the best-selling r&b discs of 1954, Charles had begun to make drastic changes in his music. Instead of crooning, he began to preach, and along with the standard twelve-bar blues that made up much of his repertoire, he began performing original numbers that were set in the eight-bar and sixteen-bar mold of gospel music.

Charles, a proud man, has denied that Guitar Slim influenced him to move in this direction, but the evidence contradicts him. Wexler says that Charles "was very much taken with Slim's perfervid, impassioned, preach-blues style," and it was only toward the end of 1954, after "The Things I Used to Do" had become a huge hit, that Ray recorded his first overtly gospel-based single, "I've Got a Woman." During the same period he also recorded a version of "Feelin' Sad" that makes his debt to Guitar Slim even more apparent—it's a very close imitation of Slim's Bullet original, yet it's also, unmistakably, Ray Charles. It seems that, like so much else in American popular music, the enormously influential Ray Charles style—a style that effectively broke down the musical barriers between gospel and pop and is generally considered the prime source of modern soul music—was inspired by yet another Delta bluesman.

Slim never recorded another big hit, but for a time, in the mid-fifties, he was a popular concert attraction across the country. He's been described as the most flamboyant of the period's blues guitarists; he would get his band rocking, climb onto the shoulders of a burly retainer, and allow himself to be carried through the adoring throngs and into the street, where he soloed for chorus after chorus at the end of an extra-long cord. He inspired numerous imitators, including, for a time, Ike Turner, who recorded several Slim sound-alike numbers, and New Orleans's Earl King, who has claimed that Slim's mid-fifties playing sounded a lot like the Jimi Hendrix of the late sixties. A few of Slim's Specialty recordings, most notably "The Story of My Life," include enough whining sustain and biting high-note work to lend King's story some credence. Slim recorded for Atlantic in New York during the late fifties, and he died there of pneumonia in 1959, at the age of thirty-two.

Chicago, Detroit, Memphis, St. Louis, New Orleans—only one other major city played an important role in the Delta blues diaspora of the fifties, and that was Houston, Texas. Don Robey, a black businessman who owned Houston's principal black club in the late forties and managed the popular blues guitarist and singer Gatemouth Brown, grew so disgruntled with Aladdin Records's handling of Brown that in 1949 he recorded him locally and put out the disc himself, naming the label Peacock after his Bronze Peacock Club. Early in Peacock's career Robey recorded a seminal gospel hit, "Our Father," by the Five Blind Boys of Mississippi, but it wasn't until 1952 that he made the most fortuitous business deal of his life by buying the Memphis-based Duke label—recorded masters, artists' contracts, and all. Among the artists who came to Robey with Duke were Johnny Ace, Roscoe Gordon, and Bobby "Blue" Bland, and in 1954 Herman "Little Junior" Parker joined an expanding Duke roster. Ace, the sloe-voiced balladeer, dominated the national r&b charts from 1952 until his fatal game of Russian roulette, which took place in a dressing room at Houston's Civic Auditorium while he was waiting to go onstage on Christmas Eve, 1954. It took several more years for Parker and Bland to hit the national r&b charts, Parker with "Next Time You See Me" in 1956 and Bland with "Farther Up the Road" in 1957.

Bland and a Houston jazz trumpeter named Joe Scott developed a big-band blues-ballad sound that featured massed brass and reeds and stinging lead guitar behind Bland's distinctive, gospel-influenced vocals. Bobby had always favored a sophisticated, stand-up approach to blues singing. He was basically a city stylist to begin with, and his Duke records capitalized on this tendency. Parker, who was born March 27, 1932, probably in Coahoma County, Mississippi, came from a much more down-home background. He learned the harmonica sitting on Rice Miller's knee—

literally, for he was still a child. When he was in his teens, he joined Howlin' Wolf's original band, and although several of his Sun recordings of 1953 featured a saxophonist and attained a certain polish, they were still very much in the Delta mainstream. In Houston, Parker fell in with Memphis saxophonist Bill Harvey, whose well-rehearsed jump band had already backed B. B. King, Gatemouth Brown, and other popular front men on records and in person. Pat Hare drifted down to Houston as well, and with Harvey's slick, jazzy horn arrangements and Hare's biting lead guitar supporting his country-sounding harmonica and expressive vocals, Parker (and Duke) had a winning combination. From 1954 through the early sixties, Parker and Bland toured together frequently as Blues Consolidated, building a large audience from the Southwest across the bottom half of the country to the Southeast. By the early sixties both artists were popular with black audiences in the North as well. Between 1958 and 1966 Parker cut a string of exciting blues hits for Duke, several of which—"Five Long Years," "Sweet Home Chicago"—were either Delta tunes or city blues first recorded by Delta artists. His last hit, "Drowning on Dry Land," climbed as high as Number Forty-eight on the r&b charts in 1971, the year he died of a brain tumor. Bland went on to become the most durable and consistently popular of modern blues-ballad singers. During the seventies he was often reunited with his friend from the Beale Streeters days, B. B. King.

One last important Delta stylist remains to be discussed—Jimmy Reed, who settled in Chicago in 1953 and recorded his first national hit, "You Don't Have to Go," in 1955. Reed was born September 6, 1925, on a plantation near the Delta hamlet of Dunleith, and he learned guitar from a childhood friend, Eddie Taylor, who was two and a half years his senior. As a child, Taylor had followed musicians like Charley Patton and Robert Johnson to house parties. Sometimes he would crawl in under the shacks and drift off to sleep while feet stomped to the guitarists' rhythms just above his head. In his youth Taylor was a wholly traditional Delta bluesman, and he and Reed would frequently play and sing Delta standards together after a day spent working in the cotton fields.

Reed says he couldn't even spell his own name when he first arrived in Chicago in 1943. After a hitch in the Navy and several more years sharecropping in the Delta, he moved north, first to

Gary (where he gigged with Albert King) and then to Chicago, where he played a kind of primitive one-chord blues with a friend named Willie Joe Duncan, a virtuoso on a homemade one-stringed instrument. In 1949 Eddie Taylor arrived in Chicago, and he and Reed began working together in a succession of tough, low-rent South Side taverns. In 1953, after flunking an audition for Leonard Chess, they began recording for the new Vee Jay label, and in 1955 Reed's "You Don't Have to Go" made it to Number Nine on the r&b charts.

Reed played harmonica mounted on a rack while he strummed his electric guitar. It was Eddie Taylor who provided the music's crisp shuffle figures, a legacy of his early admiration for Robert Johnson. Their music was very traditional, very country, but there was something about it that appealed to a broad spectrum of people—white country and rock and roll fans as well as blacks who usually preferred blues with a more uptown flavor. Maybe it was the insinuatingly lazy way Reed sang, and maybe it was the uncluttered Delta guitar shuffles, which provided a relaxed alternative to the more frenetic rhythms of rock and roll. Maybe it was Reed's lyrics, which were straightforwardly sexy but too amiably delivered to be threatening. In any event, Reed became one of the most popular blues stars of the fifties and early sixties, and probably Vee Jay's most consistent hit maker. One classic followed another—"Ain't That Lovin' You Baby" in 1956, "Honest I Do" in 1957, "Baby, What You Want Me to Do" in 1960, and the one-two knockout punch of "Big Boss Man" and "Bright Lights, Big City" in 1961. At this point, a relative handful of American whites had heard of B. B. King or Muddy Waters, but they bought Reed's Vee Jay discs in quantity, and the records got airplay on stations with white disc jockeys and rock and pop formats. Vee Jay's promotional muscle helped enormously, but, as the record business truism has it, you can't promote a stiff. Somehow, Reed reached people in a way no other Delta bluesman had been able to do, and only his increasingly debilitating alcoholism and erratic behavior on- and offstage prevented him from claiming the enormous audience he would have commanded once the English Invasion of the early and middle sixties made blues chic.

There are still professional and semiprofessional blues bands in the Delta. Many of them, including Frank Frost's popular Jelly

Roll Kings, play music that sounds a lot like Jimmy Reed, while others, such as the Little Rock–based group led by Larry Davis, work in the B. B. King idiom. The area is no longer a source of musical innovation and hasn't been since the plantations automated and the northward migration that had begun before World War I finally peaked sometime in the 1950s. But Delta blues, deep blues, is still alive, especially in Chicago, where, on a jumping Saturday night, you can choose from several dozen live blues shows, most of which take place in black neighborhood taverns on the South and West sides. And of course it's alive in California and New York and London and Paris and Stockholm and Moscow—wherever Delta bluesmen tour and Delta expatriates live, wherever, for that matter, people play or listen to blues-derived rock and roll.

EPILOGUE
The World Boogie

"The rock and roll, this hurt the blues pretty bad," says Muddy Waters. "We still hustled around and made it and kept goin', but we were only playin' for black people when rock and roll came along, and it got so we couldn't play any more slow blues. The people just wanted to 'bug. But we survived out of that." For a year or two, beginning in 1955 when Chuck Berry, Bo Diddley, Little Richard, and Fats Domino all became immensely popular with both young blacks and young whites, Muddy put down his guitar. "His band was his instrument and he sang unhampered," reported the English blues aficionado Paul Oliver in a 1959 *Jazz Monthly* article, "stamping, hollering, his whole body jerking in sheer physical expression of his blues. He would double up, clench his fists, straighten with a spring like a flick-knife, leap in the air, arch his back and literally punch out his words whilst the perspiration poured down his face and soaked through his clothing."

The younger crowd might be flocking to rock and roll package shows, but Muddy held on to his audience. Throughout the middle and late fifties he worked six or seven nights a week around Chicago, mostly at Smitty's Corner, Thirty-fifth and Indiana, with regular Wednesday excursions to a large dance hall in Gary, Indiana. The only breaks in this routine were tours, which occasionally took Muddy and his band (featuring Pat Hare, Otis Spann, and James Cotton) to the East or West Coast but more often traversed the Deep South. It was there, Muddy told Paul Oliver in 1958, that he drew his most enthusiastic response: "People there, they *feel* the blues and that makes me feel good. They come from miles around to hear us, and if we get less than six-seven-eight hundred people, believe me, that's a bad house! And it ain't cheap to hear Muddy Waters! They pay two, three dollars a time to come in; mebbe they don't eat the next day, but, man, the place is really jumpin'!"

Muddy, Wolf, and B. B. King worked regularly throughout the first years of the rock and roll explosion, while old-timers like Sonny Boy and Robert Nighthawk drifted back and forth between Chicago and the Deep South, and a number of important bluesmen, most notably Jimmy Rogers, dropped out of music altogether. One way or another, the strong survived, and it was Muddy, the strongest of the lot, who first broke through to a white audience. In the fall of 1958 he unexpectedly received an offer to tour England along with a popular English traditional jazz group led by Chris Barber. Big Bill Broonzy, who'd been one of the friendliest and most helpful of the blues stars from the thirties when Muddy first arrived in Chicago, had paved the way. During the late forties, when Muddy's gritty electric music weaned black blues fans away from the older Bluebird style, Broonzy discovered the nascent American folk revival. He'd been introduced to New York at the 1938 Spirituals to Swing concert when producer John Hammond was unable to locate Robert Johnson, and, a decade later, he was a fixture on the emerging lower Manhattan folk scene, where a left-wing and generally naive young audience accepted him, along with Leadbelly, Sonny Terry, and Brownie McGhee, as true folk artists. Broonzy's dozens of Bluebird records with bass, drums, and jazz band backing were conveniently forgotten, and he played the role of the folk bluesman fresh from the cotton fields to the hilt.

Broonzy made his first European trip in September 1951, and he was an immediate hit in both London and Paris. He returned early in 1952 along with Blind John Davis, the blues and jazz pianist who'd been one of Bluebird's busiest session musicians in Chicago during the thirties and forties. From then on, he was an established European concert draw. Early in 1958 his health began to fail. Before he died that August, he recommended to some of his English fans that they bring over Muddy Waters, and though Muddy was something of an unknown quantity there, a modest tour was arranged. There wasn't enough money for Muddy to bring his band, so he decided to travel with Otis Spann, who was his pianist, straw boss for his band, and his brother-in-law.

Muddy couldn't have known very much about the audience he was going to play for. It was a young crowd that had been attracted to the blues not through rock and roll but through trad jazz and skiffle. Trad jazz was, of course, British dixieland, and out of the trad jazz movement had come skiffle, a kind of English version of American "folk blues." The skiffle craze began early in 1956 when Lonnie Donegan, formerly the banjoist with Chris Barber's trad band, became an overnight star with a hit record called "Rock Island Line." It was a songster ballad Donegan had learned from a Leadbelly recording, and Donegan had performed it in a kind of jug band style, with acoustic guitar and bass, washboard percussion, and kazoo leads. These were the basic ingredients of skiffle. Its appeal was that anybody could afford the instruments and learn a few old blues off Leadbelly and Josh White records, and throughout the late fifties, while rockers with leather jackets and greased pompadours bopped to American rock and roll and its various British imitators, another large segment of England's youth packed the concert halls to hear their favorite skiffle artists. Until Muddy arrived in England, all the black bluesmen who'd performed there—Broonzy, Josh White, Terry and McGhee—had played acoustic music in a style the skiffle fans could easily relate to. Muddy, innocent of this audience's expectations, cranked up his amplifier, hit a crashing bottleneck run, and began hollering his blues.

SCREAMING GUITAR AND HOWLING PIANO is the way Muddy remembers the next morning's newspaper headlines. "I had opened that amplifier up, boy, and there was these headlines in all the papers. Chris Barber, he say, 'You play good, but don't play your amplifier so loud. Play it lower.' 'Cause, see, I'd been playin' here in Chicago with these people who turned theirs up." Paul Oliver noted wryly in *Jazz Monthly,* "When Muddy Waters came to England, his rocking blues and electric guitar was meat that proved too strong for many stomachs," but the tour turned out well after Muddy toned down a bit. He was more than willing to be accommodating. "Now I know that the people in England like soft guitar and the old blues," he told *Melody Maker*'s Max Jones shortly before he left to return to Chicago. "Next time I come I'll learn some old songs first."

Muddy's success in England attracted the attention of white jazz and folk fans in the United States, and at the urging of Atlantic Records jazz producer Nesuhi Ertegun, the Newport Jazz Festival booked him to headline a special blues program on July 4, 1960. Newport was a real jazz festival with no concessions to rock and roll, but it attracted a large, young, and sometimes rowdy crowd. On Saturday, July 3, a mob of approximately ten thousand teenagers and college-age youths attempted to break into the festival grounds, police were called in, and a full-scale riot ensued. The rest of the festival was called off by joint decision of the Newport City Council and the festival's producer, George Wein—except for the Sunday afternoon blues show, which was allowed to go on. This time the audience was a jazz crowd that wouldn't cringe at drumming and amplification, and Muddy had brought his whole band—Hare, Cotton, Spann, bassist Andrew Stephenson, and drummer Francis Clay. The set they played mixed Muddy's established crowd-pleasers—"I'm Your Hoochie Coochie Man," "Baby Please Don't Go"—with some of his newer, jump-oriented material, including his then-current Chess single, "Tiger in Your Tank," a novelty blues written by Willie Dixon.

The crowd was cheering wildly as the set neared its end, and Muddy told them, "We got one more we're gonna do. . . . I got my mojo workin', woman. D'you hear me?" Spann hit a rollicking intro and the band was off, rocking hard but with a relaxed, sinuous grace. Muddy had first recorded "Got My Mojo Working" in 1957, but rock and roll was at its zenith then and the record didn't even make the r&b charts. Live, the song had been an immediate sensation. Muddy had climaxed most of his English dates with it, calling Chris Barber's jazz band back onstage to help him put it over, and by 1960 it was his obligatory set closer. It drove the Newport crowd wild. He had to sing it all over again after the cheering had subsided. The afternoon closed with Otis Spann singing an impromptu "Goodbye Newport Blues," written out on the back of a Western Union telegram blank by the poet Langston Hughes following the announcement (false, as things turned out) that, because of the rioting, this would be the last Newport Jazz Festival. But moving as this final slow blues was, the young crowd went away whistling the catchy "Got My Mojo Working."

Chess was quick to capitalize on Muddy's emerging reputation outside the black community, and an album of his Newport performances was issued. It sold surprisingly well and was particularly influential in England. There, young blues enthusiasts like Alexis Koerner and Cyril Davies, who'd hung on Muddy's every word and guitar lick when he visited in 1958, had begun playing music that was harder and rougher than the predominant skiffle and trad jazz. Their various nightclub ventures and groups bred a still younger crop of English musicians and blues enthusiasts, including the future Rolling Stones, Yardbirds, and Animals, who were ready and waiting when Muddy returned to England in 1962—with an acoustic guitar and a repertoire of older, "folk" blues learned especially for the occasion. "The first thing they wanted to know," he remembers, laughing, "was why I didn't bring the amplifier. Those boys were playing louder than we ever played."

Soon after he returned from his second English trip in 1962, Muddy was booked into the Jazz Workshop in Boston, and there he took on a young manager, Bob Messinger, who was convinced that he could sell Muddy to white folk and jazz crowds. But this aspect of his career didn't really pick up steam until around 1964 when English groups, especially the Rolling Stones, began recording their own versions of his songs and of other Chicago blues and telling American interviewers that Muddy Waters was among their favorite musicians, though few reporters or Rolling Stones fans had heard of him. "Before the Rolling Stones," says Muddy, "people over here didn't know nothing and didn't *want* to know nothing about me. I was making race records, and I'm gonna tell it to you the way the older people told it to the kids. If they'd buy my records, their parents would say, 'What the hell is this? Get this nigger record out of my house!' But then the Rolling Stones and those other groups come over here from England, playing this music, and now, today, the kids buy a record of mine, and they listen to it. Fifteen years ago, after Newport, at some of my gigs, I might have a few kids from the university, but if it wasn't some school date I was playing, if it was just in a club in Chicago, it would be maybe one percent, two percent white. I play in places now don't have no black faces in there but our black faces."

Muddy and his band frequently share concert billings with white blues or blues-influenced rock bands. From time to time they play shows with several other popular black bluesmen—B. B. King, Albert King, Bobby "Blue" Bland. These shows tend to attract both black and white fans. Occasionally Muddy gets to work alongside one of his peers, or with a younger bluesman like Otis Rush whose music is deeply rooted in the Delta tradition, but that doesn't happen often. "Ain't too many left that play the real *deep* blues," he said the last time I talked with him. "There's John Lee Hooker, Lightnin' Hopkins—he have the Texas sound, and Texas blues is very, very good blues—and, let's see, who else? Ain't too many more left. They got all these white kids now. Some of them can play *good* blues. They play so much, run a ring around you playin' guitar, but they cannot vocal like the black man. Now B. B. King plays blues, but his blues is not as deep as my blues. He play a type of blues that can work in a higher class place, like to a higher class of peoples—they call 'em urban blues. Bobby 'Blue' Bland, the same thing. Albert King play a little deeper blues than they do, Otis Rush is deeper. . . . I don't want to put down nothin' that'll make anybody mad, but it's the truth. There ain't too many left sings the type of blues that I sing."

I wondered if this state of affairs made Muddy nostalgic for the old days, for Mississippi or for Chicago in the fifties. He snorted derisively. "I'm out there workin' as much as I want to, turnin' down jobs I could be doin', and the money's up," he said. "These records I'm makin' now, that Johnny Winter's producin', they're sellin' better than any of my old records ever did. We got that Chess sound, too. I'll tell you the truth: This is the best point of my life that I'm livin' right now." I asked how he felt about having taken so long to get to this point, and he looked at me like I was a plain fool, his eyes glinting ironically. "Feels good," he said. "Are you kiddin'? I'm glad it came before I died, I can tell you. Feels great."

MUDDY'S EARLY VISITS TO ENGLAND opened the way for other Delta bluesmen, and one of the first to follow him was Rice Miller, who was invited to take part in a 1963 American Folk Blues Festival tour that stopped in France, Holland, Germany, Denmark, Sweden, and England. Memphis Slim was playing piano on the tour, and when it was over, Sonny Boy and Slim toured Poland and returned to England for further engagements. By this time, there were "beat clubs"—places where young electric blues and r&b bands like the Stones, Yardbirds, and Animals played for dancing—in various English cities, and Sonny Boy found these clubs much to his liking. The beat club crowd didn't expect him to be a "folk artist," rustic and reserved—he could front an electric band, holler, and stomp. While he was in England in 1963, and during a second tour in 1964, he performed and recorded backed by both the Yardbirds (with Eric Clapton on lead guitar) and the Animals. He also took to English haberdashery, affecting a bowler hat, a natty black umbrella, kid gloves, and some suits he had made by a London tailor that were half charcoal gray and half black in a kind of harlequin design. He would show up for club engagements with his scruffy young accompanists carrying a fancy leather attaché case full of harmonicas and amuse his audiences by mimicking the airs and accent of an English gentleman.

After his 1964 European tour, Sonny Boy surprised most of his old friends by returning to Helena, where he once again took over King Biscuit Time. KFFA had moved out of the Floyd Truck Lines building and into a modern, carpeted studio on the top (fifth) floor of the tallest building in town. During broadcasts thick drapes were drawn across the windows, but before and after the live shows, one could open them and look out at the levee, the old Illinois Central tracks, the big, leafy elm and sycamore trees along the edge of the river, and the ferry landing almost directly below.

Announcer Sonny Payne wondered why the irascible old harp man had come back after all these years, bowler hat, attaché case, two-tone suits, and all. "Sonny Boy," he said one day after a broadcast, "I thought you were having a ball over there in Europe."

"Yes, sir, I was."

"Why'd you come back?"

"I just come home to die. I know I'm sick."

"How do you know you're going to die?"

Sonny Boy looked Payne right in the eye. "We're just like elephants," he said. "We knows."

At least that's the way Sonny Payne tells it. The story sounds heavily romanticized, but apparently it isn't. Houston Stackhouse says Sonny Boy told him, "Well, Stack, I done come home to die now."

Stackhouse was unconvinced: "I thought he's just talkin'. I carried him to Greenwood, two or three times. We had some plays down there, and I'd go down there with him, and we'd play. So he had me to carry him all around where he used to be, all up and down them roads and things. One day comin' back . . . I knowed it was somethin' funny about him then. . . . He just wanted to see every place that he had used to be down there. Sometimes we'd be two or three miles out off the highway. We'd go on around. He'd say, 'Carry me way on up in here. I got to see these people.' Or just go look at the spots, anyhow. He didn't live long behind that."

Early in 1965, five young white rockers were staying in a Helena motel and performing at night at the Delta Supper Club, a large roadhouse run by the local businessman who owned the ferry. They were well known in the area because they'd been through dozens of times as the Hawks, rockabilly singer Ronnie Hawkins' backup group and probably the most widely imitated white band in the Midsouth. Levon Helm, the drummer, had grown up around Helena, but the rest of the musicians—Robbie Robertson, Rick Danko, Richard Manuel, and Garth Hudson— were Canadians. They'd left Hawkins a couple of years before and were making a living, if not a spectacular one, as Levon and the Hawks, churning out tough, loud cover versions of the latest rock and roll and r&b hits at roadhouses and frat parties from Louisiana to Ontario, West Texas to New Jersey.

"Levon had grown up listening to Sonny Boy on King Biscuit Time," Robbie Robertson recalled years later, after the Hawks had become The Band, perhaps the most respected of all American rock groups. "We were in Helena, just hanging out and talking about the music, and we thought about Sonny Boy. Somebody said, 'Maybe he's here.' So we went down to the holler—Levon knew where everything was—and we asked some people if Sonny

Boy was around. They said, 'Yeah, he's playing down at the café.' We went down there, and there he was—a big tall man in a bowler hat, white hair, and a white goatee, wearing a suit he'd had made in England that was gray on one side and black on the other, and the reverse on the back. He looked kind of . . . fine.

"Levon introduced himself and said, 'Can we go somewhere to play some music?' So he took us to these friends of his. This woman had a place where she sold bootleg corn liquor. Well, that stuff is outrageous. We got drunk, *drunk*, and we all played. And, man, he played the harmonica inside out. He'd put the whole thing inside his mouth and play it. As time went on, I kept noticing him spitting in this can. I thought maybe he was chewing tobacco or something. I was wandering around at one point, *really* drunk, and I happened to look in the can, and it was blood. He was spitting blood.

"Things got a little weird there. There were all these young black guys around trying to hustle us. They were afraid of Sonny Boy. He was the only legend around the neighborhood, and it was also a known fact that if you fucked with him, he would cut you. But eventually there were just too many people. So we all left, and we smuggled him into our motel—they wouldn't let any black people in there, you understand—and we just played and played, and he couldn't believe it. He'd been playing in England with the Yardbirds and some other groups, and he told us, 'They're awful. They want to play the blues so bad, and they play it so *bad*. . . .' We really got on with Sonny Boy, made all these plans. We were gonna tour with him, be his backup band. Then we were playing in New Jersey, and we got this letter from Helena saying Sonny Boy had passed." It wasn't long after that that the Hawks got a call from New York asking them to back up a young folksinger named Bob Dylan.

"Carrie Wilkins said he was fishin' that Monday," Stackhouse reports, "and Sonny Boy didn't say three words, just sat on the river fishin' down there. Said he was just sittin' there just lookin' into the water, just unconcerned, just fishin', and wasn't talkin' or nothin'. And so the next day [May 25, 1965] he was dead. When they got ready to broadcast, he hadn't showed up. Peck went back from the radio station and went upstairs there where he was livin' and found him dead. . . . He didn't lie about he'd come back home to die. But he sure had a lot of people at his funeral. He was well thought of through that country."

Nighthawk was back in Helena after a last attempt to establish himself in Chicago in the mid-sixties. He took over King Biscuit Time for a short while, with Peck on drums and James Starkey on piano, but it wasn't long before he found a more remunerative gig in Memphis. He was increasingly debilitated by heart trouble, and two years later, on November 5, 1967, he died in Helena Hospital. He'd consulted a root doctor first, but she said she couldn't cure him, that he had "dropsy," and "it done run too long."

King Biscuit Time continued, but with recorded music instead of live musicians. As of this writing, it's still on the air three days a week. Sonny Payne handles the announcing and plays Sonny Boy's recordings between the commercials for King Biscuit Flour and Sonny Boy Meal. "I get requests," Payne said when I visited Helena in 1979, "from all around this area. And at least once or twice a month, somebody from one of the two white beauty shops in town will call and say, 'Have you got King Biscuit Time on?' 'Yeah, it's on.' 'Well, wait'll I turn it up. Play us a song. Don't say who it's for. Just play us one.' These are well-to-do white women listening. *I* listen, every day when I'm doing the show, for the simple reason that there's something there. They're trying to *tell* you something, and if you think hard enough and listen hard enough, you will understand what it's all about."

IT WAS A BITTERLY COLD NIGHT on Chicago's North Side entertainment strip. Otis Rush, the best of the city's modern, B. B. King–inspired bluesmen, was leaving the bandstand after a tepid first set—five or six finely crafted but low-keyed instrumentals and an indifferently sung blues shuffle. The crowd in the Wise Fools Pub, a noisy little storefront bar with a reputation for presenting some of Chicago's finest blues talent, began to thin out a little, and the blues fans I was sitting with were debating whether to stay or to walk a few blocks up the street to another club, where Jimmy Rogers and the brilliant but erratic harmonica virtuoso Big Walter Horton were co-leading a band. "I caught their first set,"

someone said, "and it was great right up to the end. But they were
getting real drunk, and Walter started playing in a different key
from everybody else. I don't think the rest of the night's gonna be
too hot."

Dick Shurman, a serious aficionado who's usually able to sniff
out the hottest blues sets on any given night, looked over at the
bar, where Rush was nursing a drink and staring moodily at the
floor, his lacquered rooster hairdo glinting in the amber light.
"When Otis gets like this," Shurman said, "there's no telling
what he'll do. But I don't think he's gonna do much tonight. We
oughta give Jimmy and Walter a try." Everybody trooped off into
the snow but me; I don't get to Chicago that often, and at that
point Otis Rush hadn't been to New York since the sixties. Not
long after my friends left, a lovely Japanese girl walked in, and
Rush brightened. He'd toured Japan to great acclaim and recorded an inspired live album there in 1975, and blues gossips had
told me a female fan followed him back to Chicago and moved in
with him, vastly improving his outlook on life (which has never
been notably positive or predictable). Otis and the girl exchanged
a few pleasantries, and then he returned to the bandstand.

The set that followed was devastating. The first tune rocked,
with Otis snarling the words out of the side of his mouth, and then
he settled down to slow, minor-key blues, an idiom in which nobody can touch him. "He's *so* good, man," Muddy Waters had told
me, and Muddy doesn't dispense praise lightly. There are indications of how good Rush can be on his records, beginning with "All
Your Love (I Miss Loving)," "Double Trouble," and the other
sides he made for the Cobra label between 1956 and 1958, continuing with his sporadic appearances on local labels and his more
recent albums. All of these records have been flawed by lackluster
backup or uneven performances from Rush himself, but all of
them have contained at least a glimmer of sheer genius. That
night at the Wise Fools, during one forty-minute set, Otis focused
all his extraordinary talents. His grainy, gospelish singing carried
the weight of so much passion and frustration, it sounded like the
words were being torn from his throat, and his guitar playing hit
heights I didn't think any musician was capable of—notes bent
and twisted so delicately and immaculately they seemed to form
actual words, phrases that cascaded up the neck, hung suspended

over the rhythm, and fell suddenly, bunching at the bottom in anguished paroxysms.

The performance, if you could call it that, was shattering and uplifting all at once, the way blues is supposed to be. I had heard bluesmen play and sing with comparable intensity and technique, but Otis Rush had something else—an ear for the finest pitch shadings and the ability to execute them on the guitar, not as mere effects but as meaningful components in a personal vocabulary, a musical language. He was playing the *deep* blues. After the set I passed him at the bar and told him how overwhelmed I'd been, but he was being moody again. "Yeah," he mumbled, "thanks." "By the way," I added, "I've been out interviewing Muddy Waters, and he said if I saw you tonight to be sure and send you his regards." Rush smiled brightly for the second time that night. "I tell you," he said, warmly wringing my hand, "I love that man."

Otis Rush arrived in Chicago in 1948 at the age of fourteen. He'd sung in church choirs, and he'd been fooling with the guitar since he was eight, but the countryside near Philadelphia, Mississippi, where he grew up, didn't offer much inspiration in the way of live music; what little Otis learned he picked up from two older brothers who were amateur guitarists and from records. After he settled in Chicago, he began listening to Muddy, John Lee Hooker, and other Delta bluesmen, and by the early fifties he was working as Little Otis ("Everybody was 'Little' at that time—Little Walter, Little Otis, Little Milton") at various ghetto clubs, duplicating, as best he could, blues hits by Muddy, Hooker, Walter, and other popular artists. Gradually, he progressed from playing and singing mostly in a Muddy/Hooker vein to the idiom of younger performers like B. B. and Albert King—high-note string bending, biting single-note lines. And he began listening carefully to jazz guitarists like Kenny Burrell, George Benson, and Chicago session man Reggie Boyd, who gave him some lessons.

In 1956 a West Side businessman named Eli Toscano launched his new Cobra label with Rush's "I Can't Quit You Baby." It was a medium-slow, steady-rocking shuffle, with Otis shouting the gospel blues and playing rapid-fire bursts of high-note guitar paced by bass-string riffs that still retained a little of the Muddy Waters feel. During the next few years, Cobra introduced two more young guitarists, Magic Sam and Buddy Guy, who together with Otis became the leading practitioners of what's been called the West Side blues style. Sam, whose real name was Sam Maghett, had a background that strikingly paralleled Otis's. Born in Grenada, Mississippi, in 1937, he learned to play guitar mostly by listening to the early recordings of Muddy Waters and Little Walter, moved to Chicago at the age of thirteen, and began working in the West Side taverns with his uncle, the harmonica player Shakey Jake. Buddy Guy was born in Lettsworth, Louisiana, in 1936 and also learned to play from records (Hooker, T-Bone Walker), but he'd had a few years of professional experience before he arrived in Chicago. Otis and Magic Sam were playing a "Battle of the Blues" at the Blue Flame Club at Fifty-fifth and State when Buddy walked in off the street and floored them by playing and singing in a similar style but with even more intensity and showmanship. It was Sam who arranged for Guy's first recording contract, with Cobra's Artistic subsidiary.

The young West Side guitarists introduced a number of innovations into Chicago's still heavily Delta-oriented blues community, including slow, gospel-tinged blues sung in minor keys (an idea taken up with great success by Bobby "Blue" Bland a year or two after Otis' and Sam's first successes with such material) and probably the earliest use on blues records of the new electric bass. Rush actually initiated both trends, the first with "I Can't Quit You Baby," the second with his working bands of the period. He had Greenwood-born guitarist Willie D. Warren playing bass lines on the four bottom strings of his regular guitar before Fender began marketing the four-stringed bass guitar. But the Cobra venture that had begun so promisingly soon went downhill. Toscano was an inveterate gambler who began gambling away the money that was due his artists, and he ended up heavily in debt. In 1959 his labels folded.

Otis went on to record for Chess and Duke, but they released only a few singles and kept his career in limbo until the mid-sixties when he participated in sessions for Vanguard Records' *Chicago—The Blues—Today!,* the first anthology of modern Chicago blues aimed specifically at a white folk and rock audience. From that point on, Otis became a favorite of numerous white blues and rock guitarists, including Duane Allman, Mike Bloomfield, and Eric Clapton. But his recording career was erratic. He made an overproduced album for Atlantic in 1968; a set recorded for Capitol in 1971 went unreleased until the small Bullfrog label bought the tapes and put them out in 1976; and since then, there have been two albums on Delmark and a handful of European and Japanese releases.

Rush remains a suspicious, introverted man. He almost never works in Chicago's black clubs—he once commented that he'd seen too many people knifed or gunned down while he was playing—and when he travels to the East or West Coast, he usually goes as a single, picking up local musicians for his various club dates and rehearsing them on the bandstand. His music, and the music of contemporaries like Buddy Guy, has grown closer to rock in certain ways—long instrumental solos are emphasized more than the songs and the singing, and fast-paced, rocking tempos are mandatory for opening and closing numbers. But even in his more involved instrumental workouts, Otis retains the expressive essence of deep blues.

In 1978 Rush made a triumphant return to New York, bringing a tight Chicago band with him and packing the Village Gate for three weeks. Less than a year later, he showed up for an opening set at New York's Lone Star Café missing a front tooth and tanked to the gills—not a state he's often in. He proceeded to turn in an embarrassingly erratic, self-indulgent performance, backed by an incompetent pickup band that hadn't been able to rehearse with him and apparently had never heard any of his records. After the set, he got into a violent argument with his Japanese lady friend, who ran out of the club in tears and attempted to commit suicide by prostrating herself in the middle of Fifth Avenue. Onlookers dragged her out of the path of the oncoming traffic, and Otis got through the rest of the gig, more or less, but his rejuvenated career as a New York club attraction seemed to have come to a premature end.

A year later I went to hear Rush at another New York club, Tramps. The band was a local pickup group with a decent rhythm section and little personality, but Otis showed up radiating confidence and played a magnificent two-hour set during which he managed to keep the audience riveted on his every move while teaching the band most of the material they'd be doing for the remainder of the engagement. The next few times I saw him at Tramps, he'd whipped his backup band into shape and his music was almost up to the standards he'd set that unforgettable night in Chicago.

Magic Sam suffered a heart attack in 1969, just as he was about to attract a substantial white following, which would have meant breaking out of the grind of low-paying ghetto bar work. Buddy Guy is still going strong, often in partnership with the West Memphis–born harmonica player and former Muddy Waters sideman Junior Wells. Like Otis Rush, these musicians are playing *Chicago* blues—a music shaped by the Delta heritage but very much a music of the city, a music of today. Chicago's black blues clubs seem to be about as active as ever, and new blues performers continue to find their way out of ghetto anonymity and onto record albums and festival stages. Many of these newcomers are middle-aged or older, but some are still in their thirties, and a few, like the sensitive guitarist Lurrie Bell, are still in their early twenties.

IT WAS ANOTHER CHICAGO WINTER, and at five in the afternoon the street outside the Wise Fools Pub was already dark. Inside, the Son Seals blues band was waiting apprehensively for Seals, who was driving over from his apartment on the South Side through a rapidly developing snowstorm. The studious-looking rhythm guitarist was sitting in the middle of the Pub's tiny stage restringing his instrument, the bassist was running through his extensive repertoire of funk licks, and the drummer was sitting with veteran blues saxophonist A. C. Reed at a corner table, discussing some fine points having to do with drinking and the weather. "It's okay to drink when you're running around in this kind of cold," Reed was saying, "but the thing is, you got to keep *on* drinking."

Seals made his entrance briskly, his black overcoat flapping behind him, his guitar already out of its case and ready for action. As usual, his round, expressive face was caught halfway between a cocky grin and a bad-ass glare. Though he was still in his thirties (he'll turn forty in 1982), he was the hottest blues guitarist in Chicago, with a string of international club and festival appearances to his credit and two albums on the independent Alligator label that had drawn extravagant critical praise ("Chicago's most exciting new blues voice in a decade"). On this particular night he was to begin recording a new live album, but things weren't going right. His amplifier—he used the bottom of a bass amplifier to get his fat, sizzling sound—was acting up, his pianist hadn't shown up for the rehearsal earlier that afternoon, and the weatherman was predicting Chicago's heaviest snowfall in ten years. The preceding weeks had been plagued by other mishaps. The van Seals and his band traveled in broke down in the middle of nowhere; his onstage wardrobe was stolen. That's the blues.

Son Seals was born into the blues, and not just in a figurative sense. His father, Jim Seals, ran the Dipsy Doodle in Osceola, Arkansas, and the family lived in a frame house attached to the club. Son, whose given name is Frank, was born August 11, 1942, and he says that "blues is the first thing I ever heard. When I was a kid, it seemed kind of like a dream. Blues was all we had on the jukebox—Muddy Waters, Jimmy Rogers, Elmore James. Guys like Robert Nighthawk, Joe Hill Louis, and later Albert King would play in the Dipsy Doodle on the weekends." When Son showed an early interest in percussion, his father brought him a drum set; by the time he was in his mid-teens, he was playing at the Dipsy Doodle and other spots around Osceola behind Nighthawk and Rice Miller, among others.

There was a larger black club on the outskirts of Osceola, the T-99, and before long Son was in demand there, too. "Guys like B. B. King, Junior Parker, and Rufus Thomas would come into town on a weekend to play the T-99," he remembers, "and a lot of times, they would call before they came over and ask would I play with 'em. But I learned guitar along with the drums, learned it from my father, and for a while there I was playing guitar all around Arkansas during the week and drums on the weekend. I wanted to get my own band together, and when my father saw that I was interested, he pitched in, helped us get a couple of amps, a guitar, stuff like that. So I got some guys together and started working around town, in Blytheville, up at the Arkansas-Missouri state line, and in 1959 I took this band over to Little Rock to work at the Chez Paris."

The Chez Paris was on Ninth Street, the main thoroughfare of

Little Rock's black community. Most of the bluesmen who'd worked there in the early fifties were gone—Driftin' Slim was in California, Rice Miller was spending a lot of time in the North—but local entrepreneur Jim Lindsay was still running clubs in Little Rock and in North Little Rock across the Arkansas River, and Seals, now concentrating on guitar, found plenty of work. Son and his band would play at the Chez Paris until after midnight, then pack up and race across the bridge to one of Lindsay's North Little Rock clubs, where the law was lenient and the joints kept rocking until four or five in the morning. "I played some rock and roll," Son notes; he still plays slashing renditions of "Johnny B. Goode" and other Chuck Berry songs. "We'd play in schools around there for a bunch of kids, and they wanted to hear Little Richard or the Platters. I had a guy singing with me who could sing like Sam Cooke, too. Playing Chuck Berry stuff was fun, 'cause he had that blues touch all the time, even though he spoke in rock and roll. But basically, rock and roll wasn't what I was used to. We had to learn to play some of everything, but when I had the chance, I'd always fall back into the blues."

During the early sixties Son also took occasional road gigs as a drummer, most notably with the former Robert Nighthawk student Earl Hooker and his Roadmasters. He visited Chicago briefly in 1962, and there he met Hound Dog Taylor and several other Delta musicians, but the mid-sixties found him back in Osceola, taking care of his ailing father. The town had changed, and so had the Dipsy Doodle. "See, my father's place was right in the middle of town," says Son. "He was living right in the community, people all around. Well, they gets a new chief of police, and he comes down, says, 'You all can't do this, and you gotta cut that out.' So my father couldn't have no bands. He had to cut out a lot of entertainment. Now the T-99 was out of the city limits, so the bands could still play over there. But right across the highway from my father's place was a bunch of whites living in that area, and they'd complain, blah blah, this and that all night long. So for a while my father had just a piano player, and then it was the jukebox."

Albert King grew up around Osceola, and Son had been listening to him for years. "He always had that sound, man. Back then, you could walk up outside a joint, and you could say, 'That's Albert in there. That's so and so on piano.' You could tell the difference

even a mile away if they were playing in one of those wood buildings. Albert may have developed a little more technique, but even
then you could tell him from all the rest." In 1966, King found
himself desperately in need of a solid blues drummer, and he
called Son, who temporarily put his guitar away and spent the
next couple of years on the road. That's Son drumming on King's
Live Wire Blues Power album, recorded at the Fillmore West in
1968. These were the years that found Albert, B. B. King, and
other bluesmen breaking out of the grind of chitlin circuit one-
nighters to play for white rock audiences, a development Son
found interesting. But in 1968 he returned to Osceola, where his
father was now seriously ill. Jim Seals died in January 1971, and
Son, now almost thirty and a veteran of the road, decided the only
place to go was Chicago.

"Not too long after I got to Chicago and got me a day job," he
says, "I went down to where Hound Dog Taylor was playing. I
hadn't seen him since I was up visiting in 1962, but he remembered me. He said, 'Hot damn, there go Son Seals.' His other guitar player had quit him, and he said, 'Man, I'm sure glad to see
you. I can use you.' He was playing at the Expressway Lounge
over on Fifty-fifth Street. So we worked together there and some
other places. Three or four places around town we'd make during
the week and then do the Expressway on the weekends. Then
Hound Dog started making records for Alligator and getting more
out-of-town work, and it got to where he couldn't hold down the
job at the Expressway Lounge. So he said, 'Why don't you take
it?' "

Taylor had been playing basic Delta blues in the Elmore James
style, but once Son took over, the music got more modern. The
main thrust of his playing was derived from Albert King's work,
but there were strong reminders in it of everything he'd done,
from the early days backing Nighthawk and other traditional
bluesmen to the rock and roll gigs in Little Rock. He also had his
own songs, some with strikingly original lyrics—"Your Life Is
Like a Cancer," for example. It wasn't long before a dedicated
Chicago blues fan named Wesley Race excitedly telephoned Alligator Records' Bruce Iglauer from the Flamingo, Seals's regular
Thursday-night gig, and held the telephone outside the booth so
that Bruce could hear the raw, rocking music. "Who the hell is

that?" Iglauer asked. He thought he knew the Chicago blues scene pretty well, but this was somebody he hadn't encountered before. "That," said Race proudly, "is Son Seals." Iglauer came down and decided to make an album strictly on the basis of Seals's playing and singing. Son astonished him by showing up at the first rehearsal for the album with a stack of his own songs.

During the rest of the seventies Alligator grew from a shaky one-man operation into the most successful modern blues label, with worldwide distribution and a booking office for all its artists. Son began working more and more out-of-town gigs, and his second Alligator album, *Midnight Son,* really opened things up for him—appearances at some of the country's major rock nightclubs, festivals, European tours. The album was a musical landmark as well. There were bright, punching horn arrangements, the rhythms were contemporary, the music's aggressive energy was pure rock and roll, but the singing and guitar playing and Son's songs were unquestionably the blues. "I want to stay on top of things," Seals says. "I want to always be able to be creative and change away from the same stuff you been hearing the last twenty or thirty years. As long as I can come up with some good lyrics, I can create a good new piece of music to go with 'em. That's what I mean by doing my own thing, and that concerns me quite a bit all the time."

We sat at a table in a dark corner of the Wise Fools, waiting for the place to fill up. The blizzard was hitting its peak, but people came straggling in by twos and threes, and pretty soon the room was packed, with more listeners crowded into the adjoining bar. Bruce Iglauer was down in the club's dank basement, his four-track recording console set up on a stack of beer cases. When Son saw the house filling, he excused himself, and before long the band hit a solid shuffle instrumental, with more than a hint of James Brown funk from bassist Snapper Mitchum. Son, now dressed in a brown suit, shirt, and hat, with a rakish feather in his hatband, pushed through the crowd to the bandstand and plugged in. He's a gravelly, authoritative singer, with a unique way of chuckling and laughing in time to the music without undercutting his carefully cultivated aura of menace. You can hear traces in his vocals of B. B. King and Ray Charles, among others, but they've been subsumed into a personal approach. And by this time, he was more than an adept Albert King imitator on guitar. The phrases came coursing out of his amp, grainy and distorted in tone like the fifties solos of Willie Johnson and Pat Hare but executed at a furious pace and with razor-sharp rhythmic acuity. With all those years as a drummer behind him, Son could make you stomp your feet and want to get up and dance even without his band, and the band was pushing hard.

Despite the blizzard, occasional squawks of static from his temperamental amp, and the frustrations of the past few days, Son turned in a spectacular night of blues playing. In his slow blues in particular, the attentive listener could hear fleeting reminders of the man's rich heritage. When he squeezed out a lagging, liquid phrase in his guitar's middle register, the sound was unmistakably Robert Nighthawk. When he played "The Sky Is Crying," running his tough, callused fingers up the instrument's neck like a metal slider, he recalled the intensity of Elmore James. There were flashes of Albert and B. B. King, of Junior Parker, even of the Muddy Waters records that were on the Dipsy Doodle's jukebox when Son was a toddler. Between sets I asked him about all the ghosts I was hearing. Were they really there? "The things that I heard and learned while being around those guys are things you can't forget," he said. "Even though you're trying to do your own thing, that basis will come out. A lot of times it may come out without me being conscious of it. You're hearin' somethin' that sounds like Robert sometimes, and somethin' that sounds like Elmore? Sure, man. It's there."

SON SEALS CAN CALL UP THE SHADES of Robert Nighthawk, Elmore James, and his other early influences with uncanny immediacy simply by attacking a note a certain way or bending a string just so. But Seals doesn't have the acute sensitivity to pitch shadings that makes Otis Rush's blues so compelling. Rush added modern jazz influences, including the idea of taking long improvised solos, to his Mississippi blues roots, and in doing so he forfeited the sort of concise sledgehammer effect Muddy Waters achieved in three-minute masterpieces like "Still a Fool." Muddy simplified Robert Johnson's busier, more diffuse rhythms, and

Johnson had already streamlined Charley Patton's earlier blues, which were predicated on a rhythmic density later blues musicians never even attempted to duplicate.

Similarly, Son Seals's most personal blues lyrics have never quite matched the self-revealing intensity of Son House's "Preachin' the Blues" or Robert Johnson's "Hellhound on my Trail." And Johnson, despite his exceptional gifts as a lyricist, never captured the look, the feel, and the complex social relationships of his time and place as vividly as Charley Patton did in blues like "Tom Rushen" and "Moon Going Down" and "High Water Everywhere."

Has deep blues been declining, falling ever so slowly from the grace of its early years? I don't think so; I think it's been in a constant state of flux. It's true that Charley Patton's blues were richer rhythmically and perhaps more telling lyrically than the blues that have come after them, but if Patton were alive today he'd probably be amazed at how fluidly and eloquently Otis Rush makes his electric guitar speak. Robert Johnson made some of the most thrilling records in the history of American music, but he didn't live to develop an ensemble music with the refined, classical balance of Muddy Waters' early band recordings, and one can't automatically assume that he'd have been able to if he'd been given a few more years. Blues has lost a lot; it's lost the sense of in-group solidarity that once tied it so closely to its core audience, its crucial context of blackness. But it's gained a new, wider context, and that isn't necessarily bad. Delta blues never enjoyed a golden age; the musicians were too busy learning and evolving and speaking their souls.

The deepest blues asks its listeners to confront their joys, their sorrows, their lusts, and, above all, their mortality. If the music has a single Great Subject, it's impermanence. "The sun's gonna shine in my back door some day," sang Tommy Johnson, hopefully. "The wind's gonna rise and blow my blues away." Willie Brown began his 1930 recording "Future Blues" with these lines: "Can't tell my future, I can't tell my past / Lord it seems like every minute sure gon' be my last." Son House sang in "My Black Mama," "It ain't no heaven, no, ain't no burnin' hell / Where I'm going when I die, can't nobody tell." Once you start remembering them, the images of loss, gain, physical movement, and metaphysical transformation accumulate in hard, diamondlike clusters. "Leaving this morning if I have to ride the blinds." "Gonna get up in the mornin', I believe I'll dust my broom." "You may bury my body down by the highway side / So my old evil spirit can catch a Greyhound bus and ride." "I'm gonna write me a letter, I'm gonna mail it in the sky / Mama, I know you will catch it when the wind goes blowing it by." "I'm goin' down to Louisiana / Baby behind the sun / Well y'know I just found out / My trouble's just begun."

But even as it's coming to terms with impermanence, the blues is asserting a permanence of its own, and it's in deep blues that that permanence is most imposing. During the eight decades that have passed since Charley Patton learned blues from Henry Sloan, a beast we call Civilization has utterly transformed our planet. Nomads and hunter-gatherers whose ancestors lived in the open and understood the language of the physical world now sit mutely in urban cubicles, watching "Charlie's Angels" and "Kojak" and "Hee Haw." Ancient civilizations have crumbled, dynasties have fallen, rivers and lakes and oceans have been poisoned, men in funny rubber suits have provided diversion by walking on the surface of the moon. Yet the music of Charley Patton, a functionally illiterate rounder who sang for common laborers in an isolated geographical pocket that most of the rest of America had forgotten or never knew existed, still informs, entertains, and moves listeners all over the world. Son Seals can still add a little pressure to his touch on the guitar strings, slide into a note just so, and instantly communicate something of the personality, the creativity, the accomplishment of a man who called himself Robert Nighthawk and learned from Houston Stackhouse, who learned from Tommy Johnson, who learned from Charley Patton, who learned from Henry Sloan—the tradition is unbroken, the language is still spoken and understood.

Leo Smith, who is a composer and trumpet player and a close associate of Anthony Braxton and other jazz avant-gardists, was raised in the Delta by a bluesman, his stepfather Alec Wallace. "Growing up in that environment made me feel that whatever I play relates to a gigantic field of feeling," he says. "To me, the blues is a literary and musical form and also a basic philosophy. When I get ready to study the mystical aspect of black people, I go to the blues; then I feel that I'm in touch with the root of black people."

A literary and musical form . . . a fusion of music and poetry accomplished at a very high emotional temperature . . . these are different ways of describing the same thing. A gigantic field of feeling . . . that's a way of describing something enduring, something that could be limitless. How much thought (to return to Miss Waddell's Clarksdale English class, May 1943) can be hidden in a few short lines of poetry? How much history can be transmitted by pressure on a guitar string? The thought of generations, the history of every human being who's ever felt the blues come down like showers of rain.

DISCOGRAPHY

I: SELECTED AFRICAN RECORDINGS

SENEGAMBIA
Wolof Music of Senegal and the Gambia. Ethnic Folkways FE 4462.
African Journey: A Search for the Roots of the Blues. Vanguard SRV
  73014/5.
Le Mali des Sables: Les Songoy. Barenreiter Musicaphon BM 30 L 2503.
The Griots: Ministers of the Spoken Word. Ethnic Folkways FE 4178.
Niger: La Musique des Griots. Ocora OCR 20.
Africa: Drum, Chant and Instrumental Music. Nonesuch H-72073.

WEST COAST
Musical Atlas: Ivory Coast. EMI Odeon (Italian) 3 C064 - 17842.
Masques Dan, Cote d'Ivoire. Ocora OCR 52.
Musique Toma Guinée. Vogue LDM 30107.
Musiques Dahoméennes. Ocora OCR 17.
Africa: Ancient Ceremonies, Dance Music and Songs of Ghana. None-
  such H-72082.

CONGO-ANGOLA
Musique Kongo. Ocora OCR 35.
Musique Centrafricaine. Ocora OCR 43.
Anthologie de la Musique des Pygmées Aka: Empire Centrafricain. Ocora
  558526/7/8.

NOTES: The Nonesuch and Folkways recordings are the most easily obtainable. Of the Senegambian recordings, *African Journey, Le Mali des Sables,* and especially *Niger: La Musique des Griots* offer excellent examples of singing and stringed-instrument styles related to blues. The west or slave coast recordings *Masques Dan* and *Musique Toma Guinée* include examples of voice masking. The anthology of Aka pygmy music includes examples of pygmy whooping and yodeling.

II: BLUES ROOTS

Afro-American Spirituals, Work Songs, and Ballads. Library of Congress AAFS L3.
Afro-American Blues and Game Songs. Library of Congress AAFS L4.
Negro Work Songs and Calls. Library of Congress AAFS L8.
Negro Religious Songs and Services. Library of Congress AAFS L10.
Negro Blues and Hollers. Library of Congress AFS L59.
Roots of the Blues. New World Records NW 252.
Afro-American Folk Music from Tate and Panola Counties, Mississippi. Library of Congress AFS L67.
Traveling Through the Jungle: Negro Fife and Drum Band Music from the Deep South. Testament T-2223.

NOTES: *Afro-American Spirituals, Work Songs, and Ballads* includes a ring shout. *Afro-American Blues and Game Songs* includes two of Muddy Waters's Library of Congress recordings (collected in full on *Muddy Waters: Down on Stovall's Plantation,* Testament T-2210). *Roots of the Blues* is a fine collection of 1959 field recordings from northern Mississippi by Alan Lomax. The last two albums named are field recordings by David Evans and document extensive African survivals in black folk music from Mississippi.

III. RECOMMENDED BLUES COLLECTIONS

Really! The Country Blues. Origin Jazz Library OJL-2.
Country Blues Encores. Origin Jazz Library OJL-8.
Goin' Up the Country. Rounder 2012.
Let's Get Loose: Folk and Popular Blues Styles from the Beginnings to the Early 1940's. New World Records NW 290.
Black Cat Trail. Mamlish S3800.
Home Again Blues. Mamlish S-3799.

NOTES: The two OJL albums include pre–World War Two recordings from the Delta and elsewhere in the South and remain the definitive country blues anthologies. *Goin' Up the Country* is a collection of outstanding field recordings made in Mississippi and Louisiana in the 1960s, and *Let's Get Loose* is an exceptionally wide-ranging anthology, including early white blues, vocal-group blues, and other styles, assembled by Evans. The two Mamlish albums are excellent collections of early electric blues from Mississippi, Chicago, and elsewhere, recorded in the late 1940s and early 1950s.

IV. BLUES FROM THE DELTA, AND RELATED TRADITIONS

Charley Patton: Founder of the Delta Blues. Yazoo L-1020.

Patton, Sims, and Bertha Lee. Herwin 213.

The Famous 1928 Tommy Johnson/Ishman Bracey Session. Roots RL-330.

Jackson Blues 1928–1938. Yazoo L-1007.

Jackson Blue Boys 1928–1940. Policy Wheel PW 4593.

The Mississippi Blues 1927–1940. Origin Jazz Library OJL-5.

The Mississippi Blues No. 2: The Delta, 1929–1932. Origin Jazz Library OJL-11.

The Mississippi Blues No. 3: The Transition, 1926–1937. Origin Jazz Library OJL-17.

Mississippi Blues, Vol. 1. Roots RL-302.

Mississippi Blues, Vol. 2. Roots RL-303.

Mississippi Blues, Vol. 3. Roots RL-314.

Delta Blues: Skip James/Son House/Charley Patton/Robert Johnson. Roots RL-339.

Blues Roots/Mississippi. Folkways RBF-14.

Mississippi Blues 1927–1936. Yazoo L-1001.

Mississippi Moaners 1927–1942. Yazoo L-1009.

Lonesome Road Blues: 15 Years in the Mississippi Delta 1926–1941. Yazoo L-1038.

William Harris, Blind Joe Reynolds, Skip James: Delta Blues Heavy Hitters, 1927–1931. Herwin 214.

Mississippi Bottom Blues. Mamlish S-3802.

Bullfrog Blues. Mamlish S-3809.

Mississippi Delta Blues Vol. 1. Arhoolie 1041.

Mississippi Delta Blues Vol. 2. Arhoolie 1042.

The Sound of the Delta. Testament T-2209.

Blind Lemon Jefferson/Son House. Biograph BLP-12040.

Son House: The Legendary 1941-1942 Recordings in Chronological Sequence. Arhoolie/Folklyric 9002.

Son House, Willie Brown, and others: Walking Blues. Flyright LP 541.

The Legendary Son House, Father of Folk Blues. Columbia CS 9217.

Son House: The Real Delta Blues. Blue Goose 2016.

Robert Johnson: King of the Delta Blues Singers. Columbia CL 1654.

Robert Johnson: King of the Delta Blues Singers, Vol. 2. Columbia C 30034.

Calvin Frazier and Sampson Pittman: I'm in the Highway Man. Flyright LP 542.

Muddy Waters: Down on Stovall's Plantation. Testament T-2210.

Tommy McClennan. French RCA/Bluebird PM 42040.

Big Joe Williams: Early Recordings 1935-1941. Mamlish S-3810.

David "Honeyboy" Edwards: I've Been Around. Trix 3319.

David "Honeyboy" Edwards: Mississippi Delta Bluesman. Folkways FS 3539.

Blues from the Delta. Matchbox SDM 226.

High Water Blues: Field Recordings of Mississippi and Louisiana Blues, 1965/70. Flyright LP 512.

South Mississippi Blues. Rounder 2009.

Roosevelt Holts and His Friends. Arhoolie 1057.

Fred McDowell and Johnny Woods. Rounder 2007.

Mississippi Fred McDowell: Delta Blues. Arhoolie F 1021.

Sounds of the South. Atlantic 1346.

Roots of the Blues. Atlantic 1348.

The Blues Roll On. Atlantic 1352.

Mississippi River Blues. Flyright-Matchbox SDM 230.

The Mississippi Sheiks: Stop and Listen. Mamlish S 3804.

Walter Vinson: Rats Been On My Cheese. Agram AB 2003.

Sam Chatmon: The Mississippi Sheik. Blue Goose 2006.

Bo Carter: Greatest Hits 1930-1940. Yazoo L-1014.

Bo Carter: Twist It Babe 1931-1940. Yazoo L-1034.

Bo Carter: Banana in Your Fruit Basket, Red Hot Blues 1931-36. Yazoo L-1064.

It Must Have Been the Devil: Mississippi Country Blues by Jack Owens and Bud Spires. Testament T-2222.

Skip James: Early Blues Recordings 1931. Biograph BLP 12029.

Skip James: Devil Got My Woman. Vanguard VSD 79273.

Skip James: Today! Vanguard VSD 79219.

Memphis Shakedown. Magpie PY 1810.

Memphis Jug Band. Yazoo 1067.

South Memphis Jug Band. Flyright LP 113.
Memphis Blues, Vol. 1. Roots RL-323.
Memphis Blues, Vol. 2. Roots RL-329.
The Memphis Area 1927–1932. Roots RL-307.
Low Down Memphis Barrelhouse Blues. Mamlish S 3803.
The Blues in Memphis 1927–1939. Origin Jazz Library OJL-21.
Ten Years in Memphis 1927–1937. Yazoo L-1002.
Frank Stokes' Dream: The Memphis Blues 1927–1931. Yazoo L-1008.
Memphis Jamboree 1927–1936. Yazoo L-1021.
If Beale Street Could Talk . . . A Selection of Pre-War Memphis Blues Favorites 1928–1939. Magnolia 501.
Jumping on the Hill: Memphis Blues and Hokum 1928–1941. Policy Wheel PW 459-1.
Jim Jackson: Kansas City Blues. Agram AB 2004.
Frank Stokes: Creator of the Memphis Blues. Yazoo L-1056.
Blues Classics by Memphis Minnie. Blues Classics 1.
Memphis Minnie Vol. 2. Blues Classics 13.
Memphis Minnie and Kansas Joe McCoy 1929–1936. Paltram PL-101.
Sleepy John Estes, 1929–1940. Folkways/RBF 8.
The Blues in St. Louis 1929–1937. Origin Jazz Library OJL-20.
Good Time Blues! St. Louis 1926–1932. Mamlish S 3805.
Hard Time Blues: St. Louis 1933–1940. Mamlish S 3806.
St. Louis Blues: The Depression 1929–1935. Yazoo L-1030.
St. Louis Town 1927–1932. Yazoo L-1003.
Leroy Carr: Blues Before Sunrise. Columbia CL 1799.
Leroy Carr and Scrapper Blackwell: Naptown Blues 1929–1934. Yazoo L-1036.
Peetie Wheatstraw 1930–1936. Flyright 111.
Blues Classics by Kokomo Arnold/Peetie Wheatstraw. Blues Classics 4.
Roosevelt Sykes: The Country Blues Piano Ace 1929–1932. Yazoo L-1033.
Roosevelt Sykes and His Original Honey Drippers: Boogie Honky Tonk. Oldie Blues OL 2818.
Bluebird Blues. RCA Victor LPV-518.
Big Joe Williams and Sonny Boy Williamson. Blues Classics 21.
Blues Classics by Sonny Boy Williamson. Blues Classics 3.
Blues Classics by Sonny Boy Williamson, Volume 2. Blues Classics 20.
Blues Classics by Sonny Boy Williamson, Volume 3. Blues Classics 24.
"Sonny Boy" Williamson, Vol. 1. French RCA FXM1 7203.
"Sonny Boy" Williamson, Vol. 2. French RCA PM 42049.

NOTE: The above albums are by John Lee Williamson, "Sonny Boy I."

Big Maceo: Chicago Breakdown. RCA/Bluebird AXM2-5506.

Arthur "Big Boy" Crudup: The Father of Rock and Roll. RCA LPV-573.

Lake Michigan Blues 1934–1941. Nighthawk 105.

Windy City Blues 1935–1953. Nighthawk 101.

Chicago Slickers 1948–1953. Nighthawk 102.

Chicago Boogie 1947. Barrelhouse bh 04.

Chicago Blues: The Beginning. 12 Previously Unissued 1946 Recordings in the Newly Developed Modern Blues Styles by Muddy Waters, Johnny Shines, Homer Harris and James Clark. Testament T-2207.

On the Road Again: An Anthology of Chicago Blues 1947–1954. Muskadine No. 100.

Blues is Killing Me. 14 Rare Performances, Many Previously Unissued, from the Golden Age of Chicago Blues. Juke Joint 1501.

Chicago Blues: The Early 1950's. Blues Classics 8.

Tampa Red: Guitar Wizard. RCA/Bluebird AXM2-5501.

Tampa Red 1932–1953. Oldie Blues OL 2816.

Tampa Red: The Guitar Wizard 1935–1953. Blues Classics 25.

Genesis: The Beginnings of Rock. English Chess 6641047 (4 lp's).

Genesis Vol. 2: Memphis to Chicago. English Chess 6641125 (4 lp's).

Genesis Vol. 3: Sweet Home Chicago. English Chess 6641174 (4 lp's).

Blues from the Windy City: Chicago in Transition 1946–1952. Flyright 4713.

Drop Down Mama. Chess 411.

After Midnight: Chicago Blues 1952–1957. Delta Swing 379.

Goin' To Chicago Blues: 1949–1957. Negro Rhythm 107.

Chicago Blues Anthology. Chess 2CH 60012.

Blues in D Natural. Red Lightnin' RL 005.

Sweet Home Chicago. Delmark DS-618.

Blues Southside Chicago. Flyright LP 521.

Electric Blues Chicago Style. Buddah BDS 7511.

Chicago Jump. JSP 1004.

J.T. Brown and his Boogie Boys: Rockin' with J.T. Flyright LP 4712.

J.T. Brown: Windy City Boogie. Pearl PL-9.

Robert Nighthawk: Bricks in My Pillow. Pearl PL-11.

Masters of Modern Blues Volume 4: Robert Nighthawk/Houston Stackhouse. Testament T-2215.

Robert Nighthawk: Live on Maxwell Street. Rounder 2022.

Sultans of the Slide Guitar. Blues Ball 2003.

Slide Guitar Classics. Chicago Slide CS-005.

Chicago Guitar Killers. Blue Night BN 073-1669.

Johnny Shines and Robert Lockwood: Dust My Broom. Flyright 563.

Johnny Shines/Big Boy Spires with Johnny Williams: Chance Vintage Blues/R&B Crops Vol. 1. Japanese P-Vine Special PLP 705.

Johnny Shines: Too Wet to Plow. Blue Labor BL 110.

Robert Jr. Lockwood: Steady Rollin' Man. Delmark DS-630.

Robert Jr. Lockwood: Contrasts. Trix 3307.

Robert Jr. Lockwood Does 12. Trix 3317.

Robert Jr. Lockwood and the Aces: Blues Live in Japan. Advent 2807.

Elmore James/Walter Horton: Cotton Patch Hotfoots. English Polydor Super 2383 200.

Resurrection of Elmore James. United US-7787.

Elmore James: Original Folk Blues. United US-7743.

The Legend of Elmore James. Kent KST 9001.

Elmore James/John Brim: Whose Muddy Shoes. Chess 1537.

Elmore James/Eddie Taylor: Street Talkin'. Muse MR 5087.

History of Elmore James. Trip TLP 8007 (2).

History of Elmore James Volume 2. Trip TLX 9511.

Muddy Waters: Sail On. Chess 1539.

McKinley Morganfield a.k.a. Muddy Waters. Chess 2CH-60006.

Muddy Waters: Back in the Early Days, Volumes 1 and 2. Syndicate Chapter S.C. 001/2.

Muddy Waters: Good News, Volume 3. Syndicate Chapter S.C. 002.

Muddy Waters/Little Walter/Howlin' Wolf: We Three Kings. Syndicate Chapter S.C. 005.

They Call Me Muddy Waters. Chess CHLS 276.

Muddy Waters at Newport 1960. Chess LP 1449.

Muddy Waters Folk Singer. Chess LP 1483.

Muddy Waters "Live." Chess CH 50012.

Muddy Waters: Hard Again. Blue Sky PZ 34449.

Muddy Waters: I'm Ready. Blue Sky JZ 34928.

Muddy "Mississippi" Waters Live. Blue Sky JZ 35712.

Bo Diddley/Muddy Waters/Little Walter: Super Blues. Checker LPS-3008.

Howlin' Wolf/Muddy Waters/Bo Diddley: The Super Super Blues Band. Checker LPS 3010.

The Legendary Sun Performers: Howlin' Wolf. Charly CR 30134.

Howling Wolf: Original Folk Blues. United US-7747.

Howlin' Wolf: Heart Like Railroad Steel. Blues Ball 2001.

Howlin' Wolf: Can't Put Me Out. Blues Ball 2002.

Howlin' Wolf: From Early 'Til Late. Blue Night BN 073-1667.

Howlin' Wolf: Going Back Home. Syndicate Chapter S.C. 003.

Chester Burnett AKA Howlin' Wolf. Chess 2CH 60016.

Howlin' Wolf: Evil. Chess 1540.
Howlin' Wolf: The Real Folk Blues. Chess 1502.
Howlin' Wolf: Change My Way. Chess CHV 418.
Howlin' Wolf: Live and Cookin' at Alice's Revisited. Chess CH 50015.
Jimmy Rogers: Chicago Bound. Chess 407.
Jimmy Rogers. Chess 2ACMB-207.
Little Walter: Boss Blues Harmonica. Chess 2CH 60014.
Little Walter: Confessin' the Blues. Chess CHV 416.
Little Walter: Hate to See You Go. Chess CH-1535.
Little Walter: Blue and Lonesome. Le Roi du Blues 33.2007.
Little Walter: Southern Feeling. Le Roi du Blues 33.2012.
Little Walter: Blue Midnight. Le Roi du Blues 33.2017.
Sonny Boy Williamson: King Biscuit Time. Arhoolie 2020.
Sonny Boy Williamson: This Is My Story. Chess 2CH 50027.
Sonny Boy Williamson. Chess 2ACMB-206.
Sonny Boy Williamson: Bummer Road. Chess 1536.
Sonny Boy Williamson and Memphis Slim. GNP Crescendo GNP-10003.
Sonny Boy Williamson: A Portrait in Blues. Storyville SLP 4016.
Sonny Boy Williamson: Final Sessions 1963–4. Blue Night BN 073-1668.
J.B. Lenoir/Sunnyland Slim/Lazy Bill: Chance Vintage Blues/R&B Crops, Vol. 3. Japanese P-Vine Special PLP-707.
J.B. Lenoir: Mojo Boogie. Flyright FLY 564.
J.B. Lenoir: Natural Man. Chess 410.
J.B. Lenoir. Chess 2ACMB-208.
Homesick James: Chance Vintage Blues/R&B Crops Vol. 2. Japanese Peavine PLP-706.
Snooky Pryor. Flyright LP 100.
Detroit Blues: The Early 1950's. Blues Classics 12.
Detroit Ghetto Blues 1948–1954. Nighthawk 104.
Blues Guitar Killers! Detroit, the 1950's. Barrelhouse BH 012.
John Lee Hooker: Detroit Special. Atlantic SD 7228.
John Lee Hooker: Folk Blues. Crown CST 295.
The Blues Came Down from Memphis. Charly CR 30125.
Memphis and the Delta—1950's. Blues Classics 15.
Memphis Blues. United US-7779.
Blues for Mr. Crump. English Polydor Super 2383 257.
706 Blues. Redita lp-111.
Lowdown Memphis Harmonica Jam 1950–1955. Nighthawk 103.
Sun—The Roots of Rock. Volume 1: Catalyst. Charly CR 30101.
Sun—The Roots of Rock. Volume 2: Sam's Blues. Charly CR 30102.
Sun—The Roots of Rock. Volume 3: Delta Rhythm Kings. Charly CR 30103.

Sun—The Roots of Rock. Volume 6: Sunset Soul. Charly CR 30106.

Sun—The Roots of Rock. Volume 7: Sun Blues. Charly CR 30114.

Sun—The Roots of Rock. Volume 11: Memphis Blues Sounds. Charly CR 30126.

Sun—The Roots of Rock. Volume 12: Union Avenue Breakdown. Charly ER 30127.

Mississippi Blues. United US 7786.

Down South Blues 1949–1961. African Folk Society #3428.

Packin' Up My Blues: Blues of the Deep South 1950–1961. Muskadine No. 102.

Blues from the Deep South. United US 7781.

Arkansas Blues. United US 7784.

Dr. Ross: His First Recordings. Arhoolie 1065.

Earl Hooker: His First and Last Recordings. Arhoolie 1066.

Joe Hill Louis: The One Man Band. Muskadine No. 101.

Joe Hill Louis, Big Boy Crudup and Others: Going Down to Louisiana. White Label LP 9955.

The Legendary Sun Performers: Roscoe Gordon. Charly CR 30133.

The Legendary Sun Performers: Junior Parker and Billy Love. Charly CR 30135.

Billy the Kid Emerson: Little Fine Healthy Thing. Charly CR 30187.

Sun Sound Special: Shoobie Oobie. Charly CR 30148.

Ike Turner Rocks the Blues. Crown CST 367.

Ike Turner's Kings of Rhythm: I'm Tore Up. Red Lightnin' RL 0016.

B.B. King: 1949–1950. Kent KST 9011.

B.B. King: Live at the Regal. ABC ABCS-724.

The Best of B.B. King. ABC ABCX-767.

Albert King/Otis Rush: Door to Door. Chess 1538.

Albert King: Travelin' to California. King KSD 1060.

Albert King: King of the Blues Guitar. French Atlantic 40494U.

Albert King: Live Wire/Blues Power. Stax STX 4128.

Driftin' Slim and his Blues Band: Somebody Hoo-Doo'd the Hoo-Doo Man. Milestone MSP 93004.

Frank Frost. Jewel LPS 5013.

The Jelly Roll Kings: Rockin' the Juke Joint Down. Earwig LPS 4901.

Joe Willie Wilkins and his King Biscuit Boys. Adamo ADS 9507.

Little Milton: Raise a Little Sand. Red Lightnin' RL 0011.

Billy Boy Arnold: Blow the Back Off It. Red Lightnin' RL 0012.

Memphis Slim and His House Rockers, featuring Matt "Guitar" Murphy: Memphis Slim—U.S.A. Pearl PL-10.

Memphis Slim: Mother Earth. Buddah BDS 7505.

Johnny Young and Big Walter: Chicago Blues. Arhoolie F 1037.

Chicago Ain't Nothin' But a Blues Band. Delmark 624.

I'm Jimmy Reed. Vee Jay LP 1004.

Jimmy Reed: Rockin' with Reed. Vee Jay LP-1008.

The Ultimate Jimmy Reed. ABC Bluesway BLS 6067.

I Feel So Bad: The Blues of Eddie Taylor. Advent 2802.

Eddie Taylor: Bad Boy—A Long Way From Chicago. Japanese P-Vine Special PLP 3501.

John Littlejohn's Chicago Blues Stars. Arhoolie 1043.

Otis Rush and Magic Sam: The Other Takes. Flyright LP 562.

Magic Sam: Magic Rocker. Flyright LP 561.

Magic Sam Blues Band: West Side Soul. Delmark DS-615.

Magic Sam Blues Band: Black Magic. Delmark DS-620.

Otis Rush: Groaning the Blues. Flyright LP 560.

Otis Rush: Right Place, Wrong Time. Bullfrog 301.

Otis Rush: Cold Day in Hell. Delmark DS-638.

Otis Rush: Troubles Troubles. Sonet SNTF 756.

Otis Rush: So Many Roads. Delmark DS-643.

Junior Wells: In My Younger Days. Red Lightnin' RL 007.

Junior Wells: Blues Hit Big Town. Delmark DL-640.

Junior Wells' Chicago Blues Band with Buddy Guy: Hoodoo Man Blues. Delmark DS-612.

Junior Wells: Southside Blues Jam. Delmark DS-628.

Junior Wells: On Tap. Delmark DS-635.

Buddy Guy: In the Beginning. Red Lightnin' RL 001.

Buddy Guy: I Was Walking Through the Woods. Chess 409.

Eddie C. Campbell: King of the Jungle. Mr. Blues MB 7602.

Buster Benton: Spider in My Stew: Japanese P-Vine Special PLP 3502.

Fenton Robinson: The Mellow Blues Genius. P-Vine Special PLP-9001.

Fenton Robinson: Somebody Loan Me a Dime. Alligator 4705.

Fenton Robinson: I Hear Some Blues Downstairs. Alligator AL 4710.

The Son Seals Blues Band. Alligator 4703.

Son Seals: Midnight Son. Alligator AL 4708.

Son Seals: Live and Burning. Alligator AL 4712.

Big Walter Horton with Carey Bell. Alligator 4702.

Walter Horton and Floyd Jones: Do Nothing Til You Hear from Us. Magnolia MLP 301.

Hound Dog Taylor and the House Rockers. Alligator 4701.

Hound Dog Taylor and the House Rockers: Natural Boogie. Alligator 4704.

Hound Dog Taylor and the House Rockers: Beware of the Dog! Alligator AL 4707.

J.B. Hutto and the Hawks: Hawk Squat! Delmark DS-617.

J.B. Hutto: Slidewinder. Delmark DS-636.
Eddie Shaw and the Wolf Gang: Have Blues, Will Travel. Simmons ES-1815.
Chicago/The Blues/Today! Volumes 1, 2, and 3. Vanguard VSD 79216/7/8.
The Best of the Chicago Blues. Vanguard VSD 1/2.
Living Chicago Blues, Volumes 1, 2, and 3. Alligator AL 7701/2/3.
Chicago Blues at Home. Advent 2806.
Chicago Breakdown. Takoma TAK 7071.
Rare Blues. Takoma TAK 7081.
Chicago Blues Live at the Fickle Pickle. Flyright LP 549.
Johnny Jones with Billy Boy Arnold. Alligator 4717.
Meat & Gravy from Cadillac Baby, Volume 1: "Records Was Cheap to Make Then." Red Lightnin' RL 0019.
Meat & Gravy from Cadillac Baby, Volume 2: Hits That Missed. Red Lightnin' RL 0020.
Meat & Gravy from Cadillac Baby, Volume 3: Trying to Make a Living. Red Lightnin' RL 0021.

NOTES: The above is a more or less complete list of the albums I used as recorded source materials for this book, including both Delta blues and "related materials"—blues from areas contiguous to the Delta or areas with a significant concentration of migrants from the Delta. The records are listed in an order that reflects the organization of the text, but with obvious subgroupings—the collections of contemporary Chicago blues are grouped at the end, for example. While it is long, the list is by no means exhaustive. Essentially, it's a list of my own collection of relevant albums, and since much of the material has appeared in different guises, and often on different labels, over the years, I've simply given the label and catalogue number of the version I own. A number of these albums are rare, out-of-print, or otherwise difficult to acquire, so I've also made up the following list, a much shorter selection of what I consider the essential recordings in the field. At present, all the albums in the following list are in print (somewhere in the world, at least). The most reliable source for recordings of this nature is Down Home Music, 10341 San Pablo Avenue, El Cerrito, California 94530; 415-525-1494.

V. DELTA BLUES AND RELATED TRADITIONS:
THE ESSENTIAL RECORDINGS

Charley Patton: Founder of the Delta Blues. Yazoo L-1020. This double album collects the cream of Patton's recordings. *Patton, Sims and Bertha Lee* (Herwin 213) is a worthwhile companion volume and includes several of Patton's sung sermons.

The Mississippi Blues 1927–1940. Origin Jazz Library OJL-5. This album includes important early recordings by Son House and Willie Brown, among others. Its companion volumes (OJL-11 and OJL-17) are worthwhile as well.

Blues Roots/Mississippi. Folkways RBF-14. This superb sampler, still in the Folkways records catalogue, is the most readily available source for three of Tommy Johnson's classic recordings; *The Famous 1928 Tommy Johnson/Ishman Bracey Session* on Roots is just as highly recommended, if you can find it. The RBF collection also includes great performances by Joe Williams, Robert Johnson, Tommy McClennan and (oddly, since he was from Tennessee) John Lee "Sonny Boy" Williamson.

Lonesome Road Blues: 15 Years in the Mississippi Delta 1926–1941. Yazoo L-1038. Early Delta blues enigmas like Freddie Spruell and Sam Collins, Robert Petway's "Catfish Blues," and Skip James's "I'm So Glad" are the highlights of this collection.

Blind Lemon Jefferson/Son House. Biograph BLP-12040. Miserable sound quality, but it boasts Son House's 1930 classics on one side and some first-rate Texas blues by Blind Lemon Jefferson on the other. The collection of 1941–1942 Son House recordings on Arhoolie/Folk Lyric is also highly recommended.

Son House, Willie Brown and others: Walking Blues. Flyright LP 541. The 1941 recordings of Son House and his band collected here, including the devastating six and a half minutes of "Walking Blues," are not to be missed, and the album also includes a rare Willie Brown solo appearance and five fine selections by a young Honeyboy Edwards.

Robert Johnson: King of the Delta Blues Singers, Volumes 1 and 2. Columbia CL 1654 and C 30034. These are the essential Robert Johnson collections. For those who want more, *Delta Blues* (Roots RL-339) includes an entire side of Robert Johnson alternate takes that are as good as (and sometimes better than) the versions on the Columbia albums.

Muddy Waters: Down on Stovall's Plantation. Testament T-2210. If you can't find this riveting and well-rounded portrait of young Muddy two of the best performances on it are on *Afro-American Blues and Game Songs,* Library of Congress AFS L4.

Lake Michigan Blues 1934–1941. Nighthawk 105. This collection sketches in the Chicago blues scene on the eve of Muddy's arrival, with classic performances by John Lee "Sonny Boy" Williamson, Robert Nighthawk, and Robert Jr. Lockwood.

Chicago Slickers 1948–1953. Nighthawk 102. A fine album of early Delta-style Chicago blues by Johnny Shines, Floyd Jones, and the early Little Walter. *On the Road Again* (Muskadine No. 100) and *Chicago Blues: The Early 1950's* (Blues Classics 8) cover the same ground, perhaps equally well, and there is no duplication. Just as essential, but out of print and very hard to find, are *Chicago Boogie* (Barrelhouse bh 04), which includes the early Maxwell Street sessions by Little Walter and Jimmy Rogers, and *Chicago Blues* (Testament T-2207), with Muddy's earliest Chicago recordings.

Robert Nighthawk: Bricks in My Pillow. Pearl PL-11. This album collects the early fifties Nighthawk recordings, with the best sound quality and detailed liner notes. A rawer but, at its best, wonderful additional choice would be *Robert Nighthawk Live on Maxwell Street* (Rounder 2022).

Johnny Shines and Robert Lockwood: Dust My Broom. Flyright 563. Early-fifties recordings by Robert Johnson's outstanding disciples, Shines in country-style performances (with the best Big Walter Horton blues harmonica on records) and Lockwood, typically, with a small jump band.

The Legend of Elmore James. Kent KST 9001. This album was also available as a budget lp on United. It's probably the best early Elmore collection, though the first *History of Elmore James* (Trip TLP 8007) is also very fine, and any of the James albums listed offers a representative sampling of his work.

Muddy Waters: Sail On. Chess 1539. As of this writing, the immense Chess catalogue is moribund in the U.S., but this album, also issued as *The Best of Muddy Waters,* is available in several European countries and through Down Home Music. It's the essential collection of Muddy's Chess masterpieces and is nicely supplemented by *McKinley Morganfield A.K.A. Muddy Waters* (Chess, out of print) and the three reissues on the English Syndicate Chapter label, *Back in the Early Days* being particularly fine.

Muddy "Mississippi" Waters Live. Blue Sky JZ 35712. This recent live album on Columbia proves Muddy is still a commanding blues performer.

Howlin' Wolf: Going Back Home. Syndicate Chapter S.C. 003. This bootleg from England was originally intended to supplement the readily available Chess collections of Wolf's music, but as of this writing it's the best anthology of his Chess recordings (including sides made for Sam Phillips in Memphis) that's readily available. The best single collection, if you can find it, is *Chester Burnett A.K.A. Howlin' Wolf* (Chess 2CH 60016) with *Evil* (Chess 1540), *Original Folk Blues* (United US-7747), and *The Legendary Sun Performers: Howlin' Wolf* (Charly CR 30134) also highly recommended. The last two consist wholly of pre-Chicago performances by Wolf's West Memphis band.

Jimmy Rogers: Chicago Bound. Chess 407. Definitive, if you can find it.

Little Walter: Boss Blues Harmonica. Chess 2CH 60014. Ditto.

Sonny Boy Williamson: King Biscuit Time. Arhoolie 2020. Ditto, except you can find it. These are early Mississippi recordings by Rice Miller, the "second" Sonny Boy Williamson, made with musicians from the *King Biscuit Time* radio show. The two Chess double albums by this Sonny Boy (2CH 50027 and 2ACMB-206) are also excellent.

John Lee Hooker: Detroit Special. Atlantic SD 7228. This is a fine collection of vintage Hooker. It doesn't contain his original hit "Boogie Chillen," which is available on several anthologies on the Kent and United labels.

The Blues Came Down from Memphis. Charly CR 30125. Here are the classic Sun blues recordings from the early fifties, including James Cotton's "Cotton Crop Blues" (with super-distorted electric guitar by Pat Hare) and Dr. Ross's "The Boogie Disease." *Memphis and the Delta— The 1950's* (Blues Classics 15) is equally fine and more wide-ranging, with selections by Arkansas' Drifting Slim and Junior Brooks plus vintage Elmore James, Joe Hill Louis, Boyd Gilmore ("Rambling On My Mind"), Sunnyland Slim, and others.

Ike Turner's Kings of Rhythm: I'm Tore Up. Red Lightnin' RL 0016. These are the rocking mid-fifties Federal recordings of the Kings of Rhythm in their prime, with Ike Turner's explosive, jangling guitar solos and gritty vocals by Billy Gayles and Jackie Brenston, whose "Rocket 88," along with some of the best early Muddy Waters and Sunnyland Slim and other essential recordings, was last available on the English Chess Genesis boxed sets, now impossible to find.

B.B. King: Live at the Regal. ABC ABCS-724. This is the standard B.B. King album, and one of the classic live lp's along with James Brown's *Live at the Apollo. B.B. King 1949–1950,* on Kent and United, is also highly recommended for its picture of King at a more formative stage.

Albert King: King of the Blues Guitar. French Atlantic 40494U. You can trace Albert's earlier work, heavily influenced by Elmore James and other Delta stylists, on *Door to Door* (Chess 1538, good luck) and *Travelin' to California* (King KSD 1060), but this finds Albert in his prime, on

Stax in the mid-sixties. His *Live Wire/Blues Power* (Stax STX 4128, available through Fantasy records) is another fine live recording, bearing comparison with B.B. King's *Live at the Regal.*

The Ultimate Jimmy Reed. ABC Bluesway BLS 6067. Reed's Vee Jay recordings have been packaged by several labels under numerous guises. This is the best single collection and can still be found in some stores.

Otis Rush and Magic Sam: The Other Takes. Flyright LP 562. The B.B. King–influenced blues style that developed on Chicago's West Side is well represented by these seminal Cobra recordings.

Otis Rush: Cold Day in Hell: Delmark DS-638. This is an excruciatingly uneven album, but its best selections (the slow blues) demonstrate Rush's depth better than any other items in his discography.

Junior Wells: Blues Hit Big Town. Delmark DL-640. These are early-fifties performances by Wells, then a teenage harmonica virtuoso, with stellar support by Elmore James and Muddy Waters, among others.

Son Seals: Midnight Son. Alligator Al 4708. With nasty, snarling guitar, popping horns, and funk rhythms, this is the definitive *contemporary* blues album, and Seals's best so far.

Chicago/The Blues/Today! (Vanguard VSD 79216/7/8) and *Living Chicago Blues* (Alligator Al 7701/2/3) are sets of three albums (each album being available separately) chronicling what were, at the time of recording, relatively little known Chicago blues talents. The Vanguard set included performances by Junior Wells and J.B. Hutto (Volume 1), Otis Rush and James Cotton (Volume 2), and Johnny Shines and Walter Horton (Volume 3) and was a revelation when it was originally released back in the sixties, though virtually all these artists have recorded better performances since. All three of the Alligator albums include fine performances, but Volume 1 is the best.

BIBLIOGRAPHY

I: BOOKS

Ashmore, Harry S. *Arkansas: A History*. New York: Norton, 1978.

Bascom, William R., and Herskovits, Melville J., eds. *Continuity and Change in African Cultures*. Chicago: University of Chicago Press, 1959.

Bebey, Francis. *African Music: A People's Art*. New York: Lawrence Hill, 1975.

Berkow, Ira. *Maxwell Street: Survival in a Bazaar*. Garden City, N.Y.: Doubleday, 1977.

Botkin, B. A. *Lay My Burden Down: A Folk History of Slavery*. Chicago: University of Chicago Press, 1945.

Charters, Samuel. *The Legacy of the Blues*. New York: Da Capo Press, 1977.

————. *Sweet as the Showers of Rain*. New York: Oak Publications, 1977.

Chernoff, John Miller. *African Rhythms and African Sensibility*. Chicago: University of Chicago Press, 1979.

Cohn, David L. *Where I Was Born and Raised*. Boston: Houghton Mifflin, 1948.

Courlander, Harold. *Negro Folk Music U.S.A*. New York: Columbia University Press, 1963.

Curtin, Philip D. *The Atlantic Slave Trade: A Census*. Madison: University of Wisconsin Press, 1969.

Daniel, Pete. *Deep'n As It Come: The 1927 Mississippi River Flood*. New York: Oxford University Press, 1977.

d'Azevedo, Warren L., ed. *The Traditional Artist in African Societies.* Bloomington: Indiana University Press, 1973.

Dundes, Alan, ed. *Mother Wit from the Laughing Barrel.* Englewood Cliffs, N.J.: Prentice-Hall, 1973.

Epstein, Dena J. *Sinful Tunes and Spirituals: Black Folk Music to the Civil War.* Urbana: University of Illinois Press, 1977.

Escott, Colin, and Hawkins, Martin. *Sun Records: The Brief History of the Legendary Record Label.* New York: Quick Fox, 1980.

Evans, David. *Tommy Johnson.* London: Studio Vista, 1971.

Fahey, John. *Charley Patton.* London: Studio Vista, 1970.

Ferris, William. *Blues from the Delta.* Garden City, N.Y.: Doubleday, 1978.

Garon, Paul. *Blues and the Poetic Spirit.* New York: Da Capo Press, 1978.

———. *The Devil's Son-in-Law: The Story of Peetie Wheatstraw and His Songs.* London: Studio Vista, 1978.

Genovese, Eugene D. *Roll, Jordan, Roll: The World The Slaves Made.* New York: Pantheon Books, 1974.

Georgia Writers' Project. *Drums and Shadows.* Garden City, N.Y.: Doubleday/Anchor, 1972.

Gert zur Heide, Karl. *Deep South Piano: The Story of Little Brother Montgomery.* London: Studio Vista, 1970.

Gleason, Judith. *A Recitation of Ifa, Oracle of the Yoruba.* New York: Grossman, 1973.

Godrich, John, and Dixon, Robert. *Blues and Gospel Records 1902–1942.* London: Storyville Publications, 1969.

———. *Recording the Blues.* London: Studio Vista, 1970.

Groom, Bob. *The Blues Revival.* London: Studio Vista, 1971.

Handy, W. C. *Father of the Blues.* New York: Macmillan, 1941.

Harris, Sheldon. *Blues Who's Who.* New Rochelle, N.Y.: Arlington House, 1979.

Herskovits, Melville J. *The Myth of the Negro Past.* Boston: Beacon Press, 1958.

———. *The New World Negro.* Bloomington: Indiana University Press, 1966.

Hurston, Zora Neale. *Mules and Men.* Bloomington: Indiana University Press, 1978.

Keil, Charles. *Tiv Song.* Chicago: University of Chicago Press, 1979.

———. *Urban Blues.* Chicago: University of Chicago Press, 1966.

Leadbitter, Mike. *Delta Country Blues.* Sussex: Blues Unlimited Publications, 1968.

———, ed. *Nothing But the Blues.* London: Hanover Books, 1971.

————, and Slaven, Neil. *Blues Records 1943–1966*. New York: Oak Publications, 1968.

Levine, Lawrence W. *Black Culture and Black Consciousness*. New York: Oxford University Press, 1977.

Miller, Jim, ed. *The Rolling Stone Illustrated History of Rock & Roll*. New York: Random House, 1980.

Mitchell, George. *Blow My Blues Away*. Baton Rouge: Louisiana State University Press, 1971.

Napier, Simon A., ed. *Back Woods Blues*. Sussex: Blues Unlimited Publications, 1968.

Nketia, J. H. Kwabena. *The Music of Africa*. New York: Norton, 1974.

Oakley, Giles. *The Devil's Music: A History of the Blues*. New York: Taplinger, 1977.

Oliver, Paul. *The Blues Tradition*. New York: Oak Publications, 1970.

————. *The Meaning of the Blues*. New York: Collier Books, 1963.

————. *Savannah Syncopators: African Retentions in the Blues*. London: Studio Vista, 1970.

————. *The Story of the Blues*. Philadelphia: Chilton, 1973.

Olsson, Bengt. *Memphis Blues*. London: Studio Vista, 1970.

Palmer, Robert. *A Tale of Two Cities: Memphis Rock and New Orleans Roll*. Brooklyn, N.Y.: Institute for Studies in American Music, Brooklyn College, 1979.

Percy, William Alexander. *Lanterns on the Levee: Recollections of a Planter's Son*. Baton Rouge: Louisiana State University Press, 1973.

Ramsey, Frederic, Jr. *Been Here and Gone*. New Brunswick, N.J.: Rutgers University Press, 1960.

Roberts, John Storm. *Black Music of Two Worlds*. New York: Praeger, 1972.

Rooney, James. *Bossmen: Bill Monroe and Muddy Waters*. New York: Hayden, 1971.

Rosenberg, Bruce A. *The Art of the American Folk Preacher*. New York: Oxford University Press, 1970.

Rowe, Mike. *Chicago Breakdown*. New York: Drake Publishers. 1975.

Russell, Tony. *Blacks, Whites and Blues*. London: Studio Vista, 1970.

Sackheim, Eric, ed. *The Blues Line: A Collection of Blues Lyrics*. New York: Schirmer Books, 1975.

Shaw, Arnold. *Honkers and Shouters: The Golden Years of Rhythm and Blues*. New York: Collier Books, 1978.

Skates, John Ray. *Mississippi: A History*. New York: Norton, 1979.

Southern, Eileen. *The Music of Black Americans: A History*. New York: Norton, 1971.

Spear, Allan H. *Black Chicago: The Making of a Negro Ghetto 1890–1920*. Chicago: University of Chicago Press, 1967.

Thompson, Robert Farris. *African Art in Motion*. Los Angeles: University of California Press, 1974.

Titon, Jeff Todd. *Early Downhome Blues: A Musical and Cultural Analysis*. Urbana: University of Illinois Press, 1977.

Toll, Robert C. *Blacking Up: The Minstrel Show in Nineteenth-Century America*. New York: Oxford University Press, 1974.

Tryon, Warren S., ed. *My Native Land: Life in America, 1790–1870*. Chicago: University of Chicago Press, 1952.

Various Authors. *African Music*. Paris: UNESCO/La Revue Musicale, 1972.

Wachsmann, Klaus P., ed. *Essays on Music and History in Africa*. Evanston, Ill.: Northwestern University Press, 1971.

II: ARTICLES

NOTE: Although my own interviews furnished the basic materials for *Deep Blues*, I also referred to back issues of *Blues Unlimited, Living Blues,* and the more short lived *Blues World*. Almost every issue of these periodicals has included something pertinent to the present study, and it would have been impractical to list articles individually. Instead, I have listed a few articles from other periodicals that were of particular relevance. For more information on the blues, subscriptions are recommended to *Blues Unlimited* (36 Belmont Park, Lewisham, London SE13 5DB, England) and *Living Blues* (2615 N. Wilton Avenue, Chicago, Illinois 60614).

Evans, David. "Afro-American One-Stringed Instruments." *Western Folklore* 23 (1970).

———. "Black Fife and Drum Music in Mississippi." *Mississippi Folklore Register* 6 (1972).

———. "Folk, Commercial, and Folkloristic Aesthetics in the Blues." *Jazz Forschung* 5 (1973).

———. "Techniques of Blues Composition among Black Folksingers." *Journal of American Folklore* 87 (July-September 1974).

Murray, Charles Shaar. "The Blues Had a Baby . . . and they called it Rock 'N' Roll." *New Musical Express*, April 30, 1977.

Odum, Howard W. "Folk-Song and Folk-Poetry as Found in the Secular Songs of the Southern Negroes." *Journal of American Folk-Lore* 24 (July-September 1911 and October-December 1911).

Oliver, Paul. "Muddy Waters, Hoochie Coochie Man." *Jazz Monthly,* January 1959.

Peabody, Charles. "Notes on Negro Music." *Journal of American Folk-Lore* 16, no. 62 (1903).

Perls, Nick. "Son House Interview—Part One." *78 Quarterly,* 1967.

Standish, Tony. "Muddy Waters in London." *Jazz Journal,* January 1959.

Wardlow, Gayle Dean, and Roche, Jacques. "Patton's Murder—Whitewash? Or Hogwash?" *78 Quarterly,* 1967.

INDEX

"Bird Nest Bound," 83–85
Bivens, Cliff, 213
Black, Bill, 241
"Black Angel Blues," 195, 209
"Black Spider Blues," 178, 181
Blackwell, Scrapper, 109–10, 114, 181
Blair, Sonny, 239
Bland, Bobby "Blue," 102, 229, 230, 237, 250, 251, 260, 267
Blind Blake (Arthur Phelps), 107, 108, 110
Bluebird label, 135, 145
Bolton, Antra, 157
"Boogie Chillen," 243–44
"Boogie Disease, The," 239
"Boogie in the Park," 228
Boogie-woogie, 106–107, 130–31, 150
Booker, Charley, 239
"Boom Boom," 245
"Booted," 234
"Born under a Bad Sign," 246
Boyd, Eddie, 146–47, 155, 156
Brenston, Jackie, 221, 222, 240
"Bright Lights, Big City," 252
Brim, John, 165
Broonzy, Big Bill, 124, 130, 135, 145, 256–57
Brown, Bill, 223
Brown, Charles, 155
Brown, Gatesmouth, 250
Brown, J. T., 214
Brown, Lee, 155
Brown, Othum, 159, 203
Brown, Robert (Washboard Sam), 135
Brown, Roy, 230, 248
Brown, William, 126
Brown, Willie, 58, 59, 61, 62, 78, 79, 82–84, 108, 112–14, 126, 129, 275
Buchanan, Roy, 236
"Bumble Bee," 87, 110, 111
Bunch, William (Peetie Wheatstraw), 114–16, 127, 135
Burlison, Paul, 235, 236
Burnett, Chester (Howlin' Wolf), 35, 61–63, 110, 117–19, 161, 174, 182, 207, 231–37, 256
Burnette, Dorsey, 235
Burnette, Johnny, 235
"Bye Bye Bird," 185

Calaway, W. R., 86–87
"Caldonia," 201–202
Call and response, 28–29
Callicott, Joe, 243–44
Calt, Steve, 79
Campbell, Little Milton, 238, 245, 247
Canned Heat, 244
Cannon, Gus, 46–47
Cannon, Viola, 57
"Carrier Line, The," 42
Carr, Leroy, 109–10, 111–12, 114, 181
"Catfish Blues," 104, 165, 214
Catlett, Big Sid, 135
Charles, Ray, 81, 167, 248–49
Chatmon family, 51
Chess, Leonard, 157–60, 161–65, 167, 210, 223
Chess, Phil, 157
Chess brothers, 223
Chess label, 98, 214–16, 223, 234–37, 259
Chicago, Illinois, 11–14, 137–47
Chicago blues, 16, 125, 134–35, 163, 210, 211, 267, 269
Chicago Defender (newspaper), 138–39
Chisholm, Malcolm, 162, 163
Christian, Charlie, 197, 198, 228
Clapton, Eric, 125, 128, 129, 246
Clay, Francis, 168, 258
Cleighton, Peter (Dr. Clayton), 154
"Clouds in My Heart," 168
Cobra label, 166–67
Cohn, David L., 92, 139–41, 225
Cole, Nat "King," 155
Collins, Crying Sam, 123
Columbia Records, 109, 135, 156
"Come on in My Kitchen," 117
Cotton, James, 237, 256, 258